Making Death and Life in Palestine

"In this important edited volume, two pioneering figures in Social Reproduction Theory, Tithi Bhattacharya and Sue Ferguson, extend their framework beyond the working-class struggle for life in advanced capitalist societies, accounting for the specificity of settler colonial capitalism. The essays they have assembled here urgently address the contemporary case study of Palestine in the horrific era of the Gaza genocide. They reveal the intensity of the battle between the exterminationist death-making force of Israeli colonialism and the Palestinian determination to produce and sustain a flourishing and liberated collective life."

—Abdel Razzaq Takriti, Palestinian historian and Arab-American Educational Foundation Chair in Arab Studies, Rice University

"A theoretically grounded and politically urgent book that reminds us of beauty, resistance and courage at a time in which Israel's genocide wants us to succumb to despair and the feeling of powerlessness. Palestinians continue to teach us life, as they have done for over 75 years. They show us that affirming life against capital's death drive and settler colonialism in the midst of unspeakable atrocity is the only way forward. Everyone should read this book!"

—Sara Farris, Department of Sociology, Goldsmiths, University of London

Mapping Social Reproduction Theory

Series editors Tithi Bhattacharya, Professor of South Asian History and Susan Ferguson, Associate Professor Emerita, Wilfrid Laurier University

Capitalism is a system of exploitation and oppression. This series uses the insights of social reproduction theory to deepen our understanding of the intimacy of that relationship, and the contradictions within it, past and present. The books include empirical investigations of the ways in which social oppressions of race, sexuality, ability, gender and more inhabit, shape and are shaped by the processes of creating labour power for capital. The books engage a critical exploration of social reproduction, enjoining debates about the theoretical and political tools required to challenge capitalism today.

Also available

Social Reproduction Theory:
Remapping Class, Recentering Oppression
Edited by Tithi Bhattacharya

A Feminist Reading of Debt
Luci Cavallero and Verónica Gago

Women and Work:
Feminism, Labour, and Social Reproduction
Susan Ferguson

Going Into Labour:
Childbirth in Capitalism
Anna Fielder

Disasters and Social Reproduction:
Crisis Response between the State and Community
Peer Illner

Social Reproduction Theory and the Socialist Horizon:
Work, Power and Political Strategy
Aaron Jaffe

Eros and Alienation:
Capitalism and the Making of Gendered Sexualities
Alan Sears

The Contested Domain:
Selected Writings on Marxism and Feminism
Lise Vogel
Edited by Kirstin Munro

Making Death and Life in Palestine

Social Reproduction in Settler Colonialism

Edited by
Tithi Bhattacharya and Susan Ferguson

Foreword by
Ruth Wilson Gilmore

PLUTO PRESS

First published 2025 by Pluto Press
New Wing, Somerset House, Strand, London WC2R 1LA
and Pluto Press, Inc.
1930 Village Center Circle, 3-834, Las Vegas, NV 89134

www.plutobooks.com

British Library Cataloguing in Publication Data
A catalogue record for this book is available from the British Library

ISBN 978 0 7453 5106 3   Paperback
ISBN 978 0 7453 5108 7   PDF
ISBN 978 0 7453 5107 0   EPUB

This book is printed on paper suitable for recycling and made from fully managed
and sustained forest sources. Logging, pulping and manufacturing processes are
expected to conform to the environmental standards of the country of origin.

Typeset by Stanford DTP Services, Northampton, England

Simultaneously printed in the United Kingdom and United States of America

EU GPSR Authorised Representative
LOGOS EUROPE, 9 rue Nicolas Poussin, 17000, LA ROCHELLE, France
Email: Contact@logoseurope.eu

Contents

Figures

Foreword
Emancipation in Rehearsal

Ruth Wilson Gilmore

Social reproduction theory (SRT) focuses our attention on detailed dynamics of beautiful life-making. Life-making in the abyss of genocide requires creative aggression, which is what these chapters militantly model from the ground up. In these pages, imperialism's victims are also, relentlessly, history's protagonists. There's no outside to the social – which is the existential given from which SRT's strength and flexibility draws energy.

What does the energy power? Our analytical capacity to recognise the creative aggression that shapes a variety of models (not a single blueprint) working towards emancipation. In other words, SRT illuminates political abolition as a process of becoming – in other words, as emancipation in rehearsal.

To emphasise the variety of models is not to suggest emancipation is a strictly local struggle. To the contrary, creative aggression is fundamental to the ongoing struggle of becoming internationalist from below. The forces of murder, destruction, and displacement that are concentrated in Palestine extend systemically throughout the world, not only because of the coordinated interdependence of powerful élites, but also because the summary objectives of contemporary imperialism are land-grabbing, time-grabbing, and life-grabbing.

I'll discuss these three aspects of imperial activity in a moment, but for now let's reflect further on this volume's lessons. Persistent life-making otherwise already exists in fragments of the coming social reality that emancipation seeks to realise: where life is precious, life is precious. The multiple aspects of social reproduction, including shifting spatial dimensions, oppose organised abandonment and organised violence *in practice by making something else.*

That "something else" is abolition geography – frequently geometrically discontinuous yet tending towards connection into the socio-spatial sinews and visions of small-c communism. In other words, geography is an antagonistic contradiction not contained by borders or skin, although the combined ascriptive power of those limits, as seen "from above", can lead to the confusing notion that those distinctions are battlements to be defended rather than interfaces to be reworked.

Imperialism churns the planet in multiple yet interlocking forms of expro-priation. Frictions that arise from people, places, and things being forced into motion spark contradictions. Those sparks sometimes fire the creative aggression through which social movements, with varying modalities of experiment and precision, create social reality. I'll repeat that abolition is a model, not a blueprint. Internationalist movement depends on enhanc-ing emancipatory consciousness-in-common towards making freedom by making place. In this view, solidarity is interdependency from below.

The objective necessity for such interdependency becomes starkly apparent when we think about how contemporary fascism targets peoples for expulsion and elimination. The danger of group-differentiated vul-nerability to premature death is on the rise, as fascists seize imperialism's weapons and institutions – especially the anti-state state – to renovate and make extensive *afresh* the particularities of land-grabbing, time-grabbing, and life-grabbing that have characterised modernity's long arc.

The grabbing, including all of Palestine, southern Lebanon, western Syria, and also Sudan, Brazil, Indonesia, Congo, the Andaman Islands, Indigenous lands, and lands overlying resources including water, and list list list, occurs through organised abandonment and organised violence. Social reproduc-tion crises are at once intimate yet visible from the satellite-studded heavens. We can see rubble, sere, craft, waiting. War kills, not only directly by the various instruments of industrialised killing perfected over centuries of cap-italist modernity, but also as always, indirectly by hunger, illness, injury, abandonment, siege, displacement, and the entire range, as we see in this book, of material, conceptual, and symbolic maldistributions.

While we are not defeated, we face the growing problem, again, of those who control the forces of organised violence also controlling the means of production and reproduction, and importantly creating the possibility to replace with machines the human labour needed to make the commodi-ties from which capitalism appropriates profit. I'm not saying humans don't work: billions do. I am saying the robotic threat under direct control of racial capitalism is an incitement for mass killing and industrialised punishment rather than a possible route towards general human well-being.

Land-grabbing, time-grabbing, and life-grabbing compel us to consider, perhaps a bit abstractly, the factors of production that these grabs distort and destroy. Social reproduction theory enables us to think these factors with grounded specificity: they are the territories where we make life and live, the resources and opportunities to mix our imaginative and physical energies with the external world, and the evidence that life is by definition spatial, viscerally experienced in human terms as the territories of selves. Time-grabbing kills. Killing takes time.

Social reproduction theory, as the editors tell us so eloquently in their introduction, allows us to think together while things are in motion, to perceive diagnostically the gorgeously delicate sturdinesses of life-making. The political horizon is what matters. These chapters help us focus, recognising continuities not only of vulnerabilities but also of strengths through which creative aggression comes into being to provisionally resolve as abolition: emancipation in rehearsal.

1

Introduction
Making Death and Life in Palestine: Social Reproduction in Settler Colonialism

Tithi Bhattacharya and Susan Ferguson

On 27 December 2024, the world witnessed a lone man in a white coat walking towards an Israeli tank in Gaza while the occupying army evacuated his hospital.[1] That man was Hussam Abu Safiya, a paediatrician and director of the Kamal Adwan Hospital in Gaza. The hospital – identified by Israel as a "terrorist stronghold" – had been attacked several times since October 2023, each assault depleting its capacities to provide medical care during a genocide. One early casualty of the constant bombardment was Ibrahim, Abu Safiya's 15-year-old-son. Ibrahim was killed in a drone strike at the entrance of the hospital, which his father refused to leave so long as he could provide any care to those who needed it most. Finally on 27 December, the Israeli army, presumably fed up with this hospital's "terroristic" commitment to providing medical care, forced an evacuation of the building at gunpoint. As the world watched, the doctor in a white coat walked away from a hospital dispensing care towards a tank dispensing death.

In this volume, we recentre and redocument Doctor Abu Safiya's steps. The book poses this contradiction between life and death that the essays to follow explore: how does social reproduction theory (SRT) as a theory about life-making shed light on what is so clearly Israel's project of death-making? The lexical order – placing the word "death" before "life" in the title – is a subtle but important recognition not only of the genocidal logic of Israel's frontal assault on Gaza after 7 October 2023, but also of the eliminatory logics expressed through Israeli settler colonialism from the outset. For to be Palestinian is to defy the death-making of the Western-backed, Zionist state machinery as the very condition of existence. The very conditions of life-making in Palestine are also a chronicle of resistance and history making.

SRT concerns itself, on the face of it, with life-making in capitalist societies.[2] It proposes that capital's very existence depends upon the daily and generational reproductive work that working-class people do – most of it performed outside the immediate circuits of commodity production – to ensure a steady flow of labour power is made available for capitalists to exploit. Yet the system can only thrive if it undermines and depletes such work in order to keep the value of labour power as low as possible. Capitalism thus has a doubled relationship to those who do the work of social reproduction, it degrades them while being dependent on them. It is precisely SRT's revelation and exploration of this dialectic that makes it a compelling lens through which to study occupied Palestine.

At the same time, the SRT framework emerged and largely developed through engaging the problem of a gendered, racialised *capitalism*. Less considered were the precise contours of and logics shaping *settler colonial* capitalist societies. We hope this book can be the beginning of those conversations while also helping to incite further empirical research.

Settler colonial ruling classes, Sai Englert has argued, can be pulled between two incompatible projects: the transformation of Indigenous people into a cheap labour force (as in South Africa, for example) and the attempt to eradicate Indigenous life (as in the USA and Canada).[3] Considered through the lens of SRT, the former – exploitation – requires some systemic (if limited) support for the social reproduction of Indigenous peoples; the latter – elimination – requires the (violent) end of Indigenous life-making.

Historically, Israeli settler colonialism has vacillated between these two logics. Englert and many others emphasise the eliminatory logic. While radically extended after 7 October 2023, with the unleashing of a US-backed Israeli war machine on Gaza, attempts to eradicate Palestinian lives had been unfolding at an uneven pace for decades prior. The crippling of Palestinian institutions and practices of life-making is evident in the multiple checkpoints that obstruct and delay Palestinians in the West Bank and Gaza travelling to schools, hospitals, work, and shops; Israeli settlements diverting water that originally flowed to Palestinian households and fields; the siege of Gaza limiting food imports to the bare minimum daily nutritional allowance for Gazan children; the escalating invasions and bombings of universities and hospitals, and the targeted murders and detentions of professors and doctors.

Even so, Palestinian life-making continued. In large part, that has to do with the sheer strength and will of the Palestinian people. Despite all odds, Palestinians commit to a personal and collective future by building and rebuilding homes, families, schools, hospitals, markets, and more. And by creating art, poetry, music, and stories. These are means not only of sustaining themselves but also of finding cracks in the systems that dominate them, and of fortifying their resistance against their occupiers. As chapter after chapter in this volume shows, Palestinians' ongoing life-making on land they refuse to leave or forget weaves together acts of survival, flourishing, and resistance.

Yet the elimination–resistance axis is not the only dynamic we need to analyse when considering the social reproduction of the Palestinian peoples. The Zionist state's eliminatory impulses have also competed with Israeli capital's efforts to turn Palestinians into a cheap, mobile labour force.[4] As Shireen Akram-Boshar notes, the numbers of Palestinian workers participating in the Israeli economy vastly expanded in the aftermath of the Israeli occupation of the West Bank and Gaza in 1967. At that time, authorities heightened Palestinians' economic dependency on Israel by using work permits as "bargaining chips to pressure families against activism and resistance".[5] Then, with the uptick in resistance during the First and Second Intifadas, the logic of exploitation receded. Palestinian workers were sent back to the West Bank and Gaza, as migrant workers from elsewhere filled their shoes inside Israel. More recently, in the latter years of the 2010s and before 7 October 2023, Israeli capital had once again started treating Palestinians in Gaza and the West Bank as a convenient, low-wage labour pool. In November of 2023, however, Israel expelled about 12,000 Palestinian workers, forcing them to walk to Gaza, where the now unmitigated exterminationist mission of settler colonialism prevailed.[6]

This nuance – Israel's vacillation between eliminatory and exploitative tendencies – is important. Along with illustrating settler colonialism's entanglement with global capitalist dynamics (and vice versa), it underlines the degree to which the work of social reproduction is freighted, even in settler colonial projects in which the threat of Indigenous genocide is ever-present. Matters are further complicated when we consider the difficult conditions and contradictions involved in socially reproducing the Indigenous peoples of Palestine in relation to the social reproduction of Israeli citizens. As a number of essays in this volume illustrate, it is not just Israeli capital that profits from the depletion of Palestinian life-making. So too do Israeli citizens – in complex and differentiated ways. That complexity is perhaps most starkly evidenced in the use Israeli settlers make of Palestinian labour to pick crops and build homes and roads, while their very settlement is premised on *eliminating* Palestinians, on erasing Palestinian life on Palestinian land.[7]

There is much for SRT to disentangle in all this, and this book – by grounding theory in the concrete history of a small but weighty place, Palestine – is a modest contribution to that effort. The essays to follow explore that history in ways that reveal and assess the continuum between life-making and death-making that characterises the Israeli settler colonial regime of social reproduction. SRT, however, does not just theorise the depletion and alienation of life-making forces. It recognises and celebrates the fact that although capital relies on workers' social reproduction, life and life-making exceed capital. *Celebrates* because it is in that excess that resistance resides. Marx guides us in this reasoning when he explains in the Paris Manuscripts that, even to complete the most basic tasks, humans employ intentional practices adhering to aesthetic standards. The struggle against domination then begins here, with our capacity as humans to make life and (re)make ourselves purposively "in accordance with the laws of beauty".[8]

Finally, it is important for us to state here that this book was written during a genocide. A genocide committed openly by the terrorist state of Israel, cheered on by the global ruling class, as the television cameras rolled to bring its minutest violent detail to the entire world. There is thus an unfinished quality to this project; a disorder that we are proud of. Many of our contributors lost friends and family during the writing of this book. As editors, we are humbled by their commitment. We are also proud to be part of the global protests that erupted in response to the genocide. All proceeds from the book's royalties will therefore be donated to the Palestinian charity *Taawon*, which has created a programme to rebuild the major universities in Gaza.[9]

As editors and contributors, we see this book both as a disobedience and a promise. We will never submit to writing history without Palestine and settler colonialism, and we make a promise here to continue to organise till Palestine is free.

This book then is also about *flourishing* – life-making over and above mere survival. It analyses and celebrates the ways in which Palestinians, despite the odds, have insisted on living, and living life fully. They have done so through their dream of return, their committed pursuit of education and healthcare, their poetry, art, dance, food, and more. They have done so through their brave and committed struggles against the Israeli state both within and beyond the borders. These are purposive, conscious labours that not only sustain themselves but, crucially, sow the seeds of resistance. They also enclose the very essence of our species being.

NOTES

1. Inlakesh, "Hussam Abu Safyia".
2. Bhattacharya, *Social Reproduction Theory*.
3. Englert, *Settler Colonialism*.
4. For accounts of the fluctuations in labour flows from the occupied Palestinian territories to Israel and West Bank settlements, see Roy, "De-Development Revisited"; Maharmeh, "Israel's Exploitation"; and Hackl, "Occupied Labour".
5. Akram-Boshar, "Recentering Indigenous Resistance". Akram-Boshar argues that Palestinian resistance has been "the key factor" in Israel's shift away from reliance on Palestinian labour.
6. Akram-Boshar, "Recentering Indigenous Resistance". After 7 October, Israel also cancelled work permits of more than 140,000 West Bank and Gaza Palestinians, detaining thousands illegally (Maharmeh, "Israel's Exploitation").
7. Just prior to October 2023, the number of Palestinian men working in illegal Israeli settlements had peaked at 27,000, employed mostly in agriculture and construction. While only a tiny proportion of Palestinian women workers are employed in the settlements, their numbers are growing at an exponential rate: from 0.7 per cent in 2018 to 3.4 per cent today. The "vast majority" of these women work without contracts, long hours under harsh conditions and for very low pay (Oxfam, "Palestinian Women", 8 and *passim*). Settlements also rely on Palestinian child labour (see Human Rights Watch, "Ripe for Abuse").
8. Marx, *Economic & Philosophic Manuscripts* (1964), 114.
9. Information about this programme can be found on the *Taawon* website, www.taawon.org/en/isnad.

2

Gaza: Care, Hope, and Genocide

Asmaa AbuMezied

It is now 18 months of the ongoing Israeli genocide on Gaza, an unprecedented event in our collective lifetime. Reports on the devastation highlight the immense loss of life and extensive destruction of infrastructure. Academic scholarship has offered frameworks such as scholasticide, urbicide, ecocide, cultural genocide, medicide, and domicide to contextualise the gravity of these atrocities. Nevertheless, the narratives shared by my family, friends and voices from Gaza on social media reveal a far more intricate reality that receives minimal attention. This chapter seeks to illuminate some of these complexities by examining, through the frameworks of necropolitical control introduced by Achille Mbembe and social reproduction theory, the systems and structures of care that have been, both historically and presently, systematically annihilated.[1] Before delving into their destruction, it is crucial to understand the foundational care structures that defined Gaza's society and its role in collective survival.

Gazan society has mainly been studied as part of the overall Palestinian society, particularly after 1948 and 1967. I draw on this larger context to explore how care structures in the twentieth century and early 2000s were shaped by both historical resilience and forced adaptation to the Israeli systematic violence. Palestinian society has long cherished a tradition of social solidarity, where community members supported one another through networks of mutual care. This solidarity originated in older rural lifestyles and village-centric social structures, which depended on and hence emphasised collective responsibility and mutual aid. However, the demographic reconfiguration of Gaza since 1948, when Israel forcibly displaced and confined over 200,000 Palestinians to the Gaza Strip – a fraction of the former Qada Gaza, which encompassed 54 villages and three major cities – socially re-engineered community relations.[2] Forced into densely populated refugee camps, particularly within the Gaza Strip, Palestinians developed an intimate communal life marked by physical closeness and national struggle for liberation. Gaza, now home to 2.3 million people within a compact area of 365 square kilometres, fosters a sense of collective experience and emotional understanding of the Israeli violence exercised over decades. Yet, it is essential not to idealise this social fabric, which is imperfect and complex, and has been subjected to sustained attacks aimed at eroding its capacity for care. This forced displacement necessitated the reimagining of care structures under conditions of settler colonialism.

Social reproduction theory (SRT) helps us understand this systematic targeting of care because it emphasises the essential structures that sustain daily life and collective well-being.[3] In what follows, I use the broad definition of "care structures" to encompass formal services like education, healthcare, and informal support systems such as social relationships, connections to land and space, as well as collective memory and imagination. This broadened perspective allows for a nuanced analysis of how Israeli policies and actions have impacted Palestinian social reproduction, particularly in light of Tithi Bhattacharya's adaptation of concepts of "life-making" and "flourishing".[4] Within this framework, the social reproduction of life in Gaza is not only a matter of economic or physical survival but also involves the continuity of community identity, memory, and collective future-building under the Israeli settler colonialism.

After the *Nakba*, dual imperatives of survival and resistance reconfigured Gaza's care structures. Historically, while the Israeli occupation deliberately targeted critical infrastructure to weaken social cohesion and disrupt daily life, Palestinians responded with innovative grassroots networks that became essential to collective survival. The First Intifada (1987–1993) serves as a pivotal example of this dynamic, where popular committees emerged to provide essential services under occupation.[5] This grassroots-led care system transcended mere survival; it nurtured the continuity of community identity, memory, and solidarity, aligning with Bhattacharya's concept of "life-making". However, these organic structures faced significant transformation in the post-Oslo period, as the rise of NGOisation replaced grassroots mobilisation with donor-driven priorities.[6] Internationally funded civil society organisations adopted professionalised frameworks that often prioritised development projects over the resistance-oriented care of the Intifada era. While NGOs played an important role in delivering services and conducting international advocacy, their increasing detachment from grassroots movements reflected broader neoliberal trends, and "antipolitics of care".[7] These shifts reshaped care networks in Palestine in general and in Gaza.

Beyond grassroots efforts, Gaza's care structures have historically relied on a constellation of actors to sustain daily life. UNRWA remains central, providing services like education, healthcare, and emergency assistance. Gaza accounts for 40 per cent of UNRWA's schools, serving over 290,000 students, and its 22 healthcare facilities in Gaza receive over 3.3 million annual visits.[8] Additionally, 67 per cent of Palestinian refugees receiving its emergency food assistance are located in Gaza, reflecting the extent to which these services, though very politicised, sustain daily life under the Israeli settler colonialism. The Palestinian household is another pivotal provider of care, shaped by traditional gendered dynamics and economic inequality, with women playing a central role in unpaid domestic labour and filling gaps created by depleted public infrastructure. Community-level mutual aid initiatives also complement household care, addressing needs in times of death, poverty, and violence. Civil society organisations, while increasingly professionalised by international donors, supplement these efforts with specialised healthcare, income-generating programmes, and emergency relief.[9] Lastly, the government also provides public facilities, managing 55 per cent of schools, 13 hospitals, and 55 primary healthcare centres. Yet, the interplay between these layers of care highlights a central tension: while care structures continue to support Palestinians' survival, they coexist with Israeli infrastructural violence and are persistently shaped by external dependency.

GAZA BEFORE 2023: INFRASTRUCTURE WARFARE AND SOCIAL REPRODUCTION

Necropolitical control in Gaza manifests through targeted infrastructure warfare, where repeated destruction of essential services systematically depletes resources critical for social continuity and daily survival. Two decades of the blockade on Gaza, and recurrent military aggressions function not just as tools of warfare but as mechanisms of control over the conditions of life itself, and function as a "genocide by attrition" as termed by Helen Fein and elaborated by scholars like Richard Falk and Ilan Pappé, who describe it as "incremental genocide."[10] This genocide by attrition inflicts slow, cumulative destruction that depletes the resources essential for life-making and social continuity.

The constraints imposed by the blockade and ongoing infrastructure destruction exemplify what Honaida Ghanim terms *Thanatopower* – the management of death and destruction, where the pervasive threat of death becomes woven into the fabric of daily life.[11] Ghanim articulates, in Gaza, "death is just on hold, again and again, from moment to moment". Yet I argue that the environment of death extends beyond mere threat, as indicated by Ghanim. Infrastructure violence makes death a continuous process that shapes daily experience, altering perceptions of normalcy and forcing life into survival mode. This ongoing Israeli management of death infiltrates and conditions every aspect of social reproduction, restructuring, through infrastructure violence, daily life, and interrupting the capacity to sustain family, community, and societal norms. In Gaza, the sounds of drones, artillery shelling, and missiles light the night sky, instilling a visceral reminder of mortality. Death manifests not only in these violent displays but also in its creeping presence in the lives of those who cannot access critical medical treatments or who are permanently impacted by disability, and as a result of Israeli aggressions. Death takes hold every second in the soul of Gaza, and its people, configuring normal life and threatening to kill their spirit.

Omar Jabary Salamanca's discussion of "infrastructural violence" as a form of spatial control and asphyxiation can shed light on the slow social reproduction depletion experienced by Gaza during the Israeli siege beginning in 2007.[12] Israel's attacks on Gaza's only power plant in 2014, which plunged the area into darkness and compounded energy poverty, exemplify this asphyxiation approach to governance. This intentional degradation of infrastructure disrupts daily life, especially for women, who are forced to restructure their routines around electricity schedules and fuel shortages. Such policies render household appliances like refrigerators and washing machines ineffective, amplifying the burden on women as primary caregivers and reinforcing gendered inequalities in domestic labour. Palestinians must continuously reconfigure their daily lives, often resorting to midnight chores, as the occupation dictates the availability of even the most basic services. Meanwhile, the continuous asphyxiation of water reserves and sanitation infrastructures left Palestinians with the only option of dumping raw and partially treated sewage in the Mediterranean Sea and Wadi Gaza, violating their relationship as custodians of nature. These structures of control alternate between slow death through deprivation and high-intensity killing, placing Palestinians in Mbembe's "world of death" where any assertion of life or resistance to passivity of victimhood risks brutal suppression. For instance, Israel's restrictions on movement, resource access, and infrastructure in Gaza function as structural violence, undermining the Palestinian ability to maintain the very care systems essential for collective survival. Through these forms of control, Palestinians' ability to manage their spaces and time is profoundly constrained.

Israel's sustained assaults on Gaza's infrastructure – both through military operations and policies of deprivation – have a devastating impact on the social reproduction of Gaza's community life. In Shuja'iyya and Khuza'a, neighbourhoods that were reduced to "deserts" during the 2014 Israeli military aggression, entire communities have faced not only the loss of family members but also the destruction of their homes, memories, and cultural sites. As Israeli soldiers recounted in interviews with Breaking the Silence, an organization of Israeli veterans that aims to expose the everyday reality of and foster public debate about the occupation, these areas were methodically targeted, rendering them inhospitable and stripping people of familiarity and ties to the land.[13] Palestinians are forced to reinvest any remaining savings into rebuilding, often indebting themselves just to restore some semblance of a safe space.

This destruction of infrastructure, accompanied by a painstakingly slow reconstruction process, drains the resources of the exhausted Palestinian population. The UN has estimated, then, that it would take 75 years to rebuild Gaza after the 2008–2009 offensive alone, which was followed by 2012, 2014, 2021, and 2022 Israeli aggressions before the 2023 genocide – all of which underscores the bleak future imposed on Gaza's residents. As infrastructure violences intensifies, the repeated cycles of destruction in areas like Beit Lahia and eastern Khan Yunis, lead to the cumulative depletion of resources, deepening Palestinian fragility and precarity. This cycle is not merely economic but affects the very foundations of social reproduction, where the community's ability to sustain life, care for its members, and maintain resilience is eroded with each new wave of aggression. Every time there is an attack, individuals are forced to use whatever limited resources they have on immediate, essential reconstruction. By the third or fourth cycle of destruction, they are operating in a state of minus resources, unable to restore even basic stability and shackled by a continual depletion of essential material and emotional reserves.

By systematically creating disabilities and health crises that make people reliant on constant care, Israeli forces effectively sap Palestinians' capacity for resistance and self-sufficiency. Israeli policies, such as targeting medical personnel or "shoot-to-cripple" tactics during the Great March of Return, are designed to incapacitate Gaza's population physically, socially, and economically. Infrastructure violence depletes the resources essential for care work and forces households and communities into subsistence, limiting their ability to organise and resist.

Despite these pervasive conditions, Palestinians in Gaza continue to create and maintain communities as acts of survival and defiance. Communitarianism in Gaza extends beyond mere support systems to become a form of resistance against attempts to reduce them to bare life. From the high rate of adopting solar energy at the household level to reduce the care responsibilities shouldered by women to the Great March of Return protests, as described by Lori Allen – which became spaces for the community to assert agency and resilience, where Palestinians established medical tents, cultural gatherings, and support structures for protestors – these acts are symbolic of a broader Palestinian refusal to acquiesce to the occupation's narrative.[14] Maintaining community in Gaza – through social, cultural, and care structures – is a deliberate assertion of life that stands in opposition to an environment of slow death.

IMPACT OF 2023 ISRAELI GENOCIDE
ON THESE STRUCTURES OF CARE

In October 2023, Israel intensified its tactics to dismantle Gaza's care structures, from healthcare system bombardments to restrictions on food and medical supplies, decimating the community's survival mechanisms. The Independent International Commission of Inquiry's report to the Human Rights Council described the reproductive violence Palestinians experience and marked October 2023 as the deadliest month ever documented for Palestinian women in Gaza.[15] Central to this campaign is the strategy of dehumanisation – a calculated effort to strip Palestinians of their personhood and, in turn, legitimise violence. This dehumanising discourse, long directed at Palestinian communities in historic Palestine, West Bank, and Gaza, as Nadera Shalhoub-Kevorkian notes in her work on Bedouin communities, has intensified in the current Israeli genocide on Gaza.[16] By labelling Palestinians as "inhuman animals", as did former Israeli UN Ambassador Dan Gillerman, Israeli officials seek to dampen international criticism of their actions and normalise brutality.[17] Other officials actively promote infrastructural violence as a form of dominance; Israeli Defense Minister Yoav Gallant declared a "complete siege" on Gaza on 9 October 2023, blocking access to basic necessities like food, water, and fuel.[18] Former Israeli Minister Moshe Feiglin went further, calling for the "complete destruction of Gaza" and comparing it to the bombings of Dresden and Hiroshima.[19] These statements reflect a deliberate strategy of calculated annihilation, an approach that views Gaza not as a region to coexist with but as a target to obliterate. Feiglin later intensified this rhetoric on social media, suggesting the need to extinguish any hope in Gaza.[20] The targeting of water resources, encouraged by Giora Eiland rhetoric to "make Gaza an impossible place to live, temporarily or permanently", exemplify the weaponisation of basic life-sustaining elements as a key tactic of what Daniel Feierstein refer to as genocidal social practices.[21]

Structural Violence on Health

During the current Israeli genocide, Gaza's healthcare system has been systematically dismantled through targeted Israeli attacks, with hospitals, clinics, and medical supplies limited to enforce a state of chronic healthcare dependency and depletion. According to a recent assessment from the United Nations, two-thirds of Gaza's structures have sustained damage.[22] This includes 297,000 housing units and severe devastation across educational facilities, with 122 schools and universities destroyed and 334 more partially damaged. Israel's focus on two pillars of Palestinian society – the healthcare sector and people's homes – reflects a strategic effort to disrupt connections vital for social reproduction and the maintenance of Palestinian identity.

In implementing these objectives, Israel has deployed a variety of tactics to obstruct initiatives essential to life-making and life-sustaining practices. By July 2024, approximately 549 Israeli attacks have been recorded against the Palestinian healthcare system in Gaza, resulting in 22 hospitals being rendered non-operational.[23] Many of these hospitals have suffered direct Israeli missile strikes or siege on their premises, cutting access and isolating patients and medical staff, with some enduring multiple Israeli invasions.[24] Furthermore, the Human Rights Council report indicated a systemic Israeli targeting of reproductive clinics and health providers such as the destruction of Al-Basma IVF clinic.[25] On 13 November 2023, the Israeli military, via its official social media channel, briefly published (and later deleted) a post labelling hospitals and ambulances as "legitimate military targets". Shortly thereafter, a senior Israeli official acknowledged that no hostages were located at Al-Shifa Hospital, framing the raid as a symbolic act to demonstrate that "no place is beyond reach".[26] This campaign of targeting hospitals and medical centres forms a critical component of the broader effort to displace Palestinians from Gaza City and the Northern governorates. It simultaneously redefines Palestinians' relationship with health spaces – from secure sanctuaries in times of violence to pathologised spaces of absolute mortality and violation after death through bioviolence and organ harvesting as reported by local authorities.[27]

Moreover, the assault extends beyond buildings to include the destruction of 133 ambulances and the deliberate targeting of medical personnel and civil defence volunteers tasked with rescuing individuals trapped under rubble. Israel has also detained many healthcare professionals, including doctors, nurses, and civil defence workers, as well as patients, from various hospitals in Gaza.[28] This approach serves a dual purpose: to immediately remove healthcare providers from the field and to disable their capacity to provide care in any future context. A harrowing account from Dr Essam Abu Ajwa, a 63-year-old physician, underscores the brutality of these measures. Dr Abu Ajwa endured sustained torture, during which Israeli soldiers repeatedly threatened to "paralyze [his] hands so [he] could never return to being a doctor". By the time of his release, Dr Abu Ajwa had lost 95 per cent of sensation in his hands. When he questioned his torturers about their perception of doctors, he was told: "You are illegal fighters".[29] This statement encapsulates a broader narrative within the Israeli military's documented communications, which categorise health infrastructure as "legitimate military targets" and reflects the vital role healthcare workers play in maintaining Palestinian existence. The calculated destruction of healthcare and educational facilities not only disrupts immediate care provision but also enforces a form of social death by severing Palestinians from essential resources for survival and collective identity.

Israel's control over the entry of medical supplies, during the past 18 months, illustrates its necropolitical policies wherein structures critical to preserving life are systemically compromised or weaponised to perpetuate a sense of inescapable vulnerability. Only minimal and often inadequate medical supplies were initially permitted, failing to meet the pressing healthcare needs in Gaza. Instead of urgently required medical equipment, shipments included items with limited utility, symbolising a form of deliberate deprivation. The entry of burial shrouds in place of essential medicines starkly conveyed a symbolic message, as if suggesting that death, rather than healing, is the expected outcome for Palestinians under the genocide.

The Israeli targeting of medical centres during campaigns designed to promote health, such as polio vaccination drives, underscores a deliberate tactic of transforming spaces of life-preservation into arenas of death and violence. For instance, Israeli drone strikes on medical centres administering polio vaccines turned efforts to protect children's health into acts of annihilation, weaponising these health initiatives as psychological warfare.[30] This tactic not only physically harms but erodes community trust in spaces of care and safety, amplifying the psychological trauma of Gaza's population. The polio vaccination campaign becomes emblematic of a broader strategy that repurposes life-saving efforts into deadly traps, profoundly undermining resilience and communal capacity to endure ongoing violence.

By systematically dismantling healthcare facilities, the Israeli military strategy enforces psychological subjugation through capitalising on the profound psychological and social significance of hospitals, which serve not only as sites of care but also as symbols of hope, through the efforts of rebuilding while the genocide is still going, within a community. The assaults serve a dual purpose: they physically deprive Palestinians of life-sustaining resources and simultaneously signal an erasure of their aspirations for a future.

In the absence of traditional healthcare structures, Palestinian households, particularly women, assume critical caregiving roles in displacement camps and tents where conditions facilitate the spread of intestinal, respiratory, and skin infections. Theories of biopolitical governance highlight how, in the context of restricted medical resources, the burden of healthcare shifts to individual households, with women's labour compensating for the enforced absence of institutional care. This imposed caregiving responsibility not only exacerbates physical and emotional exhaustion but places women on the frontline of resistance to survival, threatening conditions without adequate support. Furthermore, the deliberate restriction of food supplies contributes to a strategy of starvation as a weapon of control, increasing rates of child stunting and mortality and pregnant and lactating women vulnerability to food insecurity. Meanwhile, the systematic targeting of Palestinian bodies to induce long-term disabilities – through drone attacks and sniper fire – serves as a biopolitical tool that debilitates future generations by rendering the body physically incapacitated within an environment of destroyed infrastructure. The creation of long-term disabilities leaves a legacy of constant suffering, a reminder of the consequences of resistance, and exponentially intensifies the present and future caregiving responsibilities borne by Palestinian women. These cumulative burdens deplete Palestinian women's mental and physical resources, cementing a cycle of intergenerational trauma and systematic disempowerment that further compounds the devastating impacts of structural violence.

DISPLACEMENT AND SOCIAL FABRIC DYNAMICS

Displacement in Gaza not only uproots families physically but deeply under-mines the social bonds that form the core of communal resilience, leading to fragmentation that hinders collective survival and resistance. Feierstein's examination of genocide as a form of social practice provides a critical framework for understanding the systematic logic aimed at annihilating Pal-estinian society. In this view, displacement is not merely about territory but about dissolving social bonds, communities, and collective identity.

In Gaza, the Israeli act of forcibly removing Palestinians from their neigh-bourhoods severs decades-old relationships, fragments family units, and dismantles community structures as people forcibly move to new locations, creating a climate of isolation and vulnerability. This introduction to the idea of displacement as social engineering lays the groundwork for under-standing the deeply embedded and multilayered consequences of Israel's policies on Palestinian society, framing these actions not merely as isolated events but also as systematic attempts to erase the social fabric of resistance.

Israel's propaganda furthers this goal by drawing a divisive line between the people "above ground" – civilians enduring displacement and violence – and those "underneath the ground", the resistance fighters and instigating them against each other. The words of Isaac Herzog, Israeli president, encap-sulate using collective punishment as an instigating strategy: "It's an entire nation out there that is responsible. This rhetoric about civilians not aware, not involved, it's absolutely not true. They could've risen up, they could have fought against that evil regime."[31] Consequently, Israel deployed unprec-edented brutality on Palestinians in Gaza, from starvation, aid collection massacres, burning people alive, to complete obliteration of neighbour-hoods with Israeli soldiers documenting and sharing their violation of Palestinian private spaces through wearing women's lingerie. The more those "underneath the ground" resisted, and those "above ground" existed, the more severe the punishments Israel imposed on those "above ground"; Israeli army messages to People in Gaza in October 2023 and in the follow-ing months stating "everyone who hasn't evacuated from northern Gaza to the south might be treated as a member of a terrorist organization" reinforce this punishment.[32] And Israel's AI-aided system, Lavender, tracking resist-ant fighters through WhatsApp and targeting them along with their families and children, aims to undermine community and household support for resistance.[33] As such support weakens, there is a danger that Palestinians as a people lose a sense of their historical role as the bedrock and incubator of the resistance movement.

As displacement stripped Palestinian families of their resources, the aid industry – comprising both local and international organisations, along with volunteer networks – emerged as the principal provider of essential services around displacement camps. Yet, these so-called "care structures" often failed to uphold dignified standards of community care uniformly, particularly in campaigns fuelled by collective funding launched on the GoFundMe platform. The genocide created a disturbing opportunity for some to exploit global sympathy for the people of Gaza, engaging in misappropriation and manipulation in the guise of humanitarian aid, often misrepresenting or fabricating the distribution of resources to Palestinians.

In many cases, aid campaigns devolved into performative acts of charity; it became routine to photograph Palestinian recipients with their aid packages and prompt them to record thank-you videos to satisfy the expectations of those who donate, ensuring continued contributions. Such practices, under the pretext of care, in reality strip Palestinians of their dignity, transforming acts of humanitarian assistance into displays of "beneficiary" dependency. This dynamic, as highlighted in Linda Polman's book, *The Crisis Caravan*, underscores the paradox within the aid industry: while these campaigns claim to uphold care, they frequently prioritise the optics of generosity over the actual well-being and autonomy of those they purport to assist, thereby perpetuating a cycle of exploitation that ultimately undermines the very dignity and agency of the displaced.[34]

The Palestinian household persists as a crucial site for survival amid the ongoing tactics of displacement designed to destabilise and fracture this essential social unit. Scholars such as Mohandise and Teitelman have examined the household as a "site of oppression", particularly in its gendered dimensions, a phenomenon keenly observed in Gaza.[35] Yet, settler colonialism, exemplified in Israel's systematic policies, intensifies this oppression by repurposing the household into a tool of social engineering, eroding the stability of Palestinian society through displacement and the imposition of transient, impermanent shelters. Rather than homes, these temporary structures foster physical and psychological instability, as families are forced to seek refuge in the remaining intact buildings of friends and extended family, creating extreme overcrowding – often with upwards of a hundred individuals sharing a single household.

Such forced cohabitation under intense trauma, as Shalhoub-Kevorkian's research underscores, disrupts traditional social dynamics and imposes a strain on familial relationships, impeding the household's function as a nurturing environment. The high density and scarcity of resources drive new, intimate interactions that are often fraught with tension, giving rise to conflicts over basic needs, space, and privacy. Daily life thus becomes laden with friction, as trivial disputes escalate in these high-stress conditions. This fracturing of the household fabric reflects what Cinzia Arruzza identifies as the disintegration of social reproductive capacities under capitalist and colonial pressures, whereby the household, once a source of relative stability and mutual support, becomes a site of social disintegration and conflict.[36]

The damage to social cohesion is not merely a temporary response to the current crisis, nor another layer in accumulative fractured social fabric, but risks long-lasting repercussions on Palestinian social fabric expediting their "social death". Relationships are strained to the extent that, as some individuals confess, through personal discussions, they anticipate severing ties with family members once the current intensification of genocidal violence ceases, evidencing a rupture in relational continuity that may take years to repair, if at all. This erosion of the household's connective tissue weakens the ability of families to provide mutual care and support, compromising the very framework through which collective resilience has traditionally been nurtured.

This dynamic further pushes the Palestinian community towards "social death", limiting its ability to function as a caring social unit. The systematic erosion of both physical and social infrastructures not only depletes resources but also erases vital spaces of gathering and support, fraying the communal bonds essential for collective survival. Social death here manifests as the gradual dissolution of the structures and relationships that sustain life, as residents are prevented from maintaining the routines, connections, and shared resources that define community life. Consequently, the community's capacity to resist, recover, and rebuild is strategically weakened, rendering it perpetually vulnerable to successive aggressions.

IMAGINARY: THE ARTICULATION OF LIFE AND DEATH

The Arabic inscription on one of Gaza's wall, "ومات من نجا. نحن صامدون" "لقد نجا من مات،") ("Those who died survived, and those who survived death died. We are here steadfast"), profoundly reflects the complex existential reality Palestinians in Gaza have come to embody after enduring prolonged genocide. This sentiment, captured beside a Palestinian woman from Gaza weeping amid the rubble, conveys a philosophical and lived perception of life and death shaped by systemic Israeli violence. The Israeli policies over the past eight decades have effectively denied Palestinians the possibility of a life of dignity. Instead, they are presented with a brutal choice between a gradual death through the siege, deprivation of fundamental rights, and a swift death from the military technologies supplied by global arms networks; or between "genocide by attrition" and swift-killing genocide. Within this framework, death paradoxically becomes a form of liberation from the intensifying violence that those left alive are forced to endure daily.

The normalisation and acceptance of death in Gaza is not a rejection of life or a devaluation of its meaning; rather, it is an assertion of autonomy amid unspeakable brutality and global passive complicity. Palestinians' profound love for life manifests at every available opportunity, yet they are forced to confront death as a pathway to agency – a repudiation of the relentless violence inflicted upon them. This response echoes Naji Al-Ali's iconic Handala, the cartoon figure who embodies a rejection of imposed solutions and an insistence on dignity, symbolising Palestinians' refusal and resistance to enforced suffering. Through this acceptance, Palestinians in Gaza assert agency over their fate by being okay with the idea of death, reclaiming a modicum of control amid structures designed to strip them of it.

Bhattacharya's concept of "life-sustaining labour" complements this discourse, as Palestinians' actions in striving for normalcy – planting trees, reopening markets, or simply walking through their neighbourhoods – constitute efforts to sustain life against genocidal obliteration. Such acts of life are inherently political, a testament to resistance, but are also subjected to targeted violence aimed at severing these expressions. This dynamic, termed by Ghanim as "giving death and bargaining living",[37] defines a reality in Gaza where each semblance of life and every gathering space are deliberately struck by violence to reinforce the illusion that death is inevitable and omnipresent.

THE CONNECTION WITH THE LAND: RE-ENGINEERING OF THE SPACE

Israel's long-standing reshaping of Palestinian connections to their land is embedded in its agricultural and economic policies, continually restructuring Palestinian relationships with the land towards dependency, dispossession, or outright removal. However, the current escalation reveals an intensified erasure: Israel's bombing campaign renders Gaza's neighbourhoods unrecognisable, stripped of the familiar smells, vibrant streets, food, cherished locales, beaches, and deeply rooted memories that define Palestinian life. This transformation has led to a collective mourning as people share images of Gaza from before October 2023 or post long descriptions of the painstaking efforts invested in building their homes, tending to the herbs they grew, and the sounds that once filled their spaces. The loss of these places – a physical and emotional extension of their identities – leaves Palestinians in an enduring state of grief.

The attack on Gaza is not only on its infrastructure but on the essence of the land itself. The process of re-engineering familiar spaces, with towns like Jabalia obliterated to the point where returning residents cannot recognise their neighbourhoods, is emblematic of an intention to dismantle Palestinian continuity with their land. Infrastructure annihilation, a core element of Israel's policies, recalls the ideology of Israel's founder, Theodor Herzl, who stated, "If I wish to substitute a new building for an old one, I must demolish before I construct".[38] Advertisements by Israeli real estate companies promoted the selling of beach houses on Gaza's land illustrate the extent of this vision – not just replacement, but the elimination of any connection between Palestinians and their land, with the latter embodying Palestinian identity and heritage.[39]

This manufactured disconnection includes the Israeli deliberate targeting of agriculture and the brutal destruction of farming communities, actions aimed at breaking Palestinians' physical and cultural bonds with their environment. The systematic devastation of farmland, orchards, and gardens attacks the Palestinians' means of survival, intensifying the paralysis of grief they endure. While they were also forced to cut the remaining trees to build tents, light fires, and obtain wood for cooking, it continues to fracture Palestinians' relation with the land and their historical role as its guardians.

Despite facing "thanatopolitics", Palestinians resist with efforts rooted in life-making and sustenance. An example of this is Yousef Abu Rabee's grassroots campaign, "Northern Gaza Produces", which mobilised the community in a grassroots effort to repurpose all available seeds, cultivating homes and shelters to promote self-sustenance through local food production. Yousef's work was not only to combat starvation but an act of commemorative resistance, aimed at restoring Beit Lahia's legacy as a life-giving, green area; to transfer the land that became a desert due to the Israeli army bombing and bulldozing agricultural lands.

Yousef's life and work in Beit Lahia embodied a deep-rooted resistance to erasure, illustrating how survival in Gaza becomes an act of cultural and existential defiance. Even as they faced continuous threats, Yousef and his colleagues persisted in cultivating land, as he and other farmers transformed scorched land into over 200 dunums of life-bearing crops like eggplant and zucchini – turning soil ravaged by bombardment into a symbol of renewal, hope, and memory. Israel's assassination of Yousef and his colleagues while working in his nursery, where they produced 150,000 seedlings, underscores the extent to which its strategies seek to eradicate life-sustaining practices that nurture community resilience and cultural continuity.

Palestinians have developed resistant senses – a set of embodied sensory skills honed under Israeli settler colonial conditions, where survival has become an assertion of life in the face of structural violence. This adaptive response is more than resilience; it is a deep-seated, necessity-driven *resistance* that affirms life in an environment that continually imposes threats of annihilation. In Gaza, where Israeli military actions sustain perpetual death, these sensory skills represent a cultivated form of survival knowledge – a set of practices born not necessarily from a space of "resilience"[40] but from an unyielding will to live.

Palestinians' interaction with their militarised surroundings is reflected in what Edward Soja and Henri Lefebvre describe as "spatial survival literacy", where space actively shapes human survival tactics and behaviours.[41] Palestinians in Gaza, therefore, develop an acute awareness of environmental cues, distinguishing between the sounds of drones, F-16s, and F-35s, while performing acts of self-preservation like covering their ears to lessen the impact of missile blasts or keeping onions nearby to counteract the effects of white phosphorus. This "spatial survival literacy" becomes a learned response, embedded in everyday life, through which Palestinians engage in a perpetual struggle against the technologies of death that dictate their environment.

Such resistant senses are not individual but collective, cultivated across generations and forming part of Gaza's communal survival fabric. These adaptive practices are woven into the social fabric as intergenerational knowledge, transferred from parent to child as a necessary skill set – a toolkit for navigating a landscape shaped by structural violence. Each new Israeli military technology requires that Palestinians modify these practices, recalibrating their sensory responses to evolving threats. The use of "silent bombs", which obscure any auditory indication of origin or target, adds a new layer of vulnerability, necessitating constant recalibration of survival strategies in response to changing warfare tactics. This process of reproducing survival knowledge builds on Silvia Federici's discussions of communal practices and shared knowledge systems to maintain life.[42]

As the genocide continues, these resistant senses increasingly dominate, overtaking the sensory experiences that defined Palestinian life before October 2023. The familiar sounds and smells of daily life – birdsong after a rainy day, the aroma of coffee, the gentle chatter of water trucks, the scent of trees – are eclipsed by the sensory overload of genocide. Some Palestinians engage in rituals to preserve sensory memories, transferring them into digital spaces through collective acts of remembrance. Videos and images of Gaza, as it once was, are being shared widely, creating a collective archive of pre-genocide memories. For others, like my sister, the moments when internet access is available become opportunities to reconnect with life's gentler pleasures by watching videos of cooking, libraries, or everyday activities – efforts to hold on to a sense of normalcy and resist the erasure of their sensory connection to life as they knew it. These practices represent a quiet yet profound assertion of presence and identity, a refusal to let the destruction sever their ties to their past and their culture.

HOPE AND HOPELESSNESS: A TOOL OF WARFARE OR SURVIVAL

Saleem Saleem recounts a harrowing ordeal when his father was gravely injured after an Israeli missile strike targeted a neighbouring home. Hours later, his sister managed to pull their father from beneath the rubble.[43] Shortly thereafter, the Israeli army issued evacuation orders, presenting a fleeting opportunity to transfer him to Gaza City for medical treatment after the area was sealed off as a military zone. Yet, even within the confines of the hospital where his father was transferred, hope was undermined. The Israeli military attacked that medical facility in Gaza City, forcing out patients and individuals who sought refuge. Saleem's oscillation between hope and despair – embodied by his family's momentary relief followed by renewed violence – mirrors the broader Palestinian experience in Gaza, where moments of potential reprieve are consistently overshadowed.

Orouba Othman's concept of "hope as a tool of genocide" illustrates how hope is weaponised within Gaza as a means of engineered extermination, with aid and relief campaigns crafted to create the illusion of change and sustenance while concealing a deeper system of eradication.[44] Under this lens, fleeting access to food and medical aid becomes a tool of managed death, a "mirage of hope" that Palestinians chase even as it brings renewed cycles of death. Lindroth and Sinevaara-Niskanen echo this political economy of hope, revealing how hope itself becomes a pacifying force, offering brief relief to maintain allegiance to the occupying power while reinforcing dependency and vulnerability.[45]

This cyclical experience of hope tainted by orchestrated violence affects entire communities during the current genocide. As hunger deepens, the prospect of aid – symbolised by air-dropped food supplies and charity efforts – becomes a carefully constructed "mirage of hope" that Gaza's starving population chases. Othman describes how this constructed hope is not simply a form of withholding but a calculated weapon of death. Aid delivery sites become Israeli manufactured deathtraps where, under the guise of charity, young men and children, driven by starvation and responsibility to feed their families, are lured into spaces vulnerable to targeted violence. The Israeli military's exploitation of gendered roles within Palestinian society pressures men to risk their lives for the survival of their families, as noted in the "flour massacre", where approximately 112 Palestinians were killed while collecting flour in the southwest of Gaza in February 2024 by Israeli troops.[46] This strategic targeting uses hunger and deprivation as tools for selective killing and population control, turning the pursuit of aid into an encounter with death.

The manipulation of hope within Gaza not only targets immediate survival but strategically undermines the relational and cultural foundations of care, transforming the pursuit of hope into a battleground for existence. Israel has imposed a state of perpetual crisis where Palestinians are forced to exist within an "illusion of hope", only to be betrayed. This aligns with Othman's depiction of aid campaigns as instruments of control, "relieving" hunger only within narrow boundaries that sustain Israel's control over Gaza's fate. The very act of receiving food becomes an extension of colonial violence, reinforcing Israel's presence as an occupier under the guise of a benefactor, while Gaza's children, men, and women live precariously, subject to calculated deprivation and survival conditioned by Israeli. This gendered manipulation extends to the home itself, where women, children, and the elderly face heightened vulnerability. According to the UN Human Rights Council's reports, the initial phase of Israel's genocide had an alarming pattern: the vast majority of women and children who were killed inside their own homes – underscoring the extent to which domestic spaces have become lethal targets within a strategy of annihilation.[47]

Yet, amid this manipulation, Palestinians continue to wield hope as a crucial tool for psychological endurance and resistance. This duality of hope – its use by the occupier to entrench control and by Palestinians to survive – illustrates the complex role of hope in Gaza under genocide. Palestinians' cultivation of hope under occupation, even in uncertain or incremental forms, acts as a crucial counterforce against despair. This attempt to gain agency through cultivating hope resonates with Ghassan Hage's concept of endurance, and "waiting it out" when experiencing "stuckedness" during crisis.[48] Hage's "heroism of the stuck" emphasises asserting agency in the midst of its lack, a rejection of becoming a mere victim by enduring pathological states. Similarly, for Palestinians, hope enables a vital form of psychological endurance, allowing them to survive violent Israeli erasure attempts and resist succumbing to despair. This endurance is reflected through individuals anchoring themselves in attainable, albeit temporary, goals such as securing water or cooking a meal. Here, hope is less about expecting immediate change and more about a deliberate choice to sustain mental resilience, even within the confines of the Israeli occupation.

Building upon this framework of endurance, Palestinian daily lives under settler colonialism become a testament to the active cultivation of hope as an active survival strategy. The attempts to sustain psychological stamina, vital for navigating limited access to resources under genocide, often manifests as what I call a "necessary fallacy of hope". Palestinians, like my mom, hold onto the hope for a temporary ceasefire and for the genocide to end within days or weeks, creating an essential temporary buffer that guards against psychological collapse and succumbing to the paralysis of despair. Through these lenses, the duality of hope in Gaza emerges as both a tool of colonial control and an essential means of Palestinian survival.

CONCLUSION

This sustained aggression on the social, psychological, and physical dimensions of Palestinian life reflects not only an attempt to subjugate a population but also a larger strategy of cultural and communal erasure. Yet, amid these orchestrated mechanisms of control, people in Gaza continue to enact life-affirming practices, asserting their collective will to survive. Through symbolic acts of defiance, from cultivating destroyed land to archiving memories of a life now overshadowed by violence, Palestinians reject the imposed narrative of erasure. The chapter demonstrates that despite the relentless cycles of Israeli destruction and forced displacement, hope remains an intrinsic part of Palestinian resistance – one that transcends the occupation's intention to erode community spirit.

In essence, the structures of care in Gaza – although battered by a regime intent on their annihilation – persist as embodiments of survival, identity, and resistance. This survival is not romanticised or uncritical; rather, it illustrates a profound will to live and sustain life against calculated attempts to extinguish it. The Palestinian people's endurance amid systemic erasure stands as a testament to their unwavering determination to exist and resist in the face of unimaginable adversity. The reality of Gaza is thus one of both tragedy and defiance, where life itself becomes a daily act of rebellion against structures that seek its obliteration. Through this lens, Gaza's struggle reflects a broader human aspiration for dignity and self-determination – a narrative of hope and survival that defies the politics of annihilation.

NOTES

1. Mbembe, "Necropolitics".
2. Abu Al-Namel, *Gaza Strip, 1948–1967*, 34; and El Dabbagh, *Palestine, Our Homeland*, 11.
3. Federici, *Re-Enchanting the World*, 175; and Bhattacharya, *Social Reproduction Theory*.
4. Bhattacharya, "I Forgot to Die".
5. McGinn, "Non-Hierarchical Revolution".
6. Arda and Banerjee, "Governance in Areas".
7. Hanafi and Tabar, "Intifada and the Aid Industry"; and Ticktin, *Casualties of Care*.
8. UNRWA, "Health".
9. Hanafi and Tabar, "Intifada and the Aid Industry".
10. Pappé and Falk, *Gaza Strip*.
11. Ghanim, "Thanatopolitics".
12. Salamanca, "Asphyxiation".
13. See, for example, Breaking the Silence, "Out of the Entire Neighborhood, Only Two Houses Remained Standing".
14. Allen, *Rise and Fall*.
15. OHCHR, "More than a Human".
16. Shalhoub-Kevorkian, "Biopolitics of Israeli Settler Colonialism".
17. Law for Palestine, "Law for Palestine Releases".
18. Al Jazeera, "Life Under Siege".
19. Feiglin, "Moshe Feiglin".
20. Shaul, Do not leave stone.
21. Feierstein, *Genocide as Social Practice*, 11–38.
22. UNOSAT, "Gaza Strip Comprehensive".
23. WHO, *Casualties*.
24. OHCHR, "Attacks on Hospitals".
25. OHCHR, "More than a Human Can Bear".
26. Law for Palestine, "Law for Palestine Releases".
27. Yuksul, "Israel Needs to Face Trial".
28. OHCHR, "Attacks on Hospitals".

29. Al Jazeera, "They Broke My Teeth".
30. United Nations, "United Nations Warns".
31. Law for Palestine, "Law for Palestine Releases".
32. El-Kurd, Israeli Military Drops.
33. Abraham, "Lavender".
34. Polman, Crisis Caravan.
35. Mohandesi and Teitelman, "Without Reserves".
36. Arruzza, "Functionalist, Determinist, Reductionist".
37. Ghanim, "Thanatopolitics".
38. Herzl, Jewish State.
39. Wilkins, "Cashing in on Genocide".
40. "Resilience" is in scare quotes to reflect its contested use in Gaza, where it is often seen as normalising suffering rather than challenging it. Many Palestinians in Gaza reject its romanticisation and the word itself, emphasising that their persistence stems from a sheer will to live, not an imposed narrative of endurance.
41. Lefebvre, Production of Space.
42. Federici, Re-Enchanting the World, 175.
43. Al Jazeera, "Our Nakba Repeats".
44. Othman, "Gaza and the Transformations of the Structure".
45. Lindroth and Sinevaara-Niskanen, Colonial Emotions.
46. OHCHR, "UN Experts Condemn".
47. OHCHR, "More than a Human Can Bear".
48. Hage, "Waiting Out the Crisis".

3

Childhood and Social Reproduction in Palestine: They Didn't Know We Were Seeds

Mai Abu Moghli and Rachel Rosen

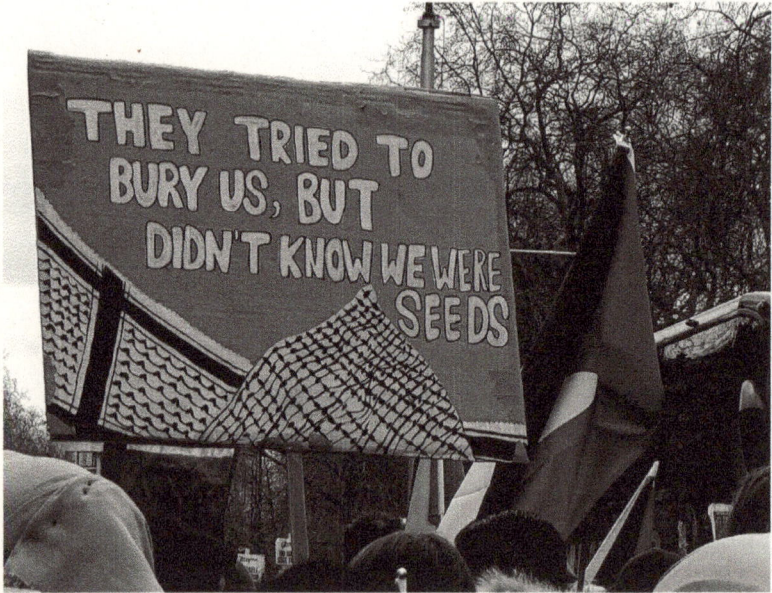

Figure 3.1 National demonstration in solidarity with Palestine (2024; London, UK). Photo by Rachel Rosen.

"They tried to bury us but didn't know we were seeds." These words, first uttered by Greek poet Dinos Christianopoulos and later taken up by the Zapatista movement in Mexico, adorned placards, banners, and walls in 2024 as people marched globally to demand an immediate ceasefire in the face of the genocide in Gaza that started in October 2023, a complete arms embargo on Israel, and an end to Western-backed Israeli settler colonialism, apartheid, and ethnic cleansing in all of Palestine. Although not written about Palestine, Christianopoulos' words hold in tension the egregious and relentless violence of the Zionist state as well as the place of hope, commitment, and fierce struggle for Palestinian liberation. The image of an insistent desire for life, embodied by seeds that refuse to be destroyed, reminds us of the importance of renewal, repair, and sustenance in movements for freedom. It is no surprise then that seeds are often emblematic of new lives and lives yet-to-come, calling up in our collective imaginaries the figure of the child. Yet, children, like seeds, like adults, need air, light, water, and nourishment – that which the violence of Israeli occupation seeks to brutally deny, withhold, and systematically destroy.

For Israeli settler colonialism operates not only through the annihilationist logic of assimilation, made infamous in the racist words of Canada's first prime minister: "kill the Indian, save the child". Palestinians are also dispossessed from childhood, as Palestinian feminist scholar Nadera Shalhoub-Kevorkian edifies through her naming and critique of the colonial practice of "unchilding".[1] Often then, Israel's version of settler colonialism is intent on physical destruction and extermination: no child is to be "saved". Israel's mode of coloniality involves as well a practice of violent appropriation, Areej Sabbagh-Khoury reminds us: the theft of Palestinian land in an effort for Israelis to "appear" as Indigenous.[2] Such incorporation is also evident in the grotesque practice of harvesting and using organs from Palestinian corpses without permission – a charge made against the Abu Kabir Forensic Institute near Tel Aviv in 2000 and again by Euro-Med Human Rights Monitor in 2023.[3] Yet, while the structural positioning of Palestinian children means they are incarcerated, killed, ignored, and denied the right to life, they are nonetheless teaching the world how to live, what it means to live for freedom, just as the strength and persistence of Christianopoulos' seeds illuminate.

What does it mean, then, to talk about social reproduction, or life-making practices, in the face of such extreme, life-denying aggression? How and why are Palestinian children so often the targets of Israeli state efforts to not only constrain life-making practices but to deny life itself? In what follows, we respond to these questions, arguing that while childhood is central to modern projects of social (re)ordering and reproduction, it assumes a prominence and particular logic in the context of the Israeli state. Zionism works through the Palestinian child in an effort to foreclose Palestinian existence – a process we call *social reproducticide* and *social deproduction*.

SOCIAL REPRODUCTION AND ISRAELI SETTLER COLONIALISM

The language of social reproduction theory (SRT) is replete with the terms of nourishment, replenishment, and regeneration. This is hardly surprising given its focus on questions of how lives are reproduced in the immediate and long term, even while it provides tools to interrogate the centrality of the reproduction of labour power for capital accumulation. As a result of this focus, social reproduction approaches have tended to give theoretical emphasis to the reproduction, and exploitation, of waged workers' labour power. Scholars in this field, however, have increasingly pointed out that racial capitalism does not just produce abstract labour power but socially differentiated bodies, including those racialised "edge" populations delineated as surplus, marginal, or disposable.[4] As Shirin Rai reminds us, reproductive labour under capitalism is not only stratified and expropriated, it can also be thoroughly depleting, requiring more resources to accomplish than are generated in the intensive processes of sustaining life.[5]

Rai's insights pull us towards an understanding that SRT may falter in the context of settler colonialism, where the appropriation of land – rather than labour – is central to its logic. "A land without a people for a people without a land", runs the infamous and thoroughly fictitious Zionist slogan. To sustain this mythology involves not only forced expulsion and historical blinkers but an ongoing genocidal practice against Palestinians to achieve the supposedly peopleless land. Shalhoub-Kevorkian refers to this as "a form of war that aims to annihilate the future generation of the Native".[6]

To date, then, social reproduction scholars offer less in the way of understanding those at the sharp edge of the nihilistic necropolitics of settler colonialism. To recognise this point is not to reject social reproduction theory but to acknowledge that its insights and theorising about regeneration and depletion must be stretched to account for a politics that condemns some to live and be replenished, even if insufficiently, and others to death.[7] Social reproduction theorists offer a starting point for this effort, stipulating that capital not only needs labour power to fulfil its drive to accumulate but must also reproduce capitalism as a system for its own survival – that which Brenner and Laslett term "societal reproduction".[8] It is instructive here that the Zionist state is part and parcel of global capitalism, for which "land theft" serves as "the *means and grounds* for Israeli and imperial capital accumulation".[9] Israel offers Western capital a "dependable partner" for its imperial interests, not least in the oil wealth and "wider regional dynamics of the

Middle East", while Western capital bankrolls Israel's settler colonial project and provides a market for Israel's weapons and technology.[10]

Palestinian life can be understood as both an impediment to Israel's project of violent appropriation via "indigenisation" and a potential source of super exploitable labour power. But, as Israel's pivot to recruiting and transporting migrant workers from South Asia post-October 2023 demonstrates, Palestinian labour power is expendable from the perspective of the Zionist state.[11] These insights about the symbiotic relationship between Israeli ethnonationalism, Israeli capital, and global capitalism help to begin accounting for what is not just a logic of abandonment, or the occasional minimal involvement of the Zionist state in the reproduction of Palestinian labour power, but one of attempted annihilation.[12] Land, and its theft, as well as labour are thus central to the settler state and its imperial backers. But, from the perspective of Zionism, labour need not be indigenous to the land. As the Israeli genocide against Gaza has shown, Palestinian labour is not just easily rendered surplus but is actively targeted for extermination.

For Palestinians, this destruction of life operates in two registers. It is at once the devastation of the means of reproducing life: the destruction of food systems, healthcare infrastructure, cultural heritage, and sites and practices of education and knowledge production, as well as the incarceration and forced (im)mobility imposed on Palestinians. But the settler state does not only destroy the means of life-making, it also operates against the reproduction of Palestinian life or, more accurately, against Palestinian existence itself. And this attempted extermination does so very clearly and directly through targeting children, despite childhood's seemingly precious and protected existence in humanitarian sensibilities.[13] We elaborate on these points below.

DESTRUCTION OF THE MEANS OF MAKING LIFE

In this section, we attempt to capture some manifestations of the systematic efforts to eradicate the means of making life, of Palestinian social reproduction, by the coloniser. We contend that these systematic attempts are life-denying aggressions and forms of *social reproducticide*.

Health

On 17 October 2023, an Israeli air strike on Gaza's al-Ahli Arab Hospital killed at least 500 people, many of whom were children. Since that massacre, the Israeli army has destroyed the healthcare system in Gaza by bombing, invading, burning, and occupying its hospitals and care centres and by abducting, torturing, and killing healthcare professionals. For instance, Dr Iyad Rantisi, the head of the women's hospital in Gaza where Palestinian women gave birth and newborn children were cared for, was detained and tortured to death in November 2024. As a result of Israeli aggression, women in Gaza report heightened miscarriages and giving birth in inhuman and horrific conditions. For those who manage to give birth, their newborn children face malnutrition, thirst, famine, and diseases as the Israeli army has blocked all access to humanitarian aid including food, water, and medicine. The destruction of the health sector and attacks on paramedics affect children's possibilities of life, let alone life-making, in other ways. On 29 January 2024, paramedics attempted to save the six-year-old Hind Rajab and her six family members who were trapped in their car as they fled Israeli bombing seeking safety. The Israeli army did not spare them, killing Hind, her family members and the paramedics who were sent to rescue the family with over 335 bullets.[14]

While the genocide has unveiled unprecedented brutality against and destruction of Palestinian health facilities, infrastructure, and personnel, this is not new. It has been happening for decades, systematically aiming to remove a main pillar and means of social reproduction for Palestinian society. Almost two decades ago, in 2002, during the Israeli invasion of the West Bank, Mai watched on TV in horror as her neighbour – a senior doctor working at the Ramallah main hospital – along with his colleagues dug graves in a small garden in front of the hospital. In the pouring rain and under months long curfew, they buried 13 young Palestinian men and women who were shot by Israeli soldiers. Today, on top of those graves, stands a stone engraved with a husk of wheat and a line from a poem written by Palestinian poet Mahmoud Darwish: "The seeds of a drying spike of grain will fill the valley with wheat".

Being a child in Palestine is to be born into colonial violence, where even the possibility of birth, the biological aspect of social reproduction, is frustrated. With so many children targeted by Israel's snipers or maimed by its bombs, the destruction of the healthcare sector forecloses the potentialities of their lives. As with adults, maiming and other forms of disability and enforced ill health make the conditions in which children attempt to make lives ever more viciously constrained. Yet, as Darwish's words remind us, Palestine and Palestinian practices of social reproduction refuse and exceed the violence of their attempted annihilation.

Education

Education is a primary target for the settler colonial project. It is perceived as a threat as it can enhance critical thinking, forge networks and communities, and create spaces for raising political consciousness and transmitting the values and tools of and for liberation. Educational spaces are regularly attacked in Palestine, not only as physical infrastructure but for what they teach (e.g. curricula and archives) and by whom (e.g. those Palestinians involved in education processes). Education has been a primary target of the ongoing genocide. All higher education institutions in Gaza have been destroyed, and over 100 university professors have been killed. Nearly 88 per cent of schools in Gaza had been destroyed or damaged by December 2024, including 275 government, 57 private and 161 UNRWA schools.[15] In September 2024, the Health Ministry in Gaza reported 10,888 students had been killed and 17,224 injured in Gaza, while in the West Bank, 113 students had been killed and 548 wounded.[16] Additionally, 429 students had been arrested. The ministry also reported that 529 teachers and administrative staff had been killed, with 3,686 injured across both Gaza and the West Bank. More than 129 staff members were detained in the West Bank.

Targeting and destroying education infrastructure and killing Palestinian students and teachers is not new. In 2009, the term "scholasticide" was coined to describe Israel's targeting of educational institutions following the destruction caused by the Israeli military aggression on Gaza called "Operation Cast Lead" as well as the systematic destruction of Palestinian academic institutions, students, and teachers since the *Nakba*. In the West Bank, due to ongoing incursions and attacks on cities, villages and refugee camps and the siege imposed on communities through closure of checkpoints and curfews, schools have been forced to close. When open, students and teachers are often unable to physically reach their schools and, if they can, face regular attacks by armed settlers and soldiers. This has resulted in a massive disruption to education, putting over half a million children at risk of losing their right to education with no viable alternatives. Schooling is also affected by the global push to dismantle UNRWA, including Israeli legislation banning the organisation and cuts to its foreign funding based on debunked Israeli allegations against UNRWA staff.[17] It is notable that this is the agency that provides schooling for Palestinian refugees in Palestine and neighbouring countries, particularly Lebanon, Syria, and Jordan. Education is therefore disrupted for Palestinian refugee children, whether they live inside or outside Palestine.

As children and young people in Gaza and the northern West Bank enter a second year of war either without schooling or with irregular access to schools and universities, international humanitarian and academic bodies are suggesting and working on well-meaning initiatives for online education. Not only does this run the risk of turning the Palestinian struggle for liberation and justice into a humanitarian issue, stripping its political core and framing it within aid and charity narratives, it threatens to further fragment and isolate communities and expose Palestinian education spaces to heightened forms of assimilatory and depoliticising censorship.

For education has historically played a central role in the social reproduction of more collectivist visions of mobilisation and organising for freedom. Palestinian educational spaces have been linked to direct action against colonisation as well as class struggle against neoliberal Palestinian Authority measures which exacerbate the societal and economic oppression of settler and global capitalism, such as partnerships with foreign donors and deals with colonial forces.[18] For instance, in 2016, parents and students joined a teachers' mass mobilisation against the PA's punitive measures against them. Children carried banners saying, "Our dignity comes from the dignity of our teachers".[19] Life-making includes nurturing political subjectivities and collective visions of freedom and has been a pillar not just of Palestinian schools but of higher education also. For example, at Birzeit University in 2016, students striking against tuition fee increases asserted the principle of "education for all", offering the potential for student activism to transcend the post-Oslo impasse through forging a space for a unified struggle that links Palestinian national liberation with class struggle. Indeed, the student movement in Palestinian universities emerged during the 1970s and has played a vital role, along with other mass organisations, in mobilising young Palestinians in resisting the occupation and struggling for liberation.[20]

(Im)mobility and Carcerality

(Im)mobility for Palestinians has always been forced: either by expulsion or, when under siege, by being denied the right to move freely within the country or across its imposed borders.[21] This is the reality under settler colonialism, and it fundamentally shapes the means of making life. Of the 2.1 million Palestinians living in Gaza before October 2023, 1.7 million were already refugees and had lived under siege for 17 years. Since October 2023, their dispossession within the small strip has heightened as they have been forced, often multiple times over, to leave their homes under heavy bombardment and shelter in tents and schools.

Gaza was described as the world's largest open-air prison well before the latest genocide. But, it is perhaps more accurate to say that the Israeli authorities have turned all Palestinians into prisoners – whether walled in or out, segregated, or enclosed in camps – not only by imposing restrictions on movement and bureaucratising apartheid through an intricate system of stratified IDs, but also by regular day and night raids on Palestinian cities and villages during which mass arrests of mainly young boys and men takes place. In October 2024, the Palestinian Commission of Detainees and Ex-Detainees Affairs reported that the number of prisoners held in Israeli prisons reached roughly 10,100, inclusive of 96 women and over 270 children. This number does not include all detainees from Gaza – estimated to be in the thousands. This number does include administrative detainees, those incarcerated in Israeli prisons without trial: 3,398 people, including 61 children. In 2016, the Israeli Knesset introduced a new law allowing children between the ages of 12 and 14 to be held criminally responsible, meaning they can be tried in court as adults and be given prison sentences.[22] According to DCI-Palestine, Israel prosecutes between 500 and 700 Palestinian children in military courts each year. In Jerusalem, hundreds of Palestinian children are arrested every year simply for their participation in the political sphere and, according to Addameer, the majority are under 14.[23] Arrest, interrogation, or house arrest can leave deep scars, affecting children's sense of self, mental health, and dignity.[24]

Siege, invasion, curfews, IDs, and checkpoints are not the only ways colonial measures strip Palestinian mobility. In June 2024, UNRWA reported that ten children per day are losing one or both of their legs in Gaza, "the biggest cohort of paediatric amputees in history", according to Dr Ghassan Abu Sittah.[25] Stripping children violently of their own limbs (what Jasbir Puar calls "debilitation") and Israel's presumed "right to maim" as a means of population control are forms of perverse expropriation via social reproduction.[26] Armaments are tested on Palestinian children, maiming them and rupturing their bodies, and then marketed as "field tested" and sold globally to be used against other children in a continuous cycle of unchilding perpetuated by the Zionist colonial project and its partners.

Controlling children's mobility is a colonial measure of *social deproduction*. Displacing children multiple times disrupts their lives and can hinder their ability to form and sustain the social connections so central to life-making. It fragments and curtails their access to education, which is so central to fostering visions and practices of liberation. At the same time, immobilising children through imprisonment puts them under the threat of torture, ill treatment, and loss of their social ties and education, all in a context where health systems are being destroyed. By attacking education spaces and infrastructures of life-making, and further fragmenting students through decontextualised and depoliticised initiatives, the settler state is attempting to complete the social reordering of its colonial project, if not through the denial of life, then through taming the Palestinian population through childhood.

A WAR ON PALESTINIAN EXISTENCE THROUGH CHILDHOOD

Calling attention to the particularly egregious nature of violence being inflicted on Gaza by Israel, in March 2024, Philippe Lazzarini, the UNRWA commissioner-general, wrote evocatively on X: "This is a war on children. It is a war on their childhood and their future". The numbers are "staggering" he added: more children had been killed in Gaza in four months than in all global conflicts in the past four years.[27] To say that this is a war on children is not simply moving but convincing. Nearly half (47.3 per cent) of Gaza's population was under 18 years of age as of 2022.[28] It is horrifying, yet unsurprising, therefore, that one year on, children made up at least 16,756 of the 41,615 Palestinians killed in Gaza, with even conservative estimates suggesting those killed in the genocide numbered closer to 186,000 in July 2024.[29] The UN's report on *Children and Armed Conflict* for 2023 draws attention to the "dramatic increase and unprecedented scale and intensity of grave violations against children" in Palestine by the Israeli state through its "armed and security forces".[30] These included: killing and maiming children; sexual violence against the young; use of administrative detention; and blockage of humanitarian aid leading to widespread starvation.

The brutal nature of this attack on Palestinian children is indisputable, and we do not disagree with these more familiar arguments about Israel's targeting of Palestinian children. But the claim we are making runs deeper. For this is not simply a war, but a genocide, part of an unceasing colonial effort to bring the mythology of Palestine as "peopleless" land into being.[31] It is also not just grave violation and violence against children, but it is an effort of extermination of Palestine through the child, a disturbing insight made possible by SRT. Social reproduction theory calls our attention to "the complex ways in which people attempt to make life worth living for themselves and for future generations".[32] In other words, social reproduction is not simply about eking out biological existence, or about how life-making is expropriated by capital, but about how existence is made meaningful and hope is nourished.

The child figure is crucial here as children are seen to embody hope, dreams, commitments, and practices that run counter to the appropriation of land, counter to their dispossession, and counter to their attempted extermination. "While the Israeli state does much to ensure that Palestinian children emerge from the womb with as much difficulty as possible, as soon as they emerge, they are the seeds of the future. They are the hope, the rain amid an arid waste", Shalhoub-Kevorkian comments eloquently.[33] Or, we might say, children exemplify Christianopoulos' seeds – their sheer existence reminding the world of Palestinians' existence and right of return. This reflection is not simply symbolic but material. Palestinian children cultivate a determination for life through practices of storytelling and memory, as well as through those banal everyday practices which SRT brings into sharp relief: cooking, cleaning, educating, and caring labour that nourishes both individual and collective subjects. Many young Palestinians also often refuse to be contained by the checkpoints and borders imposed on them within the 1948 borders officially demarcating the Israeli settler nation and in the occupied territories. They become actively involved in resistance to occupation and apartheid – a threat to the smooth operations of the settler state and therefore a key target of its aggression through the egregious act of "unchilding". This, argues Shalhoub-Kevorkian, dispossesses the young from childhood by constituting them as essentially and inherently a racialised threat and stripping them of "the very foundational rights of children to live a life without violence".[34]

We understand social reproduction as a site of struggle then, not just in the more familiar terms of who is responsible for its accomplishment and with what infrastructures, but about the ways that it may serve as a practice of regeneration and resistance in the context of racialised and colonial state violence, and likewise how this might be disorganised or destroyed by racial capitalism.[35] Seen in this light, Israel's genocide in Gaza is both a war on children and far more. If children are experienced as "rain amid an arid waste" or "seeds" of existence and resistance, we can understand how settler colonial violence works through the child in an attempt at destabilising communities. In the face of Israel's aggression, Palestinian adults are often simply not able to protect children in the way they feel they should. This can produce feelings of abjection, fracturing the possibilities of communal life as a practice of common cause involving shared memory making and building strength. In other cases, the ordering of life through the child can become a form of "collective punishment", an effort to break intergenerational solidarity and the foundation of community support for *Al Hadineh Al Sha'bieh* (community support) and collective *Sumud* (steadfastness).[36] In this sense then, killing, maiming, or detaining large numbers of Palestinian children is not just an assault on children or infrastructures of reproduction, but such attacks disrupt the replenishment of Palestinian lives and Palestinian dreams of liberated futures. That this assault operates through the child is perhaps the most aggressive form of "unchilding" – where the brutality of Israeli settler colonialism and its unchilding is an attempted "unpeopling" of Palestine.

Israel's attacks on Palestinian social reproduction are not simply an example of the depletion that happens as the marginalised and oppressed engage in the labour of life. Israel's targeting of Palestinian children is not simply a violation of their rights. We name this brutal violence against Palestinian existence through the child a form of *social reproducticide* or *social deproduction*. In so doing, we centre social reproduction approaches, stretching these by arguing for the necessity of accounting for the necropolitics that lie at the heart of settler colonial societies and their embedding in global racial capitalism. While this widespread debility stratifies the labour of social reproductive almost beyond recognition – particularly in a context where food, health, and educational infrastructures have been destroyed, Palestinian children have resisted this annihilation. They have regenerated spaces where social life can be reproduced, and the possibility of freedom nurtured, like Christianopoulos' seeds or Darwish's wheat.

Steadfastness and Refusals

The making of life for Palestinians is a contradictory process. Having experienced daily killings, expulsions, injuries, imprisonments, as well as the loss of home(s), rights, and loved ones over generations, it is perhaps astonishing that Palestinians continue to reproduce life, not only in the sense of biological reproduction but building families and communities and the means of care and well-being. For, as we watch the genocide in Gaza livestreamed in real time, it is not only the atrocities committed by the Zionist army that we see as Israeli soldiers brazenly document and celebrate their crimes for the world, we are also witnessing Palestinians coming together in care and love. Men, women, and children are digging bodies from under the rubble with their bare hands. They are documenting their own genocide in the presence of genocide-complicit mainstream media, and despite censorship and silencing from (social) media and international organisations.[37] Palestinians – including the young – are showing the world what struggling for freedom and dignified life means, while all means of life are being destroyed.

Throughout the genocide in Gaza, Palestinian children and young people have resisted international silence, by telling their stories to a global audience on social media. Palestinian children, particularly in Gaza, have refused to be reduced to images of their bodies livestreamed as they are being charred, decapitated, and shredded into pieces by Israeli missiles. Many of them have decided not only to bear witness to the genocide (*Shahid*) or succumb to their fate as a *Shaheed* (martyr), but also to reclaim the narrative, telling their stories as a form of resistance. The refusal to be silenced can be understood as a manifestation of their *Sumud*. According to Meari, *Sumud* has come to embody a whole range of significations, sensibilities, affections, attachments, aspirations, and practices.[38] It is a form of subjectivity and politics that embodies the possibility of escaping hegemonic configurations of colonial liberal politics. Children in Gaza have practised *Sumud* through signification: representing their own realities, sensibilities, and concerns by showing love to their community and land. Against all odds and unprecedented violence, they bring the dreams of their futures into the now in the service of their community. We see Lama Abu Jamous and Aboud Battah reporting as journalists, Renad Attalah as a chef and aid worker, and Ahmad Abu Sweilem as a farmer.[39] These children are producing life and practising the revolutionary act of becoming, refusing the discourse of victimhood and othering and the brutality of Israel's war of extermination. They show us that the desire for life, the labour of life, finds cracks and crevices to exceed the violence that seeks to contain, forcibly expropriate, or deny it.

CONCLUSION

The criminalisation of everything Palestinian and the colonial violence inflicted on a small population, including through egregious forms of violence directed at children, serves one goal for the Israeli settler colony and its Western backers: appropriating the maximum amount of land with the least number of Palestinians. Even the pretext of providing a semblance of social reproductive functions for an occupied population simply does not exist today in Gaza. The Israeli military is not simply a repressive arm of the state – it is precisely what the Zionist state is. As Palestinian childhoods teach us, this is an existential question that must lie at the heart of efforts to theorise and harness the political potential of social reproduction practices.

While the metaphors of wheat and seeds serve as potent reminders that renewal, repair, and sustenance are central to struggles for lives of dignity and collective liberation, they also compel us to consider the antithesis: colonial efforts to exterminate the native. The continuous support for the Israeli colonial and genocidal actions by the USA and other Western governments, and the silence or obfuscation of most media, individuals, institutions, is a form of complicity. It is a green light for the annihilation not only of infrastructures of life-making, but of life itself – nothing less than *social reproducticide.*

NOTES

1. Shalhoub-Kevorkian, *Incarcerated Childhood.*
2. Sabbagh-Khoury, "'But if I Don't Steal It'".
3. Black, "Doctor Admits Israeli Pathologists Harvested Organs"; and Euronews, "Israel 'Stealing Organs'".
4. Ferguson, *Women and Work*; the presumed marginal, disposable status of the Palestinian people is criticised by Dr. Ghassan Abu-Sittah (see his "Gaza Hospital Bombing").
5. Rai, *Depletion.*
6. Shalhoub-Kevorkian, *Incarcerated Childhood*, 17.
7. Mbembe, *Necropolitics.*
8. Bhattacharya, "Introduction".
9. Ayyash, "Colonial Racial Capitalism".
10. Hanieh, "Framing Palestine".
11. New Arab Staff & Agencies, "Indian Workers Replace Palestinians".
12. Gilmore, *Golden Gulag.*
13. Rosen and Dickson, "Exceptions to Child Exceptionalism".
14. Forensic Architecture, "Killing of Hind Rajab".
15. UNRWA, "UNRWA Situation Report".
16. Middle East Monitor, "11,000 Palestinian Students Killed".
17. Reidy, "'More People Will Die'".
18. Tayeb, "Palestinian McCity".
19. Abu Moghli and Qato, "Brief History of a Teacher's Strike".
20. Meari and Abu-Duhou, "Palestinian Student Movement".
21. Abu Moghli and Shannan, "Childhood, (Im)mobility and Care".
22. DCI, *Arbitrary by Default.*
23. Addameer, "Imprisonment of Children".
24. Moghli and Shannan, "Childhood, (Im)mobility and Care".
25. Abu-Sittah, "Gaza Hospital Bombing".
26. Puar, *Right to Maim.*

27. Lazzarini, Staggering.
28. Mohammad, "Children Make Up".
29. Chughtai and Okur, "One Year of Israel's War on Gaza"; and Khatib, McKee, and Yusuf, "Counting the Dead".
30. United Nations General Assembly, "Children and Armed Conflict", 16 and 13.
31. Pappe, *Ten Myths about Israel*.
32. Narotzky and Besnier, "Crisis, Value, and Hope".
33. Shalhoub-Kevorkian, *Incarcerated Childhood*, 18.
34. Shalhoub-Kevorkian, *Incarcerated Childhood*, 122.
35. Davis, Bhandar, and Ziadah, "Angela Y. Davis".
36. Abu Moghli and Shannan, "Childhood, (Im)mobility and Care", 199.
37. Farraj, "We Don't Want to Receive Them as Martyrs".
38. Meari, "Sumud".
39. See the following Instagram pages: www.instagram.com/lama_jamous9/?hl=en (Lama Abu Jamous); www.instagram.com/abod_bt77/?hl=en (Aboud Battah); www.instagram.com/renadfromgaza/?hl=en (Renad Attalah); and www.instagram.com/tasnemaaed8/ (Ahemd AbuSweilem).

4

"I Forgot to Die": Thinking through Social Reproduction of Palestinian Life

Tithi Bhattacharya

On Christmas morning, as my daughter slept safely in her bed dreaming of the presents piled under the tree, I did a simple google search. If a pregnant woman, let's call her Mary, were to travel today from Nazareth to Bethlehem, how many Israeli checkpoints would she have to pass through? Google returned my answer in seconds, 15. A modern-day pregnant Mary would have to cross 15 Checkpoints, complete with multiple Israeli soldiers armed to the teeth, to get from Nazareth to Bethlehem, a distance of 90 miles.

Of course, like many Palestinian women today, our modern-day Mary would have a "choice" – rather than cross multiple checkpoints she could give birth *at* a checkpoint. In 2005, the United Nations filed a report urging the UN High Commissioner for Human Rights to intervene in the "inhumane Israeli practice" of Palestinian pregnant women giving birth at Israeli checkpoints, "owing to denial of access by Israel to hospitals".[1]

As this volume takes shape, Israel's inhuman genocide against the Palestinian people, that began on 7 October 2023, continues. But before the Hamas strike on 7 October, many media sources were already calling 2023 "the deadliest year on record" for Palestinians in the West Bank. Israeli forces had killed 395 Palestinians in the West Bank that year, while settlers were responsible for 9 more killings. If murders such as these are the direct cessation of life, Israel conducts other forms of murders that either halt or impede life-making. To continue with the instance of 2023 before 7 October, last summer, at the Khalil Suleiman Hospital in Jenin, Israeli forces first launched a teargas grenade inside its emergency room, while the medical staff witnessed the obstruction of ambulances and the targeting of other parts of the facility.

For Palestinians, then, a declared war, as we are bearing witness to now, is simply a temporal and spatial escalation of an ongoing, undeclared slow war against their people. In this essay, I hope to show that the genocide unleashed by Israel since 7 October 2023 is neither arbitrary nor unpremeditated. Using the lens of social reproduction theory (SRT), I propose that inherent to the Zionist project is a twinned impulse: minimally, the disruption (through violent policies) and maximally, the annihilation (through genocide and war) of Palestinian life. Consequently, in this current cycle of violence, Israel is targeting two kinds of social reproductive capacities: one, the *institutions* of social reproduction such as schools and hospitals; and two, the future generation, that is, children. Israel wants to eradicate not just life, but the ability to reproduce a future life. A ceasefire can thus only be a baseline demand, for there to be a flourishing of life in Palestine, there needs to be more than a cessation of killing.

I develop my argument about SRT in Palestine in two interrelated ways. First, following Marx, I centre a theoretical distinction between "living" and "flourishing" as two, albeit often intersecting, modes of life-making. Second, I map the ways in which Israel, to use Jasbir Puar's powerful concept, "debilitates" Palestinian life while creating conditions for its own flourishing. Finally, I circle back to Marx's idea of species being, and argue that today Palestinian modes of life, expressions of resistance and living, captures much of the essence of humanity's species being.

LIFE, LIFE-MAKING, AND FLOURISHING: RETHINKING MARX

Social reproduction feminists have exercised the formulation "life-making" to identify the multiple ways in which human beings labour to transform nature and their surroundings to maintain themselves and satisfy their needs. The concept is a key tool for understanding the comparisons, connections, and affective outcomes between the two nodal points of Zionist violence, direct and indirect. I contend that to acknowledge the continuities between military aggression and militarised containment of Palestinian life, we need to start from the deliberate destabilisation, vulnerabilitisation, and annihilation of Palestinian capacities of social reproduction. Life-making as a concept provides us with the analytical connective tissue between the two nodes.

I take my lead from Marx in developing a capacious understanding of human labour and its relationship to life-making. In his Paris Manuscripts, Marx leads us through a careful distinction between alienated and unalienated human labour. The former, the sort of labour we perform under capitalist direction, feels "*external* to the worker", while the latter occurs when humans make "life activity itself the object of his will and of his consciousness". Simply put, as humans, we are deliberate, we do not merge with our labour (as a spider does). Ideally, our labour is a spontaneous, joyous, determination of us acting upon "the *sensuous external world*", and thereby transforming both the world and us. Too many Marxists focus on food, shelter, clothing, etc., when citing examples of the kind of products that result from humans acting upon nature. These bare necessities of biological life-making, in my view, are not only too limited as examples, but Marx himself sees them as such. Explaining the embeddedness of humans in nature, Marx specifically notes nature as providing "the *means of life* in the more restricted sense, that is, the means for the physical subsistence of the worker himself".[2]

What then is life-making in the non-restrictive sense?

Marx uses the word spiritual 22 times in the *Economic and Philosophical Manuscripts*. Importantly, he denotes human labour to be a form of activity in which "all the natural, spiritual, and social variety of individual activity is manifested". He is most struck by the deliberation with which humans "make... [their] life activity the object of... [their] will and... [their] consciousness". Even to complete the most basic tasks, humans employ intentional practices, even aesthetic standards, to follow their life-making pursuits; we work towards self-realisation "in accordance with the laws of beauty".[3]

A distinction between life-making through capitalist regimes of work and life-making under conditions of freedom is a persistent theme in Marx. He used an Aristotelian framework, mediated through Hegel, to discuss *formal freedoms*, those which are available under capitalism, and the *unfreedom and alienation*, that which lurks beneath such freedoms. Marx agreed with liberal theorists that the condition of freedom, including its definition, was historical, and that even its preliminary proceedings had to be grounded in the satisfaction of those bare necessities of biological life-making. In the third volume of *Capital*, he thus argued "the realm of freedom" to really begin, "only where labor determined by necessity and external expediency ends". In other words, only when we are not scrambling to meet our most basic needs can we contemplate and, eventually, enter the realm of freedom. His conception of "needs" is likewise historical and dynamic. Once all of humanity, through the increased productivity of labour, have transcended the basic needs of biological life-making, there can arise the potential to concentrate on the development of "human powers as an end in itself".[4] Further, as those powers expand so too do human needs and, as we satisfy those needs, we deepen our realisation of human freedom.

From the above definition of life-making, we can discern a clear distinction between *living* – a form of life-making that we are forced to do under capitalist conditions of formal freedoms but alienated labour, and *flourishing* – a form of life-making that is in our species being, that Marx is gesturing towards.

While the distinction is stark in Marx, it is also clear that within everyday *living* under capitalism, we frequently catch a glimpse of what I am calling here *flourishing*. If alienated labour is that which acts as an external force on the worker, what Marx calls serving "an alien will and an alien intelligence", then unalienated labour is that form of labour which is both freely chosen and self-determined by the worker themself.[5] Within the overall context of systemic alienation, we still nourish our plants, animals, and children; we make art and have great sex – all forms of labour that we engage in with *relative* freedom. In the *Grundrisse*, Marx refers to the composition of music as "*really free labor*", which requires "the greatest effort", and is "at the same time damned serious".[6] Thus, when Palestinian feminist poet Rafeef Ziadah writes, "We Palestinians wake up every morning to teach the rest of the world life, sir", I read that as a searing theorisation of the politics of life-making. I read that as a call to explore what happens to life-making – both in the living and flourishing sense – in Palestine.

UNDERSTANDING THE ONGOING NAKBA THROUGH A FRAMEWORK OF LIFE-MAKING

The State of Israel was established with the demographic intent to eliminate Palestinian life. Settler colonialism, a framework developed by Patrick Wolfe, has therefore been a powerful method of analysing this annihilative logic of Zionism. Since 1948, Israel has employed three broad strategies of state building vis-à-vis Palestinians – expulsion of Palestinians from within (ever-expanding) state borders, intentional generational killing of entire families, and controlling and severely curtailing Palestinian fertility. While settler colonialism, as an analytic, explains this biopolitical project of Zionism, scholars have recently argued that it does not do enough to explain the specific relationship between Zionist state building and life-making. To limit the discussion of Israeli violence to just expulsion, murder, and war is, paraphrasing Marx, to imagine life-making in "the more restricted sense" of the concept. By contrast, SRT and its expansive concept of life-making allows us to document the multiple ways in which the Zionist state tries to prevent Palestinians not only from staying alive, but also from staying human.[7]

Jasbir Puar's brilliant concept "debility" is of use to us here. Through a moving study of Black and Palestinian life, Puar offers us a theorisation of the political economy of bodily capacity. Oppressive state machineries (USA and Israel), according to Puar, put death and debility in a productive relationship with each other. States, of course, reserve the right to be the sole purveyors of death in their "right to kill", but Puar shows how not killing Palestinians is not a "humanitarian sparing of death" but rather a move to render "them systematically and utterly debilitated"; it is a "biopolitical usage and articulation of the right to maim". The Zionist project, at its core, is anchored in "the debilitating ongoingness of structural inequality and suffering" of Palestinian life. Such a process of constant debilitation creates, what Puar calls, an "asphixatory regime of power" – that threads space and time through intricate social relations of violence and occupation.

Puar's concept of debility should be extended to include in its ambit not just the injury of bodies but also the maiming of institutions of life-making. This sense is implicit in Puar, especially when she discusses "infrastructural warfare" conducted by Israel on Gaza and asserting that the assault on infrastructure is "an essential, even central, component of the biopolitical regulation of a malleable humanitarian collapse". She builds on the important work done by Omar Jabary Salamanca in this field, reproducing Salamanca's reference to the Israeli politician Dov Weissglas who claimed that Israeli policy was "like an appointment with a dietician. The Palestinians would get a little thinner, but won't die".[8]

It is this sense of *ongoingness* of assault on life-making that I hope to capture in this essay in order to show that it is not just life that is under siege in Palestine but all aspiration to flourishing, thus placing death and slow death on a continuum. The other continuum I hope to probe is the Israeli compact between the greatest of liberal values with the deepest of colonial violence. For instance, Israel is projected as the most democratic, the queerest, the most vegan, and the greatest dispenser of welfare for its Jewish citizens, while simultaneously as a genocidaire of Palestinian life and living. The question is not how these contradictions suture; the question rather is what ideological work does this suturing do? Israeli flourishing and Palestinian debility, I offer, should be seen as both a recombinant process and as a potential for anticolonial politics.

BIRTH, PROPAGATION, AND THE DIFFERENTIAL SOCIAL REPRODUCTION OF LIFE

In a recent article in the *New York Times*, conservative commentator Ross Douthat reignited an anxious, and specifically Western, discussion about the fall in birthrates in the Global North, or "the rapid graying of rich countries". While birthrates are either falling or remaining stagnant in these regions, Douthat ends the piece by quoting the demographers Morland and Pilkington, "[t]he only country in the O.E.C.D. that has chosen the 'more children' option is Israel".[9] This, however, is not new.

Israel has, since its inception, enshrined pro-natalist policies in myriad institutions. A reproductive regime has been constituted through multiple monetary rewards and committees that ensure a growing birthrate. Critical feminists such as Sigrid Vertommen and Nira Yuval-Davis have tracked these initiatives in, among others, the 1949 Heroine Award for mothers with at least ten children, the 1968 Demographic Centre with its Fund for Encouraging Birth, and more recently, the 2002 Israel Council on Demography.[10]

Israeli sociologist Meira Weiss has noted the profoundly eugenicist vein in Zionism that, historically, through a "bodily revolution" aimed to "create a new people fit for a new land". "Fit" was very much the watchword of the project. Weiss draws attention to one Arthur Rupin, a leading German Zionist, who wrote in his book, *The Sociology of Jews* (1934), that:

> while in Europe many are calling for a eugenic policy, the Jews... have never engaged in a "self-cleansing" of their race, but rather allowed every child, be it the most sickly, to grow and marry and have children like him. Even the mentally retarded, blind and deaf were allowed to marry. In order to keep the purity of our race, such Jews must abstain from child-bearing.[11]

The ideal Jewish body that emerged out of these discussions and policies was "masculine, Jewish, Ashkenazi, perfect, and wholesome", one that Weiss calls, "the chosen body".[12]

The fusion of political governance with biogovernance has outlasted Israel's moment of inception. Two kinds of technologies determine contemporary Zionist biopolitics. The first set of tools and policies are clustered around fertility and maternity, and the second, around foetal diagnostics. To the first, while Assisted Reproductive Technologies (ART) are prohibitively expensive in most countries, in Israel, they are free. In 2010, the Israeli parliament passed the controversial Law on Egg Donation which allows women to donate their ovum in return for financial compensation, thus allowing infertile women to request egg donation and its associated ART. Amendments to the law, however, stipulated that the donor and the recipient of the egg cell share the same religion, hence making it impossible for a Jewish woman to donate an egg cell to a Muslim, Christian, or Druze couple and vice versa.

The second set of technologies come into play after conception. Jewish Israeli women lead the world in birth medicalisation and foetal surveillance, with 60 per cent of them undergoing predelivery diagnostic testing of some kind. Israeli parents prefer abortion even in cases of minor bodily "impairment" such as a cleft lip, prompting Weiss to comment that the "Israeli obsession with fertility involves not just quantity but also quality".[13] Technologies are social, that is to say, they are not neutral scientific tools that arise, and are developed, abstracted from social relations. In Israel, more so than anywhere else, reproductive technologies reflect the deep Zionist anxiety against the "demographic threat" of Palestinian birth. As Golda Meir confided in the early 1970s that she was afraid of a situation in which "she would have to wake up every morning wondering how many Arab babies have been born during the night".[14]

The social reproduction of Israeli life and life-making is, of course, not limited to birth technologies alone. An entire socio-state infrastructure is maintained to ensure the *flourishing* of Israeli life and the annihilation and debilitation of the Palestinian. Methods of debilitation vary across historic Palestine. The intentional carving up of Palestine into different *regimes* of authority and control ensures a violent cat-and-mouse game between the Israeli state and Palestinians in these derecognised territories, prompting Noura Erakat's incisive assessment that Israel tries to achieve in Gaza "by warfare, what it seeks to do in the West Bank through martial law, in East Jerusalem through administrative law, in historic Palestine through civil law".[15] In the next section, I want to signpost the key ways in which Israel thwarts Palestinian life-making and promotes death-making. Detailed and rich histories exist of the different methods employed by the Zionist project, but what I aim to do here is put these different methods into a single interpretive frame, that of SRT. In so doing, I want to draw attention to two things. First, the impossibility of "reforming" the Israeli state and finding a place for Palestinian flourishing within the existing structure. This is clearly the path the Palestinian Authority is following as it tries (and fails) to "develop" certain parts of Palestine without questioning the overarching colonial project that is Zionism. Second, following from the first, the liberation of Palestine must be conceived of and created by replacing the current ethnonationalist state with a democratic one that guarantees the right to flourish for all people, Jews and Arabs, Christians and Druze.

BEYOND BIRTH: LIVING VERSUS FLOURISHING

International bodies such as the UN and World Bank use certain standard metrics for judging what they call "Development" and what I am calling "flourishing". Access to food, clean water, housing, healthcare, and education is used as the most common register of evaluation. In Palestine, each of these measures are produced through the disciplinary technologies of colonialism. Further, while such registers do form a "list" of sorts, I want to draw attention to Israel's generalisable model of operations that forms the *frame* in which they all fit. In other words, Israel organises space and human beings in particular ways, materially, affectively, and visually, ensuring the growth and consolidation of the apparatus of colonial power.

Anticolonial scholarship has taught us that landscapes are rarely "empty" but are composed of discourses and political tactics which produce nature not just as the site of human labours but also as a category of thought and imagination. Consider the place of fish in Palestinian social relations. The taste and smell of fish are in the cellular architecture of Palestinian history and memory. Folktales weave these histories into tales of fishermen and "the king of fishes", while dill, garlic, and chillies entrust this history to the physical senses. But the waters that lap Gazan shores are neither neutral, nor free from colonial frames. Gazan fishermen have only been allowed to fish six nautical miles or less offshore when most of the fish are at least nine miles out at sea, while the sea is polluted with sewage. Colonial ordering of nature and labour, thus, organises and distributes Palestinians across very specific regimes of power, visible and invisible. Oceans and deserts, rocks, and fishes can only relate meaningfully to Palestinians through Israeli control, thus creating, first and foremost, what Elizabeth Povinelli has called "geontologies" of colonial power.[16] It is through those geontologies I seek to understand the question of access to the measures of flourishing such as food and water.

In 1967, Israel, in its Military Order 158, decreed that Palestinians could not construct any new water installation without first obtaining a permit from the Israeli army. Such permits, even after nearly six decades, are impossible to obtain, thus barring Palestinians from drilling wells or installing water pumps. The Jordan River, in whose valley some of the Prophet Muhammad's most trusted Companions are buried, now functions as a wound to Palestinian life-making, as they are barred from accessing its flowing waters. According to the UN, more than 180 rural Palestinian communities in rural areas in the occupied West Bank lack access to running water.

The situation is infinitely more dire in Gaza where the drinking water, according to a resident, is "as salty as the sea".[17] Since the 2007 blockade, Israel has kept Palestinian children in Gaza on what the IDF has called a "starvation diet". According to Palestinian-American medical doctor Jess Ghannam, nearly 80 per cent of Gazan children survive on less than $1 per day (this *prior* to 7 October 2023), and consequently a significant portion of them endure hunger daily, as their access to sufficient calories has dwindled over the past 17 years of the ongoing siege. Moreover, the quality of the nutrients children consume has diminished, leading to "stunting", a medical condition resulting in lower birth weights and below average height and weight for their age group, falling far below international standards.[18]

Meanwhile, all birthing women in Israel, employed and unemployed, are entitled to maternity leave and a large number of women are entitled to a maternity allowance. If, as Doreen Massey teaches us, spatiality and place-making are intricately and profoundly connected to gender, it is important to conceive of Israeli spatiality as arising out of concrete, exclusionary social relations. Citizens of Tel-Aviv speak of the city as one "known for its pampering of new mothers". City cafés hold "daily 'Mommy and me' activities such as arts and crafts, physical therapy and massages, and nursing and sleep clinics".[19]

As a part of this flourishing, the Jewish Israeli child is assured a stellar, free, public education in a school system where 88 per cent of adults aged 25 to 64 have completed upper secondary education, higher than the OECD average of 79 per cent.[20] Palestinians form 21 per cent of Israel's population, and the letter of state laws guarantees the same rights to Arab and Jewish citizens of Israel. But the laws, *in effect*, ensure that Arab children are socially reproduced differentially and at great disadvantage. For instance, class sizes for Palestinian Arab children are larger and with fewer teachers. As the land is mutilated by and through checkpoint posts that control Palestinian mobility, many children have to travel long distances to reach the nearest school. Human Rights Watch noted, in 2000, that most Arab schools lacked basic facilities like "libraries, computers, science laboratories, and even recreation space", let alone specialised facilities such as film editing studios and theatres that many Jewish schools were equipped with. Funding-wise, Arab schools are allocated resources that are on average 40 per cent lower than Hebrew education (on a per student basis).[21] Further, in 2018, the Israeli Knesset passed the Nation State Law that stripped Arabic of its official status as language and stated clearly that the "right to exercise national self-determination in the State of Israel is unique to the Jewish people".[22] The Arab child in Israel lives an exophonic life as far as they are a "citizen" of Israel. Palestinians are thus ceaselessly reproduced as "out of place" in their homeland. A network of roads, the arteries of space, enact and secure racial exclusion. The colour of license plates determines mobility; cars with Palestinian license plates are not allowed on Israeli roads, regardless of the identification held by the driver. Such cars have restricted access even on Palestinian roads, routinely face delays at checkpoints, and are subject to regular roadblocks. An apartheid wall and multiple checkpoints help create a delirious maze of legality across the mutilated land where at each node of contact with the Israeli state, the Palestinian is juridically and emotionally reproduced as an outsider. Scholars have noted the real function of checkpoints as creating new political geographies marked by uncertainties and delays. Even World Bank researchers have shown how checkpoints reduced the number of working days, and working wages for Palestinians, while Alexandra Rijke and Claudio Minca, studying everyday life at checkpoints, have drawn attention to the long queues and the arbitrary implementation of laws, real and fictional, for the express purpose of violating, humiliating, and restricting the colonised.[23]

These differential policies towards the social reproduction of Arab and Jewish lives produce stark results: more than half of Arab families were considered poor in 2020, compared to 40 per cent of Jewish families.[24] I want to draw attention to my use of production and reproduction as verbs throughout this essay. This is because I want to emphasise the colonial relationship as productive and generative, rather than static. It reproduces itself not merely through laws and state policies but through a systemic ordering and enclosuring of the entire social body and its relationship to human and non-human nature.

"FORGETTING TO DIE"

Today, Israel expresses the quintessence of the current moment of global capitalism. The Israeli state's commitment to non-hegemonic control, its advocacy for poisoning Palestine's ecology, and its open rejection of the most basic contours of democracy capture the systemic essence of capitalism when stripped of forms of bourgeois rights. Zionism's commitment to the flourishing of Israeli-Jewish life, further contains a purpose and a function beyond the expulsion of Palestinians from the social body. Such flourishing, the beautiful avenues, the well-watered lawns, visually projects Israeli society to closely mimic the West, thus rehearsing age-old Orientalist tropes of a civilised West versus a barbaric East. Such identification also makes the West more sympathetic to Israeli life-making where, in the West's account books, the value of Israeli life continues to soar over the Palestinian. It brings to mind Ehud Barak's description of Israel as "a Villa in the Jungle".

In this essay I have tried to explain how and why the infrastructures of life-making (or social reproduction) in Palestine are currently more acutely political than anywhere else in the world and how the flourishing of Israeli life is *dependent* on the debilitation of Palestinian life-making. Ursula K. Le Guin's short story, "The One Who Walks Away from Omelas", captures the relationality of this violence. In the story, we are introduced to a fairy-tale-like city, Omelas, where life is perfect and bountiful for all its citizens. Omelas, however, inters a secret. Buried in a prison house in the city, is this society's only atrocity, a solitary child kept in constant misery, filth, and state of abjection. Once Omelas citizens are old enough, they are told this truth about their flourishing, and most come to accept this as a necessary sacrifice for their splendour. Upon learning the truth, some do walk away from Omelas, but most choose to remain. As images flood our airwaves of Israeli civilians rejoicing as they block aid trucks into Gaza, the weight of Le Guin's insight should unsettle conventional understanding of colonial violence. If this comparison with Omelas holds rather well for the Israelis, it decisively fails to represent the Palestinian condition. For Palestinians are the furthest from that abject, fictional child. Instead, they are a people who, against the greatest of odds, come the closest to Marx's definition of species being with which we began this essay.

The South African militant and artist Barry Vincent Feinberg once observed that "an unusually large number of poems stem from Palestinian poets". A Palestinian poet responding to Feinberg's comment replied, "the only thing my people have never been denied is the right to dream".[25] This is an extraordinary but consistent feature of Palestinian life, despite one hundred years of colonial violence.

The Palestinian American poet Naomi Shihab Nye concludes her poem "A Palestinian Might Say" thus:

who talks about how sad the land looks,
marked by a massive wall?
That's not a normal shadow.
It's something else looming over your lives.[26]

Nye's words, like those of many other poets, enclose a brilliant contradiction. On the one hand, Palestinian art chronicles the violent expulsion and control of Palestinians from and within the social body; on the other hand, the existence of this art in conditions of debilitation is a rejection of Palestinian deportation. Such expressions of Palestinian lives in art and daily living should prompt us to think through Marx's contention that music was "really free labor", and that such labours constituted a continuous leitmotif within and despite capitalist alienation. Palestine today, I contend, actualises this irrepressible human strain within capitalism, a reason why, like the slave rebellions in Marx's time and the resistance of the Vietnamese in the 1960s, Palestinian struggle resonates today with a wide swathe of the oppressed who see their own struggle, or their humanity, being articulated in that of the Palestinians.

The Zionist colonisers knew well the power of Palestinian humanity. General Moshe Dayan once said that reading a poem by Fadwa Tuqan was like "facing twenty enemy commandos".[27] This is how Tuqan spoke of Palestine:

our land has a throbbing heart,
it doesn't cease to beat, and it endures
the unendurable. It keeps the secrets
of hills and wombs. This land sprouting
with spikes and palms is also the land
that gives birth to a freedom-fighter.
This land, my sister, is a woman.[28]

This "dream" of Palestine is, of course, beyond formal creative energies (such as composing poetry or music) but a dream of return, of homelands, and of histories – thus indicating a set of purposive, conscious labours to sustain that "dream". Such "rational" labour is quintessentially the species being of humanity. Bertell Ollman indicates that the closest Marx comes to defining "human nature in general" is when he says: "The whole character of a species... is contained in the character of its life activity; and free, conscious activity is man's species character"; and further, "as individuals express their lives, so they are".[29] What can we call a people who constantly, ceaselessly, despite every attempt against them, continue to "express their lives?" In another time and place, we called them revolting slaves or resistant Vietnamese. Today, without a doubt, we call them Palestinians. Or a people who despite sustained violence and dispossession, continue to express the core instinct of humanity, what it is to be free. In Mahmoud Darwish's words:

A woman soldier shouted:
Is that you again? Didn't I kill you?
I said: You killed me... and I forgot, like you, to die.[30]

NOTES

1. OHCHR. "Issue of Palestinian Pregnant Women".
2. Marx, *Economic and Philosophical Manuscripts* (1977), 69.
3. Marx, *Economic and Philosophical Manuscripts* (1977), 23 and 73–74.
4. Marx, *Capital*, vol. 3, 958–59.
5. Marx, *Grundrisse*, 341.
6. Marx, *Grundrisse*, 444.
7. Chak, "Not Only to Stay Alive".
8. Quoted in Puar, *The Right to Maim*, 135.
9. Douthat, "Five Rules".
10. The Heroine Award was discontinued in 1959 when the government realised that it was mostly Palestinian mothers who were claiming the reward. See Yuval-Davis and Stasiulis, *Unsettling Settler Societies*.
11. Weiss, *Chosen Body*, 1–4.
12. Weiss, *Chosen Body*, 1–4.
13. Weiss, *Chosen Body*, 2.
14. Golda Meir quoted in Yuval-Davis "National Reproduction", 92.
15. Noura Erakat quoted in Englert, Schatz, and Warren, *From the River to the Sea*, 13.
16. Povinelli, *Geontologies*.
17. Oxfam, "Humanitarian Impact".
18. Dr Ghannam quoted in Said and Ehab, "Gaza's Kids".
19. Weinberger, "Maternity Leave in Israel".
20. OECD, "Better Life Index".
21. Human Rights Watch, "Middle East and North Africa".
22. Library of Congress, "Israel".
23. Cali and Miaari, "Labor Market Impact"; and Rijke and Minca, "Inside Checkpoint 300".
24. Khoury et al., "Five-Year Plan".
25. This exchange is reproduced in Prashad, "The Only Right that Palestinians have".
26. Nye, "A Palestinian Might Say", 90.

27. Joffe, "Fadwa Tuqan".
28. Khalidi, "This Land, My Sister".
29. Ollman, *Alienation*, 109. The quote is from Marx, *Economic and Philosophical Manuscripts* (1977), 73.
30. Darwish, "In Jerusalem", 211–12.

5

Decolonialism as Social Reproductive Class Struggle

Tal-Hi Bitton

Israel's present genocide in Palestine has constituted a thorough attack at all
levels of human life. In Gaza specifically, not only has Israel devastated the
built environments in which Gazans produce and reproduce life, it has done
so by targeting the very institutions and labourers who carry out those re/
productive activities. Considering the Gazan healthcare system specifically,
by the end of the first year of the genocide, Israel targeted 162 health institutions, rendering inoperative 80 health centres and 34 hospitals, damaging
131 ambulances, and killing 986 medical workers. Meanwhile, 1.7 million of
the 2.3 million Gazan population have suffered contagious diseases, chronic
illness, injury, cancer, and outbreaks of polio spread through wastewater.[1]
Israel has clearly met the conditions stipulated by the Geneva Convention as comprising genocide. It has decimated food systems, crop fields,
and the encompassing ecosystem; it has restricted humanitarian operations and destroyed water, sanitation, and hygiene systems.[2] In addition to
killing thousands of children physically and mentally maiming them and/
or preventing their births, Israel has arguably forcibly transferred Palestinian children by displacing Palestinians as refugees in other countries. Israel's
attack on all Palestinian life-making is "Deliberately inflicting on the group
conditions of life calculated to bring about its physical destruction".[3] The
attack on Palestinian life-*making* is perfectly embodied in the Israeli army's
use of Gazan hospitals and schools as provisional military bases and detention facilities from which to deepen the genocide. Photographs circulating
on social media that depict young Israeli soldiers, many barely 18, smiling
and waving in front of ruined Palestinian schoolyards and hospitals reveal
in a flash the degree to which Zionist death-making is not just condoned but
celebrated.[4]

Another revelatory moment is Benjamin Netanyahu's announcement that Israel plans to turn what remains of Gaza into an Israeli-controlled Free Trade Zone modelled on Singapore and Abu Dhabi. The "Gaza 2035" plan aims to "rebuild from nothing" Israeli-controlled Gaza as the hub for the India–Middle-East–Europe Economic Corridor (IMEC), itself announced at the September 2023 G20 summit in New Delhi.[5] By "deradicalising" what remains of Gaza and placing ultimate political control, euphemistically called "security", into Israeli hands, Israel endeavours to neutralise Palestinian liberation, while gaining access to Gazan oil fields and developing the area as a crucial node of the IMEC with ports, railways, and pipelines connecting Western capitalist countries to the Gulf States and India. Whether this plan is possible remains another question, but as an expression of underlying motives, it clearly aims to offer Israel's central imperialist supporter, the United States, a significant countervailing force to China's international rise. The genocide, thus, is a means for Israel to leverage and re-establish its position within the broader inter-imperialist/capitalist rivalries shaping the global capitalist system today.[6]

Amid this constellation of forces, how do we understand colonialism as an annihilation of Indigenous peoples' life-making? How does settler colonialism relate to existing capitalist interests and imperialist relations to transform Indigenous society materially? How does this understanding of material transformation illuminate the complex dynamics between Indigenous resistance, settler and Indigenous class structures, and processes of elimination, dispossession, and exploitation? How can decolonialism, as exemplified by Palestinian struggle, overcome this material transformation?

In this chapter, I develop a social reproduction account of how British imperialist and Zionist settler colonial forces transformed the prior social subsumption of nature in Ottoman Palestine into two distinct circuits: production of surplus-value and social reproduction of people. I refer to this socio-historical process as the "imperial-settler diremption of Palestine" and argue that it is the material basis for settler colonial violence against Palestinians as well as their ever-changing place as labourers under Israeli capital. To do so, I first discuss Settler Colonialism Studies (SCS) and its foundational paradigm that understands settler colonialism as based on the elimination of Indigenous peoples. I argue that this paradigm obscures capitalism's relationship to settler colonialism. I turn to Amílcar Cabral's account of imperialism as a corrective and as a basis from which to explain the imperialist-settler diremption beginning in mid-nineteenth-century Ottoman Palestine.[7] This stages the chapter's final sections, where I argue that decolonialism is a form of class struggle when understood as a social reproductive struggle to overcome the imperialist-settler diremption of human life-making from production.

SETTLER COLONIALISM: ELIMINATION OR EXPLOITATION?

Patrick Wolfe's formulation, the "logic of elimination", proposes that settler colonialism is a particular form of colonialism in which the coloniser eliminates the Indigenous community to permanently appropriate Indigenous land for their new society and state.[8] This model, further developed by Lorenzo Veracini and others, has become the dominant framework of SCS examining cases such as Australia, New Zealand, Canada, the United States, South Africa, and Israel.[9] However, the study of settler colonialism pre-dated SCS as a framework; the Palestinian Liberation Organization and its various parties, for instance, were describing Zionism as a settler colonial enterprise decades before Wolfe.[10]

The SCS approach emphasises the ongoing, eliminatory, and structural nature of settler colonialism. Settler rule continually asserts itself materially and ideologically against Indigenous peoples and their claims to sovereignty and self-determination. The justification of settler claims necessitates the absence of Indigenous peoples through elimination (be it through genocide, forced displacement, or miscegenation).[11] And it is structural in that the categories "settler" and "native" do not pre-exist but rather are created and maintained as constitutive social locations amid the settler colonial transformation.[12] In Palestine, this logic of elimination has manifested through various mechanisms, including ongoing land confiscation, settlement expansion, dispossession from homes, the institutionalisation of discriminatory legal and administrative systems (e.g. making Palestinians within Israel, or 1948 Palestinians, second-class citizens), and more.

Though SCS has provided many important insights, it has significant limitations which must be assessed in order to understand the Palestinian case.[13] One key issue is its narrow focus on elimination at the expense of understanding exploitation: Wolfe and those following him have stressed that the goal of settler colonialism is elimination, not exploitation, for these two phenomena are (supposedly) contradictory as exploitation requires the continued existence of Indigenous peoples if they are to exert their life activity in the form of labour to produce surplus. However, as recent scholarship reveals, exploitation of the colonised is a key social process alongside dispossession in various settler colonies, which complicates the class composition of settler colonies.[14]

Zionist forces have relied in the past, and continue to rely, on Palestinian labour. In the formative decades of Zionist colonisation, many Palestinians were employed in the Zionist *moshavot*, privately owned plantation settlements (which would become a flashpoint within factions of the settlers from the 1920s through to the *Nakba* in 1948). Labour Zionism, as it was promoted both by its bourgeois leaders and working-class settlers, challenged the use of Palestinian labour, advocating instead for a segregated economy and labour market in the "conquest of Land and Labor". Labour Zionism advanced its colonial expropriation of Palestinian land by setting up exclusively Jewish collectivist plantation settlements, *kibbutzim*, which often functioned as colonial outposts strategically placed on hilltops and regions outside the fertile coastal plains of Palestine where the *moshavot* operated.[15] Despite their ascendance, the *kibbutzim* and Labour Zionism never fully extricated Palestinian labour from the wider, developing Zionist colony. With the founding of Israel, Palestinian labour, while not employed across all sectors, was crucial in certain industries like construction.[16]

While this complexity is not adequately captured by the dominant SCS framework, political economic analyses show that Zionist settler colonial tendencies are often counteracted by Israeli need for cheap, exploitable, and precarious Palestinian labour. Sai Englert's recent work demonstrates how Israel's largest trade union federation, the Histadrut, and recent collective bargaining agreements won by the Israeli Construction and Wood Workers' Union have largely reproduced racialised segregation within construction sectors while counteracting more progressive labour organising by Palestinian and migrant labourers on both sides of the Green Line.[17] That construction is such an important site of contestation for Zionism's competing needs to dispossess and exploit Palestinians speaks to the importance of attending to the production and reproduction of Zionist settler colonialism. As Sobhi Samour states, "a materialist appraisal of Israel's demand for Palestinian labor would acknowledge that as long as such demand exists... Israel's settlercolonial [*sic*] strategy of elimination is kept in check".[18]

Whereas SCS assumes settler colonialism to be related to but ultimately distinct from capitalism, each social system governed by different logics, a historical materialist account needs to trace the composition of settler colonial appropriation in its historical contingency.[19] Like the "divided economy" view of Palestine and Israel, SCS posits Zionists and Palestinians as two already distinguished communities.[20] Such analytic commitments to the systematic distinctiveness of Palestinians and Zionists can instil, in Shereen Seikaly's words, "a particular formula: the Jews act, the Palestinians react".[21] Moreover, this theoretical orientation of SCS implicitly negates the precolonial relations within the Ottoman Levant, often erroneously viewed in Orientalist academic and public discourses as definitively "sectarian" rather than ecumenical, as Ussama Makdisi argues in his *Age of Coexistence*.[22]

Such analysis, assuming the separation of social systems, fails to understand the relational nature of capitalism and settler colonialism, and leaves unclear, or worse advocates for, the separateness of their attendant struggles. All this prompts anticapitalist critique to be dogmatically economistic, for both Marxists and their critics, and fails to account for the transformation of a social totality through economic *and* extra-economic means. This is especially important because Palestinian waged labour employed by Zionist capital (or subcontracted through the Zionist state) ought to be seen as a crucial mode of underdeveloping Indigenous sociality. Within settler colonial contexts, the persistence, even if discontinuous, of waged Indigenous labour, and the challenges Indigenous peoples have mounted from their waged exploitation and beyond urge us to grapple with how settler colonialism is, in certain contexts, the political form taken in capitalist development and state-building.

IMPERIALISM'S HISTORICAL DENIAL OF A PEOPLE

To better understand settler colonialism, then, we need to examine how it transforms social relations in which humans re/produce their existence. To do so requires, among other things, clarifying the general transformation imperialism and its colonial expressions induce in pre-existing social totalities. Drawing on the work of Amílcar Cabral, we can understand *the ultimate essence of imperialism* as the "denial of the historical process of the dominated people, by means of violent usurpation of the freedom of the process of development of the national productive forces" and its subsumption into the global capitalist economy and its drive to accumulate more surplus-value.[23]

Cabral argues that imperialism and colonialism, which arise from capital's ambition for globalising surplus-value accumulation, necessarily influence the development of productive forces in colonised societies. Imperialism is "piracy reorganised", which paralyses, stagnates, and even regresses the development of productive forces through many factors. Imperialism often introduces conglomerates, either privately held or colonial-state-owned. It degrades the status of the native ruling classes, while simultaneously creating a new native comprador class from their ranks. It induces urbanisation, either through force or compulsion, to populate new strata of colonial workers, state employees, and commercial and liberal professionals, while simultaneously forming urban and rural lumpenproletariat. Through these changes, colonial domination strives to transform the colonised means and relations of production by making their final cause production of exchange-values for international exchange, usurping the Indigenous people's power over the development of their form, means, and relations in which reproduce themselves. Thwarted social production, what Walter Rodney and others referred to as "underdevelopment", names the significant dysfunctionality of producing human life as social production serves the motives of capital's colonial subsumption.[24]

Against this totalising drive of settler colonialism, decolonialism proper is a phenomenon of the socio-economic whole where the social totality rejects imperialism's denial of the colonised people's historical process and capitalism's *telos*.[25] The destruction of imperialist and colonial rule is the regaining of the "historical personality" of the colonised.[26] This historical personality is centrally the formerly colonised people's resumption of social production for their sake as self-determined social metabolism with the land on which they live. This is not a recasting of simplistic readings of the Marxist conception of the economic base underlying a social superstructure.[27] Rather, it expresses the re/production of people in its material inhabitation on the land and its cultural and social idiosyncrasies that emerge from this landed social metabolism. It is, as Glen Coulthard describes, a historically specific "system of reciprocal relations and obligations" to the land which a society inhabits, and Indigenous decolonialism, a "*grounded normativity*".[28]

Cabral's concept of the "historical development of the dominated people" offers a profound existential insight on the implications of capitalist imperialism. It suggests that a society's historical development is fundamentally about the evolving organisation of a people's will to live, their life activities, their expression of freedom, forms of pre-reflective consciousness, and the meanings they fashion for their lives within their current situation. Imperialism, regardless of the pre-existing class relations, fundamentally restructures and curtails how people actualise their freedom.

THE IMPERIAL-SETTLER DIREMPTION

Although Zionist colonisation began in earnest in 1882, British imperial penetration into Palestine began decades earlier. While we must account for the internal logics of Zionism's reproduction, its initial emergence is conditioned by a historical context not of its choosing.[29] Of those historical premises, the introduction of nascent capitalist relations by way of British imperialism was crucial and decisive. Capitalist relations spread through a process Marx termed "subsumption", in which pre-existing social production is incorporated by way of being transformed into specifically capitalist forms.[30] By tracing subsumption in the context of nineteenth-century Palestine, we can better appreciate how Palestinian social metabolism was already in grave transformation, which Zionism exacerbated through major investment from European capital and influx of Jewish settler labour.[31] Thus, all human life in the geopolitical region was subjected to the life-denying contradiction between capitalist production and social reproduction which both Palestinians and Israelis faced, albeit very differently. As a shorthand, I term this process the "imperial-settler diremption" of Palestine.

This transformation began with British imperialism in the nineteenth century and was intensified through Zionist colonisation. Capitalist transformation of Palestine pre-dates Zionist colonisation by roughly 30 years during the second Ottoman *tanzimat* (reforms) period of 1856–1882. Following the Crimean War, Ottoman reforms and increasing European influence led to rapid capitalist development in the region. Palestinian production became increasingly integrated into the world market, focusing on export-oriented agrarian goods such as grains, citrus, olive oil, and cotton.[32] This economic transformation was facilitated by new legal frameworks, particularly the Ottoman 1858 Land Code and the 1878 Land Law, which privatised land and separated legal property from customary use. These changes, while initially not drastically affecting the Palestinian *fellaheen* (peasantry), became instrumental in the subsequent British imperial and Zionist colonial projects. The introduction of capitalist agriculture disrupted traditional forms of land tenure (*miri*, *mulk*, and *waqf* systems) and communal land use (*musha'a*), setting the stage for more profound transformations.[33] In this period, the *fellaheen* were not impoverished from their dispossession as they were largely allowed to cultivate the lands on which they had lived. Rather, "The fellah who was forced to transfer the title of his land to the moneylender continued to cultivate his land, though under deteriorating living conditions", some needing to work for other landowners.[34] Ultimately, though, the *fellaheen* retained usury rights to the land as their main source of their subsistence.

The establishment of Zionist colonies in 1882 only intensified the capitalist transformation of Palestine. Zionist settlements, both the privately managed *moshavot* and the collectivist *kibbutzim*, operated on capitalist relations despite socialist rhetoric.[35] These settlements, often funded by private Zionist capital or the Jewish National Fund, employed wage labour and were oriented towards surplus generation. The *moshavot*, dominant in the early period of Zionist settlement, acquired large tracts of fertile agricultural land and often employed newly proletarianised Palestinian labour, which was cheaper than Zionist labour. This process further eroded traditional Palestinian subsistence production, as *fellaheen* were increasingly separated from their means of production and forced into wage labour. The Zionist settler working class, in turn, advocated for a Jewish-exclusive economy, exacerbating the displacement of Palestinian agricultural workers and intensifying the capitalist transformation of the region's economy. The *fellaheen* keenly understood that the exchange of land as private property amounted to serious limits on their ability to survive.[36] Gershon Shafir helpfully frames the situation as a "decisive historical encounter between [...] the absolute right of private ownership on which European capitalism rested [...] and the more diffuse, but not less extensive, rights of usage in practice in many pre-capitalist societies" – struggles which persist today.[37]

These processes generated, over time and unevenly, distinct circuits in which humans produced commodities to be exchanged on the market separately from the reproduction of human life. The introduction of capitalist agriculture subsumed pre-existing agricultural labour processes at first not by changing the labour process itself but by extending the length of the workday. The pre-1882 British colonial plantations, therefore, largely formally subsumed Palestinian forces and relations of production. Already, this placed more constraints on the *fellaheen* who increasingly needed to engage in some wage labour to compensate for reduced subsistence production. What existed beyond such waged labour comprised the newly forming circuit of social reproduction, including small-scale subsistence production, and domestic and communal care. With the introduction of Zionist colonisation, and especially under the British Mandate, European and Zionist agriculture industrialised, that is, real subsumption took primacy in the development of capitalist relations, transforming the labour process to increase the production of relative surplus-value. While this was occurring within capitalist production, those forms of life-making that exceeded these processes were subsumed into capitalist forms of social reproduction.

In the Palestinian context, this diremption is manifested in various ways. Most importantly, Palestinians are separated from their land and other means of subsistence creating a metabolic rift in which Palestinian reproduction is undermined. Zionism has ultimately created a captive labour market dependent on Israeli employment or on Palestinian capital in the current era which operates within the general reproduction of Zionism.[38] Israel regularly targets Palestinian social institutions and community structures through legal, military, and economic means of strangulation or repression. The imposition of restrictions on movement, education, and healthcare disables, under-resources, and makes more time- and labour-intensive Palestinian social reproduction. This restructuring is evident in the disruption of traditional agricultural practices, the proletarianisation of Palestinian labour, and the imposition of new political and economic structures that serve the interests of the settler colonial state.

TOWARDS SOCIAL REPRODUCTIVE STRUGGLE

The diremption of production from social reproduction entails that processes of life-making are no longer the end of social production but rather, from the point of view of capital, its means. For all people dispossessed from the means of production, this separation constitutes the primary condition which disables the expanded reproduction of human beings. This condition obtains for those who are employed via a wage and those who are not.[39] Included in the latter are also the colonised who, as dispossessed from the means of production, are not (yet or fully) subsumed into the developing capitalist relations of production. These groups comprise the reserve army of labour which capitalism, as a system, requires to be reproduced to accommodate its fluctuating needs for fresh labour power. Waged labourers and non-waged, yet dispossessed peoples all compose the international working class – the class of humans in capitalist societies who have only their labour power to possibly sell. The question is: if forms of colonialism are produced capitalistically and thereby expand capitalism, in what sense is anticolonialism itself an expression or determinate form of class struggle?

Heretofore, the conceptions of class struggle SRT champions have much to do with social struggles which arise out of conditions of social reproduction to challenge those very conditions. These include struggles against land evictions, for access to clean and renewable energy, for water, fair housing, cost of living adjustments, feminist and antiracist struggles, struggles against policing (especially in its militarised form, which Israel exports internationally), and much more. However, SRT generally stresses the need to connect these struggles with struggles in the realm of production where capitalist society sets into motion its ultimate *telos*, the production of surplus-value to be accumulated.[40] What is required, in short, is a general confrontation not with individual capitalists but with the general *system* of capitalism as such. This culminates in the notion of a social reproductive strike as the general protest against the reproduction of the system that privileges profits over life-making.[41]

SRT stresses capitalism must be resisted in its various expressions, which cannot be limited to struggles with individual capitalists or sectors of the economy. These struggles can arise from within the circuit of social reproduction, which includes people who are not employed in waged labour. As such, SRT forwards as its end the unity of human life in harmony with our conditions for flourishing over and against the life-denying diremption of social reproduction from capitalist production. SRT endeavours to make intelligible these non-waged struggles as constituent expressions of class struggle. These can be considered "social reproductive struggles" insofar as they contest the diremption of production and social reproduction which is capitalism's central antisocial social relation.[42]

The concept of social reproductive struggle builds on SRT to provide a dialectical framework for understanding class struggle beyond waged labour. While I appreciate SRT's (rightful) aim in fomenting general, social reproductive strikes, all strikes must be *produced*. Some wait for opportune conditions (i.e. intolerable conditions brought about by a "Big One" crisis) to move the working class to strike. But such a position fails to take seriously capital's negative feedback loops which counteract crises' threat to the reproduction of the system at large. More importantly for my concerns here, this position takes for granted that "the existing working class is a product of capital" and acts in accordance with capital's imperatives. Are we really to believe we do not need to practise and develop our capacities for fighting *for ourselves* as a socially united class? We need to address, as Lukács saw it, the "immaturity" of the working class to engage in revolutionary struggle, be that disorganisation, political quietude, lack of class consciousness, etc.[43] As part of that, we need "conscious struggle against inherent tendencies produced by capitalism".[44]

For this, Marta Harnecker and Michael Lebowitz offer the concept of "protagonism", which means the agency members of the working class gain when they act and see themselves as causes of social change.[45] The pre-reflective lives of workers produced by capital usurps their agency over their everyday lives. However, as Marx often argued, it was by engaging in struggle that people transformed themselves, their values and self-understandings, in endeavouring to transform their conditions.[46] Engaging in struggle across various social relations fosters a confidence in those people. It also grows practical skills in solidary, community resilience, and expanding the reproduction of the working class. These are crucial for building advanced forms of struggle which require coordination, trust, and competency. This is counterposed to the passivity that often is produced through electoral processes or being handed a programme from a vanguard party (not to discount the importance of either under certain conditions). While social reproductive struggle aims at contesting the scission of life-making from production, it emphasises the need to develop our capacities as individuals of social class to force such contestations. Only then may the force of participating in a revolutionary social force be realised in the everyday lives of the masses.

Social reproductive struggle can be summarised thusly. It centrally contests the diremption of life-making from production under capitalism as life-denying. It pushes for the expanded reproduction of the total working class to develop its strength as a class. As a means for doing so, it aims to develop working-class people's capacities for protagonism. Thus, it aspires to realise at the level of skill, self-understanding, and life-making solidarity with all those within the working class. All of this aims at the abolition of capitalism, and its historically specific expressions, as privations on humanity's free, self-directed flourishing within our conscious preservation of our natural conditions for us and life generally. It is about redirecting resources and human activity away from making death (including dead labour) and towards flourishing life.[47]

DECOLONIALISM AS SOCIAL REPRODUCTIVE STRUGGLE

Decolonialism is class struggle because, in its most adequate form, it contests the separation of social reproduction and production. As Cabral has it, decolonial national liberation "is the inalienable right of every people to have their own history; and the aim of national liberation is to regain this right usurped by imperialism, that is to free the process of development of the national productive forces".[48] To overcome imperialism as the historical denial of the Palestinian people, social metabolism must be emancipated from the imperial-settler diremption. The struggle must grow its capacities to do so.

The history of the Palestinian liberation movement has both championed and, at crucial moments, weakened such protagonism. Historically, one of the strengths of the movement has been the cultivation of a spirit of resistance and resilience, *sumud*, among Palestinian communities.[49] Growing *sumud* has often meant parents bringing children to demonstrations, passing down shared history of struggle against colonisation, and building communal structures from which to organise Palestinians. In short, *sumud* expresses struggling to expand the reproduction of the Palestinian working class to strengthen Palestinian protagonism against its imperial-colonial domination.

We can take our cue from the Palestinian women who have been vital to the liberation movement since the early twentieth century. The Palestinian Women's Union, formed in 1921 in Jerusalem, organised significant protests against British rule and Zionist policies. In 1921, it helped orchestrate one of the largest demonstrations to pressure the British to cancel the Balfour Declaration. By 1929, over 300 women gathered at the first Women's Conference, drafting a programme emphasising forms of struggle such as demonstrations, conferences, leaflet distribution, and sit-ins in churches and mosques.[50]

Decades before our contemporary Boycott, Divestment and Sanctions (BDS) movement, Palestinian women organised a boycott of foreign and Zionist products, as well as demonstrations, and helped with smuggling weapons through British Army checkpoints.[51] During the Great Revolt of 1936–1939, they led a six-month-long strike and boycott of foreign and Zionist products across Palestinian cities and villages. These urban women also cared for prisoners' families, held conferences, and disseminated pamphlets, often exhibiting a more radical political consciousness than their male counterparts.[52] Against widespread dispossession and forced displacement of the *Nakba* in 1947–1948, the Palestinian women's movement expanded its services.[53] They set up first-aid centres, orphanages, and health clinics, providing financial support for poorer families. Many Palestinian women joined underground political parties in Jordan, while those in the West Bank focused on addressing changing social needs under Zionist colonisation.

The First Intifada (1987–1993) brought about new arrangements of struggle. Women organised around their classed, nationalised, and gendered oppression, all while pushing to expand the reproduction of Palestinian life. Outside of armed struggle, these groups organised women in villages and refugee camps, those whom the previous generation of Palestinian women organisers had less successfully brought into the movement.[54] They established health and education committees to combat Israeli closures of hospitals, clinics, and schools. These women's groups defended neighbourhoods from raids and settler aggression, prevented arrests, and even mediated family disputes. Additionally, they cultivated community gardens "as a token of return to land and as a means of providing food during emergency situations".[55]

Within armed struggle, women's involvement shows a contrasting picture. While some were wounded and others martyred, these women were not spared from the "feminised" task of reproductive labour.[56] Rosemary Sayigh describes how women in the militant cadres were given military training while also being set "to work in support activities that were 'natural' extensions of their domestic skills – nursing, providing food and uniforms for the fighters, setting up the social and cultural institutions that accompanied armed struggle. A rough division of labour emerged, with younger women being sent to the camps to organise and train women there and older ones directed into administration".[57] This gendered division of reproductive labour within Palestinian national struggle ultimately conformed with wider trends within Palestinian civil society, such that patriarchy permeates the liberation movement's praxis despite Palestinian revolutionaries theoretically uniting women's liberation with national liberation.[58]

While the demands of expanding working-class reproduction and protagonism were clear objectives for these women's struggles, that they were often limited to only "women's work" reflects broader limitations within the movement. One crucial moment was the Oslo process, through which Palestine was initiated into the neoliberal era thereby gravely counteracting Palestinian protagonism and social reproduction.[59] Still, the importance of social reproductive struggle cannot be understated, nor was it pushed completely back as shown by the Great March of Return and the 2021 Unity Intifada.

CONCLUSION

At stake in decolonial struggle is life: control over one's life and the collective securing of conditions to foster human life and its flourishing. Against this, imperial and Zionist capital has profited greatly through the imperial-settler diremption of Palestine. My analysis has offered a critical intervention in Settler Colonial Studies by integrating insights from social reproduction theory (SRT) to better understand the material transformation of Palestine through Zionist colonisation. The concept of "imperial-settler diremption" reveals how settler colonialism fundamentally operates as an expression of imperialism through the violent separation of production from social reproduction, reorienting both towards capitalist accumulation. This theoretical framework recontextualises Patrick Wolfe's "logic of elimination" paradigm by showing how settler colonialism functions as a specific form of capitalist development, creating conditions that undermine both Palestinian and Israeli working-class life-making, albeit in radically different ways. Through this lens, decolonial struggle emerges not merely as resistance to dispossession but as a form of class struggle that contests the very separation of production from social reproduction created by imperialism and settler colonialism. The Palestinian liberation movement's history demonstrates both the potential and challenges of such struggle, particularly through women's organising that explicitly linked national liberation with the expansion of Palestinian social reproduction. In this manner, the degree to which a social struggle contests this diremption is a crucial criterion for critiquing the revolutionary potential of various social forces – those of the Palestinian liberation movement as well as those of the reactionary Israeli working class.[60] The framework suggests that effective decolonial struggle must contest not only political sovereignty but also the very structure of capitalist social relations that both subtend and expand through settler colonial processes.

ACKNOWLEDGEMENTS

I wish to thank the editors, Tithi Bhattacharya and Sue Ferguson, for including me in this project, their encouragement, and their helpful comments which have strengthened this manuscript. I also thank Bonnie Mann and Aaron Jaffe for feedback on earlier drafts, as well as the support from Rhiannon Lindgren and especially Maxwell Cramer throughout the writing process. This research has been supported through a research grant from the University of Oregon Center for the Study of Women in Society. Any shortcomings are the fault of the author alone.

NOTES

1. Chughtai and Okur, "One Year of Israel's War".
2. IPC, "IPC Global Initiative".
3. UN General Assembly, Convention on the Prevention and Punishment of the Crime of Genocide.
4. EHRM, "Gaza". *Haaretz*, "Israeli Army Appears".
5. Barnea, "From Crisis to Prosperity"; Rizzi, "Infinite Connection".
6. For an excellent analysis of these dynamics, see Englert and Bhattacharyya, "Capital's Genocide". For a longer history of the United States' attempt to develop

free trade agreements across the Middle East and North Africa, see Hanieh, *Lineages of Revolt*.

7. Cabral, "The Weapon of Theory".

8. Wolfe, "Settler Colonialism".

9. Wolfe, *Traces of History*; Veracini, *Israel and Settler Society*; and Veracini, "Containment, Elimination, Endogeneity".

10. Sayegh, "Zionist Colonialism"; Zu'bi, "Development of Capitalism"; Abdo, "Colonial Capitalism"; and Sayigh, "Palestinian Women".

11. Wolfe, "Settler Colonialism".

12. Wolfe describes the distinct kinds of colonialism thus: "In contrast to the kind of colonial formation that Cabral or Fanon confronted settler colonies were not primarily established to extract surplus value from indigenous labour. Rather, they are premised on displacing indigenes from (or replacing them on) the land" (Wolfe, *Settler Colonialism*, 1–2). However, Fanon was deeply engaged in struggle against French settler colonialism in Algeria. And Cabral, whose thought I discuss below, held that classical colonialism, the direct domination by a foreign capitalist agent, took the form of total or partial destruction or ostensible preservation of Indigenous peoples (say, on reservations), all of which ostensibly match Wolfe's account.

13. For an excellent critique of SCS and its use of the Marxian conception of dispossession, see Davies, "World Turned Outside In".

14. This is contrasted in scholarship about South African settler colonialism; see Kelley, "Rest of Us". For further arguments of this kind, see Englert, "Settlers, Workers"; and Dunbar-Ortiz, *Indigenous Peoples' History*.

15. Asad, "Class Transformation"; Zu'bi, "Development of Capitalism"; and Abdo, "Colonial Capitalism".

16. See, for instance, Ross, *Stone Men*; and Harb, "Exhausted Circulation".

17. These recent agreements nominally cover these non-Jewish workers as well as their Jewish counterparts, yet their provisions largely benefit the stable managerial segments overwhelmingly held by Jewish Israelis. They largely fail to address the dire working conditions for low pay within the so-called wet works, that is, cementing or plastering, whose labourers are often subcontracted out. See Englert, "Hebrew Labor".

18. Samour, "Covid-19 and the Necroeconomy", 59.

19. This is analogous to how certain feminists and antiracists argued for a dual- or multi-systems approach to the connections between capitalism and patriarchy or race. For a quintessential account of a dual systems approach, see Delphy, *Close to Home*; and Guillaumin, *Racism, Sexism, Power*. For feminist socialist critiques of this style of argument, see Young, "Beyond the Unhappy Marriage"; Vogel, "Domestic-Labour Debate"; Hennessy and Ingraham, "Socialist Feminism"; Arruzza, "Functionalist, Determinist, Reductionist"; Gimenez, *Marx, Women, and Capitalist*; and Bohrer, *Marxism and Intersectionality*.

20. See, for example, Metzer, *Divided Economy*. However, as Sherene Seikaly contends, the divided economy view is made possible from the relative lack of documentation about Palestinian wages, capital, investment, etc., much of

which was destroyed or seized by the Yishuv in 1948 and subsequently in later military campaigns (Seikaly, "Men of Capital", 401).

21. Seikaly, "Men of Capital", 401.

22. Makdisi, *Age of Coexistence*, 7. Ottoman Levant enjoyed a vibrant ecumenicism where, though social hierarchies persisted, tolerance and interaction between religious and cultural groups cultivated a communal coexistence. The "ecumenical frame" lasted until the 1948 *Nakba* when European imperialism and the newly established Israeli settler state rendered it inviable. On this, see Chapter 6, "Breaking the Ecumenical Frame: Arab and Jew in Palestine", in Makdisi, *Age of Coexistence*.

23. Cabral, "Weapon of Theory", 129. This bears out as the colonised people's expression of what various competing contemporary theories of imperialism try to ascribe to its essence: either unequal exchange, super-exploitation of the Global South, an expression of monopoly, or (as I prefer) an emergent property of real capitalist competition (not perfect, idealised competition) which differentiates conditions of production and state-building across and within the Global North and South. For an excellent summary of these positions and a defence of the latter, see Post, "Explaining Imperialism Today".

24. I take this to be a general statement of the social reproductive aspects of the kind of total social transformation Fanon and Rodney argue constitutes decolonialism as an act of reshaping the world and the colonised into a new humanity. See, for example, Fanon's comments in "On Violence" as well as his discussion of reshaping relations with land, agriculture, and psyche in "Colonial War and Mental Disorders", in Fanon, *Wretched of the Earth*. As Rodney explains, "Colonialism created conditions which led not just to periodic famine, but to chronic undernourishment, malnutrition and deterioration in the physique of the African people. If such a statement sounds wildly extravagant, it is only because bourgeois propaganda has conditioned even Africans to believe that malnutrition and starvation were the *natural* lot of Africans from time immemorial" (Rodney, *How Europe Underdeveloped Africa*, 236).

25. Busk and Portella, "Contradiction between Use-Value".

26. Cabral, "Weapon of Theory", 130.

27. For an excellent critique of these simplistic dismissals of the base-superstructure conception, see Best, *Automatic Fetish*.

28. Coulthard, *Red Skin, White Masks*, 13–14. Michael Fakhri, UN Special Rapporteur on the right to food, echoes this commitment in his July 2024 UN report on food amid the present genocide: "Food sovereignty is an expression of communities' and Indigenous Peoples' power to determine how they grow, prepare, share and eat food and a reflection of their relationship to land and water. The more that power is equitably shared among all people in a food system, the more likely people will have access to adequate food; and the more that people's relationship with land and water is based on care and reciprocity, the easier it is for people to establish relationships with each other based on care and reciprocity" (Fakhri, "Starvation and the Right to Food").

29. Lebowitz, *Between Capitalism and Community*, 161.

30. Marx denotes two senses of subsumption, formal and real. Formal subsumption names the transformations in which direct producers are shaped into waged labourers employed by capitalists in a labour process which has not in itself been transformed (baring no concurrent real subsumption) but whose working day has been extended, thus capturing more absolute surplus-value. Real subsumption names the transformation of the labour process itself in which productivity is increased through mechanisation and technological innovations, thus "diminishing… the portion of the working day devoted to reproducing the labourer's wage-costs" (see, Buck, "On Primitive Accumulation", 98; and Karl Marx, *Capital*, vol. 1, Chapter 16). For an excellent overview, see de Sicilia, "Being, Becoming, Subsumption"; and for an insightful and promising extension of the distinction in examining gender and social reproduction, see Portella and Busk, "Formal and Real Subsumption". For an account of primitive accumulation that complements these approaches, see Jaffe, "History and Afterlife".

31. Schölch, "Economic Development"; Schölch, *Palestine in Transformation*; Abdo, "Colonial Capitalism"; Weinstock, "Impact of Zionist Colonization"; and Hanegbi, Machover, and Orr, "Class Nature of Israeli Society"; and Shafir, *Land, Labor*. For a discussion of alternative Palestinian class and social formations in British Mandate Palestine, see Seikaly, "Men of Capital".

32. Schölch, "Economic Development"; Schölch, *Palestine in Transformation*; and Abdo, "Colonial Capitalism".

33. Zu'bi, "Development of Capitalism", 91–95.

34. Zu'bi, "Development of Capitalism", 95.

35. Nahla Abdo presents a succinct critique of historiography that repeats the political fantasy that Zionist colonisation was an endeavour in socialism worthy of the name. See Abdo, "Colonial Capitalism".

36. In this petition from Bedouin of Khirbat Duran (east of Jaffa) in 1892, we hear both the *fellaheens'* plight and their concern for the well-being of the settlers themselves: "we have no other choice but to submit this petition to beg for the issuance of an exalted order to allow us to remain in our place of birth where we reside, based on the current arrangement and not to let the Jews chase us away and prevent us from cultivating the land in a way which will guarantee their and our rest and benefit; or else issue an exalted order to allocate us land from the imperial property, which would be sufficient for our livelihood and to sustain our families and children" (quoted in Ben-Bassat, "Rural Reactions", 353).

37. Shafir, *Land, Labor*, 201–202. Struggles around property law and the real appropriation of land are recurrent in Palestine/Israel. The year 2021 saw the violent Zionist attempt to dispossess tens of families from Sheikh Jarrah, Jerusalem, a crucial flashpoint setting off the Unity Intifada. Such struggles were prefigured in 1972, when the Sephardic Community and the General Council of the Congregation of Israel claimed that the properties of Sheikh Jarrah be released and registered to them, citing historical and religious affiliation to the land originating in the nineteenth century. As Hadeel Abu Hussein explains, these two committees supported their claims through a set of documents said to comprise registered land deeds from the Ottoman period, or *Koshan* in Hebrew. While *Koshan* have been successfully used to dispossess Palestinians in Jerusalem after

1967, in the 1972 case, the documents lacked the full description of the property as required by the Ottomans. The Israeli attorney representing the impacted Palestinian families could not locate the existing deeds in Ottoman archives, further questioning the documents' authenticity. These legal battles continued for years, ultimately resulting in a new legal precedent. The attorney, without consulting the families he represented, "negotiated an agreement... with the court that stated that his clients would not challenge the ownership claims of the committees, and would accept the status of protected tenants under the Tenant Protection Law of 1972. This status granted the families the right to continue living in the properties as long as they paid rent and observed the prohibition on all renovation works" (Abu Hussein, *Struggle for Land*, 164). Although the families challenged it, the procedural agreement has provided the precedent with which settlers have attacked Palestinians in Sheikh Jarrah, while in other cases Israeli courts have thrown out Palestinians' legitimate, verified Ottoman-era deeds. For such an example, see the case of Suleiman Darwish Hijazi in Abu Hussein, *Struggle for Land*, 166–67. Where the new precedent limited the ownership claims of Zionists, it simultaneously transformed the legal status of such Palestinians who could be dispossessed under a legal veneer, evicted on the pretence of failing to pay rents. These legal struggles are representative of Zionism's various uses of "legal work", which Noura Erakat explains as the strategic work of legal actors to interpret and reshape existing legal norms to align with their desired outcomings in a particular case. Erakat, *Justice for Some*, 7–8. Not only does Zionist legal work redraw the legal landscape through which dispossession occurs, it simultaneously attempts to conceal the settler-colonial political power behind these property relations as such.

38. For an account of the growth of neoliberalism post-Oslo in the West Bank, see Hanieh, *Lineages of Revolt*, Chapter 5.

39. The latter group includes non-waged reproductive labourers, who rely either on social provisions or the wages of other labourers, and those excluded from the production process for various reasons, such as state-designated criminals, refugees, the unhoused, children, the infirm, or the elderly. Note that it is not a necessary condition for membership in the working class that one actually sells their labour power to be in the working class.

40. Bhattacharya, "Explaining Gender Violence"; Bhattacharya, "How Not to Skip Class"; and Ferguson, *Women and Work*.

41. Jaffe, "From Social Reproduction Theory".

42. Paula Varela helpfully taxonomises three forms of what she terms "social reproduction struggle": those struggles of institutionalised (public or private) social reproduction, such as hospitals or schools; those struggles of unpaid social reproduction work, particularly but not exclusively women's work in households and communities; and finally, those struggles that contest the reproduction of life without being tied to social reproduction work as such, including demands around costs of living, demilitarisation and anti-policing, debt-based dispossession, environmental degradation, and so forth (see Varela, "Women Workers at the Heart").

43. Lukács, *History and Class Consciousness*, 295–96.

44. Lebowitz, *Capitalism and Community*, 163. Earlier, Lebowitz explains "the four critical questions [regarding protagonism] are: how to link struggles of negation to community, how to link prefigurative activities to struggles of negation, how to link separate struggles, and how to fight the tendency for hierarchy. They all pose the same problem: in contested reproduction between capitalism and community, there is no spontaneous path to community. To advance along that path, a political instrument is essential" (160).

45. Harnecker, "Ideas for the Struggle"; and Lebowitz, *Between Capitalism and Community*, 162.

46. As the late and irreplaceable Jane McAlevey wrote, "People participate to the degree they understand – but they also understand to the degree they participate. It's dialectical" (McAlevey, *No Shortcuts*, 6).

47. At this point, my reader may be inclined to ask whether "social reproductive struggle" really constitutes something other than class struggle. To this, I reply that in a sense that reaction is spot on. Insofar as this is what class struggle *should* mean, then there is no disagreement. However, insofar as class struggle often takes impoverished meanings by being relegated (by advocates and dissenters alike) to economistic conceptions, then a new field of intelligibility is needed to make sense of working-class agency that incorporates waged-labour struggles and more.

48. Cabral, "Weapon of Theory", 130.

49. Elia, "75 Years of Sumud"; and Elia, *Greater than the Sum of Our Parts*.

50. Kuttab, "Palestinian Women in the 'Intifada'", 70.

51. Kuttab, "Palestinian Women in the 'Intifada'", 70–71.

52. Al-Hamdani, "Palestinian Women".

53. Kuttab, "Palestinian Women in the "Intifada'", 71.

54. Kuttab, "Palestinian Women in the 'Intifada'", 79–82. However, where Palestinians – especially rank-and-file civilians – have found success, Zionists have been keen to counteract such promise. By disbanding these popular neighbourhood formations in the early period of the Intifada, Israel undercut the women who primarily led and organised these localised groups. And, further, Israel directly counteracted the democratic, mass basis of Palestinian struggle surging at the time. Kuttab describes how Israel's "forced elimination of these committees prevented the accumulation of a creative and democratic experience", that is, skills and sensibilities that they could be protagonists against their oppression (Kuttab, "Palestinian Women in the 'Intifada'", 80). While these committees lasted, they afforded Palestinian women, still primarily those within cities and of better socio-economic status, with many opportunities for enhanced participation different than those presented at the national level for the liberation struggle.

55. Kuttab, "Palestinian Women in the 'Intifada'", 80.

56. Sayigh, "Palestinian Women", 883; and Kuttab, "Palestinian Women in the 'Intifada'", 71.

57. Sayigh, "Palestinian Women", 883.

58. Abdo, "Gender and Politics", 40–41.

59. By entering the Oslo process, the Palestinian Liberation Organization had to recognise Israel's sovereignty claims, a major departure from the earlier analyses of
liberation. Moreover, the process ultimately established the parastate Palestinian
National Authority (PA) that was tasked with development and state-building,
which, if successful, would come to be recognised by Israel. However, nothing
of the sort has materialised. Israel has consistently undermined the capacity of
the PA to build itself as a full state all while breaking up and producing atomism
among Palestinian populations. Moreover, while Israeli capital embraced
neoliberalism in the mid-1970s, the PA enshrined neoliberal policy in its governance. This has amounted to a privileging of the national question over and
above the social and economic concerns of Palestinians. Neoliberalism within
Palestine in conjunction with Israel's economic strangulation of the West Bank
and Gaza have countered the expanded reproduction of the Palestinian working
class in an attempt to stifle its mass basis. See Erakat, *Justice for Some*, Chapters 4
and 5; Hanieh, "Class, Economy"; Hanieh, *Lineages of Revolt*, Chapter 5; Khalidi
and Samour, "Neoliberalism as Liberation"; and Khalidi, "Nation and Class".

60. While Jewish Israelis receive many benefits from settler colonialism and the
Zionist state, working-class Israelis' exploitation in waged labour, expropriated
social reproductive labour, and the systematic generation of un-met need all
presuppose capitalism's diremption which Zionist occupation has enshrined as
its political economic basis. That means, whether working-class settlers struggle
against Israeli capitalists individually or wholesale, or wage limited reproductive
struggles for housing or other conditions of life-making, without motivating that
struggle against the imperial-settler colonial control over production and social
reproduction, they will fail to contest their life-denying exploitation and unfreedom. For more on the reactionary nature of the Israeli working class, see Thier,
"Not an Ally"; Englert, "Smoke and Mirrors"; and Englert, "Hebrew Labor".

6

Scholasticide and Social Reproduction in Palestine

Susan Ferguson

I threw a poem at the conquerors' car, and it blew them up.
Mahmoud Darwish, *Journal of an Ordinary Grief*

After 7 October 2023, it took just 30 days of Israel's bombs falling on Gaza for authorities to suspend classes for 625,000 primary and secondary school students. And it took only 100 days for those bombs to turn Gaza's 15 universities to rubble. By September 2024, 85 per cent of school buildings were damaged or destroyed and 10,119 students and 413 educational staff had been killed, many in targeted murders.[1] This is *scholasticide* – Karma Nabulsi's apt term for "the systematic destruction of Palestinian education by Israel" – in its most naked form.[2]

It is not, however, its only form. As Nabulsi and others stress, Israel has long pursued a policy of containing and obstructing Palestinians' education – routinely invading campuses, confiscating and destroying costly computers, lab facilities, and student union documents; arresting and detaining thousands of students, teachers, and faculty (torturing many, including children); banning books and maps; imposing lengthy school closures; denying travel passes to attend conferences and access professional training placements; rejecting visa applications for guest lecturers; outlawing collaborations among institutions; erecting checkpoints on roads in and out of schools and campuses, forcing children to walk exceptional distances, delaying their arrival or preventing school attendance altogether.[3] What is more, police and military sit by while West Bank settlers sic dogs on Palestinian children walking to school, block school entranceways with their cars, and set fire to the buildings.[4]

And yet, against all odds, Palestinians' commitment to studying, training, and teaching persists. They honour their martyred scholars; repair and rebuild damaged buildings; restore fractured relations and create new ones. When forced from their homes in 1948, Palestinians prioritised schooling in refugee camps. Two years before the first UNRWA school opened, refugee children attended classes in tents, shelters, and under the open sky.[5] During the First Intifada, when Israel closed schools for months on end, Palestinians again took matters into their own hands. Popular Committees – formed in the 1970s to coordinate, among other things, neighbourhood alerts of Israeli attacks and clandestine storage and distribution of food during prolonged curfews – established classrooms in homes, mosques, churches, and gardens in nearly every West Bank community. When Israel outlawed the committees in 1988 and raided the makeshift schools, popular education continued underground.[6]

History shows us that Palestinians find ways not just to survive within settler colonial rule, but *to flourish* – to socially reproduce themselves as an educated population, a people steeped in and productive of philosophical, literary, artistic, mathematic, scientific, and social scientific knowledge. Such determination explains the exceptionally high literacy rates in the West Bank and Gaza – 98 per cent of 15-year-olds and older can read and write according to 2022 World Bank figures. And it explains why those in the occupied Palestinian territories (oPt) lead the Arab world in rates of primary school completion (94 versus 82 per cent) and enrolment in secondary school (87 versus 64 per cent).[7] With remarkable persistence, Palestinians have turned education into a tool for asserting control over life-making—and in so doing, fostering hope for future generations. This is a sentiment Palestinians express over and over to education scholars. In the words of one man: "Education is life for [us]".[8]

Education is seen by people everywhere as enriching individual life, preparing them for economically viable futures as well as facilitating the pursuit of creative passions and instilling confidence. And it is equally understood as a means of forging a *collective* identity and future, cultivating in students a sense of belonging to and pride in a wider community (be it that of the school itself, the city, or the nation-state). In Palestine, that collective future involves throwing off the yoke of Israeli settler colonialism. Indeed, it is this potential that drives Israeli scholasticide. As Nabulsi observes: "The role and power of education in an occupied society is enormous. Education posits possibilities, opens horizons. Freedom of thought contrasts sharply with the apartheid wall, the shackling checkpoints, the choking prisons… [Israeli authorities] cannot abide it and have to destroy it."[9]

And yet, *education systems* rarely prioritise broadening students' horizons. Formal schooling tends, rather, to channel bodies and minds into adapting to and perpetuating the status quo.[10] That is, insofar as education is organised "from above" – by a state that, through its control over public resources, sets the conditions of life-making – it is integral to upholding structures of domination. For that reason, public schools almost everywhere are organised hierarchically, imposing practices that tend to narrow horizons and disempower students and teachers.

It is a core tenet of social reproduction theory (SRT) that this life-depleting dynamic exists alongside and in contradiction to education's life-affirming potential – for capitalism both needs human life (since humans are bearers of labour power) *and* systematically undermines its reproduction by devaluing and regulating it. Historically, the capitalist state has leaned heavily on formal schooling to navigate this contradiction. Through mandatory attendance laws, tight control over curriculum design, teacher training, class schedules, and more, capitalist states aim to ensure that a regular supply of workers is available for capital to exploit – workers who are not only educated and skilled but also disciplined and socially differentiated.

Yet life-making is not so easily subsumed. At its core is the work required to promote growth and development, work that involves meeting human needs and desires. While needs and desires can be disciplined, of course, they are also often unruly, and unresponsive to legal and bureaucratic demands. Schools – even when organised "from above" (by capitalist states) – bring together students, teachers, and others in the promise of engendering hope in the future, in creating lives worth living. To a considerable degree, they foster mutual engagement and collective learning and development, the ends of which cannot be fully known in advance. Thus, insofar as school-based life-making occurs beyond the *direct* oversight of a boss or militia, there is always scope in state-run schooling for resisting and challenging systemic limits, for expanding the horizons of what is possible.[11]

To suggest that school systems navigate capitalism's contradictory dependence on human labour power, however, falls short as an explanation when we consider the history of formal education in the oPt. The reproduction of Palestinians *as workers* has always only ever been a weak goal of the region's education policies and, over time, it has been sidelined altogether. This is because the oPt (and many other settler colonial societies) is grounded in a logic of dispossession by a settler class whose own social reproduction pivots upon appropriating Indigenous peoples' land and living. And unlike in South Africa, for example, where settler capitalists relied on the exploitation (and thus social reproduction) of Black South African labour, in the oPt, Palestinian labour has grown increasingly peripheral to settler ambitions. As a result, the endgame of Zionism is the elimination, *not* the social reproduction of Palestinians.[12]

Rarely, however, is this deadly logic *fully* realised. First, Indigenous peoples fight back – creating ways not simply to exist, but ways to enrich their lives with art, music, education, sports, and more. Crucially, they reproduce themselves collectively, as a *people*, with social and political claims tied to the land on which they live, and on which their ancestors have survived before them.[13] Second, settler colonial ruling classes operate within a wider geopolitical context – one that enables the eliminationist logic (by providing military, infrastructural, and diplomatic support) but that also checks it in certain ways. In Israel's case, the threat of Arab countries retaliating is one important check; the political stability required to attract international investment has been another.

Although rarely fully realised, however, the eliminationist logic is ever-present. A pulse beating just below the surface, it can break through at a moment's notice.[14] It is because Indigenous peoples' life-making threatens this logic that settler colonial societies subject it to specific and devastating forms of violence. These include mass incarceration, displacements onto reservations and townships, pass systems and checkpoints, and, of course, genocidal wars – measures that advance settlers' territorial ambitions. Scholasticide is one such measure, a form of dispossession with eliminatory intent that has long beat below the surface in Palestine, breaking through in periods of militant resurgence, most brutally so after 7 October 2023.

This chapter aims to deepen our understanding of the dynamics of Palestinian social reproduction by analysing how scholasticide evolved, and how it has operated in tandem with the provision of public education. In what ways did the Mandate period prepare the ground for it? How does scholasticide play out alongside and through certain seemingly progressive developments within the Palestinian education system (specifically the establishment of UNRWA schools and the Palestinian Authority's control of curriculum after 1994)? And why? That is, short of total annihilation, what does scholasticide achieve from Israel's perspective? To this last question, I propose that scholasticide specifically targets *collective* life-making. In severing individuals from reproducing themselves *as* a people – as part of a unique and specific cultural formation – scholasticide undermines the bonds that support human flourishing and hope. And, through this, it aims to undercut resistance. That Palestinians continue, where possible, to recreate and enrich those bonds is a testament to their commitment to, as Rafeef Ziadah puts it, "teach life".[15]

MANDATE PALESTINE: "SEPARATE AND UNEQUAL" SCHOOLING

The education system in historic Palestine passed through many hands – until 1994, none of them Palestinian. Ottoman control over formal schooling in the late nineteenth century gave way to British in 1917, which after al-Nakba in 1948 gave way to Jordanian (West Bank) and Egyptian (Gaza) control. Then, in 1967, the Israeli military took charge until the Oslo Accords led to the creation of the Palestinian Ministries of Education and Higher Education.[16]

In 1917, the British inherited a relatively new and patchy public education system, with only 16 per cent of school-aged boys and 4 per cent of girls attending.[17] Palestine differed from other Class A Mandates (Iraq, Syria, and Lebanon) in that responsibility for education remained with the colonial power.[18] While the Mandate government's Department of Education (DoE) integrated many kuttabs/maqtabs (elementary schools imparting an Islamic education) into the public school system, other private schools run by religious authorities, foreign missions, and charities continued to operate – this robust private school system rationalising the paltry public education budget.[19]

The British approached their mission in Palestine as they did elsewhere, as a venture in "civilising" a "backward" people. They did so mindful of lessons learned in India, Egypt, and Nigeria where, they believed, an English-language curriculum that was "too ambitiously literary" and hostile to Indigenous religions fuelled anticolonial sentiments.[20] In Palestine then, DoE authorities imposed a basic European-influenced curriculum – a reform broadly supported by contemporary Muslim and Jewish modernisers – replacing Turkish with Arabic as the language of instruction. They reined in secularising impulses, judging that studying Islam was likely to depoliticise students by inspiring obedience and emphasising character formation over nationalism.

Like the Ottomans before them, the British prioritised primary over secondary education. By 1948, Palestine had only ten public high schools (including two for girls), three teacher-training colleges and not a single university.[21] Schools were crowded, the school day short, staffing levels woefully insufficient, and the curriculum limited. While urban high schools prepared students for low-level civil service jobs, teachers' college, and manual trades, village primary schools introduced boys to modern crop management and farming-related mechanics. Girls' schools, meanwhile, focused on "housewifery, infant welfare, and sewing", with "little time... 'wasted' on subjects like history, geography, or classical Arabic".[22]

To be sure, such schooling socially reproduced Palestinians as workers, just not as workers for the sorts of industrial, urban capitalist societies seen in the seats of colonial power. Rather, Mandate-era public schools aimed to reproduce Palestinians primarily as self-sufficient subjects of empire – as people who would forego national aspirations and acquiesce to foreign rule while providing for themselves (as peasants, tradespeople, and homemakers) or as waged functionaries of the colonial state. Beyond cultivating a small "elite" of government workers, the DoE aimed to "keep the *fellahin* on the land", away from what were considered radicalising urban centres.[23] Because Palestinian life-making was not considered essential to reproducing an industrial working class, public schooling was fundamentally an exercise in social control of, what was essentially in British eyes, a "surplus" population.[24] Of central concern in this regard was containing resistance – and in so doing repressing the collective flourishing of a people.

The levers of control varied. Teachers were tightly regulated, prevented from publishing without government approval and from joining nationalist groups. Books about British rule in Palestine, Zionism, and Arab nationalism were banned, and the curriculum was scrubbed of much Arabic culture and almost all Arabic history. Despite (or likely due to) these efforts, schools were key sites of anticolonial resistance, mounting strikes in 1925 and 1929, and serving as organising hubs in the 1936–1939 Arab Revolt.[25] Such a history confirms the potential for schools to foster hope, community, and resistance despite and alongside their role in reproducing domination.

Curtailing resistance through curriculum design and the oversight of teaching, however, only partially explains how the British prepared the ground for Israeli scholasticide. The legal and administrative context shaping the Palestinian education system must also be considered. For the Mandate government operated within the context of the Balfour Declaration, committing the British to prepare the population for "the establishment in Palestine of a national home for the Jewish people".[26] In hewing to such terms, the DoE ultimately created a "separate and unequal" system of public education, a proto-apartheid structure that systemically undermined Arab Palestinian life-making in the same measure that it supported the social reproduction of Jewish Zionist subjects.[27]

At least two aspects of the British colonisers' approach to public education are pertinent here. First, the British abandoned their pledge to universal education, passing no mandatory school attendance laws during their rule.[28] Because nearly all Jewish children attended school by the 1920s, the government focused on Palestinian Arabs, opening about 75 schools a year. But those efforts waned within a few years as funding and political will dried up. Later, in the early 1940s, a DoE plan to extend schooling to all children living in villages of 300 people or more was greeted by Home Office scepticism (where would the teachers and funds come from?). By 1948 then, only a minority of Arab children attended public or private schools, and only 22 per cent of *all* children attended public schools (up from 12 per cent in the Ottoman period).[29]

Second, despite pronouncing it "undesirable for 'two races' of radically different educational levels to inhabit the same lands", the British abandoned their equalisation policy, instituting in its place an ethno-racially segregated education system.[30] From the beginning, Palestinian public schools welcomed students from all recognised religions (Jewish, Muslim, Christian, Druze, and Bahá'í faith). When the Mandate began, however, most Jewish children were already attending private Jewish schools, many of which fell under the auspices of the World Zionist Organization's office in Jerusalem. To preserve and spread Zionism and Hebrew (most Jews indigenous to Palestine spoke Arabic), the Zionist Organization appealed to the British High Commission, obtaining public funds for their schools in 1927. The same courtesy was not extended to schools run by the Supreme Muslim Council (or other religious authorities) on the grounds that the public system functioned in Arabic.

However much DoE officials may have embraced it or not, equalisation from this point on was moot policy.[31] The "Hebrew Public System" (originally "Zionist Public School System") was not only *separate*, it was also *exclusive*, admitting only Jewish students, and *privileged*, granted advantages over the Palestinian public system (or "Arab Public System"). We see this in the funding system: per-capita grants were based on the pretence that all Jewish students attended Zionist Organization schools when in fact one-third of Jewish students attended other private and public schools. International donations complemented this generous public funding, making a more robust public system of education available only to Jewish students. As well, although the Hebrew public system was legally accountable to DoE policies, in practice, it operated independently. Decisions about curriculum, school management, and more were made in consultation initially with the

Zionist Organization, and later, with the Jewish Agency and the Va'ad Leumi (National Council). Rather than colonial institutions answerable to a British Empire that aimed to quell national sentiment and resistance (as were Arab public schools), Hebrew public schools during the Mandate period were answerable to an incipient state aiming to consolidate national power, in part by shaping the citizens of tomorrow.

It bears emphasising that these developments were not inevitable. Prior to 1917, while schools were generally divided along sectarian lines, some privileged Arab and Jewish students attended the same schools. After the Mandate, a few Zionist educators contested school segregation and "advocated a kind of colonial humanism like the European colonial discourse at the time", while a few Arab intellectuals saw Palestinian admission to elite Hebrew schools as a form of racial uplift.[32] Moreover, British DoE officials did not generally trust or favour a Zionist-controlled curriculum. They and MPs at home regularly lamented in strong terms – but, notably, did nothing about – the "watertight compartments" of the Hebrew and Arab systems.[33] Yet, according to historian Yoni Furas, British hopes for integration dissolved in the face of Arab resistance to colonialism; and it was only after the 1929 strike that the British dropped plans for an Arabic-language university.[34] Ultimately, social control of a "surplus" population – not equalisation or universal schooling – proved the more powerful impulse. Britain consolidated a segregated system whose purpose was to *deny* communal life-making among Arab Palestinians while, at the same time, providing Zionists with the resources to promote the same among Jews in Palestine. As such, the DoE prepared the ground for the forces of Israeli scholasticide to follow.

POST-1948 EDUCATION: PALESTINIAN LIFE-MAKING UNDER SIEGE

The 1936–1939 uprising did much to consolidate a *Palestinian* national identity that had been taking shape since the turn of the twentieth century.[35] Arab student and teacher unions proliferated in the 1940s, and some Arab educators and bureaucrats pushed for greater autonomy in directing public education.[36] After 1948, however, responsibility for the system shifted. UNRWA was charged with running schools for Palestinian refugees in Grades One through Nine. They did so in compliance with the education policies set by host countries Jordan, Syria, and Lebanon, while in the West Bank and Gaza Strip, Jordanian, and Egyptian policies prevailed, respectively. Only those Arab schools within Israel's new borders and in East Jerusalem fell to the Israelis to administer directly. Yet throughout historic Palestine and the Diaspora, teaching Palestinian history and culture was either banned or neglected. And although more Palestinians than ever were now attending schools, the priority remained primary education, supplemented by teacher training and a few vocational colleges. Those who could afford it (or who qualified for limited UNRWA grants) travelled abroad for university.[37]

When Israel took control of the West Bank and Gaza Strip in 1967, UNRWA continued to run refugee camp schools. Elsewhere within the oPt, Palestinians attended government or private schools. *All* schools were now overseen by the Israeli military (in 1982, authority transferred to the Israeli Civil Administration) – and directly subject to the dictates of the Israeli government. In one respect, the new colonisers simply continued the practices of the old, adopting the Mandate's separate but unequal system that enabled underfunding and neglect of Palestinian public education. Under Israeli control, Palestinian schools lacked furniture; buildings were not maintained; teachers were underpaid; curriculum was outdated and secondary education neglected.[38]

In another respect, the sheer intensity of Israeli repression altered the very nature of public education in Palestine after the Mandate. Zionist authorities censored thousands more books, sometimes simply because they contained the word "Palestine", referenced Arab unity, or featured the colours of the Palestinian flag. They permitted only maps identifying Palestine as Israel to be displayed in classrooms. As well as deepening restrictions on curriculum, administrative relations took on a new character: teachers and students were regularly transferred, or they were suspended and arrested for political activity – a portend of the targeted killings of scholars and school officials over the years since.[39]

In hugely intensifying the repressive features of British colonial education policy, the Israelis sharpened the nihilistic features of the school system, incorporating them into the broader eliminatory logic of Zionist settler colonialism. We might think of it in these terms: public education under the Mandate aimed to reproduce Palestinians as self-sufficient and politically quiescent subjects of empire, seeing schools as enabling that formation in part through repressing the emergence of Palestinian identity and nationalism while nonetheless furnishing individuals the skills and knowledge required to keep the colony afloat. The Israelis, on the other hand, aimed to establish a Zionist homeland that held no room for Indigenous Palestinians. They were not interested in Palestinians *qua* subjects, self-sufficient or not. The Israeli economy was only lightly dependent on Palestinians as a source of low-waged labour (while about half of Palestinian workers were employed inside Israel in the late 1960s).[40] But more than this, Palestinians – as a self-conscious community occupying land the Israeli state laid claim to – constituted obstructions to Israeli goals. Collectively, they posed an existential threat to the Zionist project.

Thus, the Israeli approach to Palestinian schooling certainly involved containing resistance, but it also involved destroying the very promise of education – hope in the future, a Palestinian future. At the same time, Israel relied upon and needed to retain the support of the international community (especially the USA, Britain, and to some extent, the UN), and to navigate relations with its Arab neighbours. For these reasons, it could not – at that moment anyway – completely devastate public education. Rather, scholasticide's deadly logic broke through in bits and starts, gaining greater momentum as Israel responded to periods of heightened resistance, when collective Palestinian life-making was at its strongest: during the two intifadas and after 7 October 2023.

Despite – and because of – this attack on their subjecthood, Palestinian resolve that education was key to building a collective future hardened. In 1972, the Palestinian Liberation Organization (PLO) drafted an educational philosophy aimed at "construct[ing] a united cognitive educational framework for the Palestinian people".[41] The three-page document tasks education with cultivating Palestinians' duty to the collectivity. It endorses democracy, gender equality, religious and racial inclusion, and armed struggle against Zionism and imperialism.[42] Essentially, for the PLO in 1972, education was to serve Palestinian liberation – a philosophy that was broadly embraced and disseminated through the organisation's Higher Education Council comprising education professionals, trade unionists, and university presidents, among others. The Council helped to launch a Palestinian higher education sector that explicitly promoted nationalist aims. To this day, Birzeit University in Ramallah boasts that it has been "a thorn in the side of the occupation" since it offered its first Bachelor of Arts programme in 1972.[43] Five more universities welcomed students before the decade was out.[44] Meanwhile, in primary and secondary schools, many Palestinian teachers found creative ways to introduce students to their cultural and political histories. According to historian Elizabeth Brownson, teachers often circumvented the regulations as "there was no power able to control all their activities all the time".[45] This is an important point that I return to below.

Schools, however, were hardly hotbeds of nationalism, an accusation Israelis regularly flung particularly at UNRWA schools. For one thing, the Israelis heavily surveilled all Palestinian schools, and teachers endorsing anti-Zionism or Palestinian nationalism risked being fired or arrested. Moreover, UNRWA schools are accountable to and reliant on international funders who show little tolerance for Palestinian nationalism.[46] But, beyond such practicalities, Palestinians generally value education for more than its potential to foster collective identity, nationalism, and resistance. As most people do everywhere, they also see it as offering an escape from poverty and hardship, "a means for securing a white-collar job with steady income, and to enhance social status, in a predominantly peasant society".[47]

This dual promise of education – personal growth and well-being wrapped in the potential of collective self-determination and individual economic success – can animate a mixed consciousness among the oppressed. Tejendra Pherali and Ellen Turner draw on W.E.B. Du Bois' image of "two warring ideals in one dark body" to explain:

Here, the oppressed group is forced to view themselves and the world around them through the lens of ongoing subjugation which denies their own self-conscious view of reality. Double consciousness emerges as the Palestinians are forced to embrace status quoist, hegemonic ideas that constantly cultivate individualistic, material aspirations, normalising the repressive political space, while their collective sense of liberatory aspirations and the romanticized "Palestine" is deeply entrenched in the other side of the consciousness. The dilemma emerges from the inability to dwell upon either consciousness, the disconnection between and the failure to reconcile the two.[48]

If and how this dilemma is resolved depends upon whether schools nurture personal advancement as part of a commitment to collective enrichment and liberation, or if they serve a more radically individualist ideal of personal development disconnected from social goals and values. The balance schools strike in this regard depends on wider economic and political forces, as the experience of Palestinian education during and after the First Intifada shows.

LIBERATION AND ACCOMMODATION:
SCHOOLING'S CONTRADICTIONS

In early 1988, Israel closed all West Bank educational institutions (including kindergartens) and imposed strict curfews in Gaza that prevented normal school operation. A pattern of re-openings and closings followed, with younger students forfeiting 35 to 55 per cent of class time each year of the Intifada. Meanwhile, all institutions of higher education were closed from 8 January 1988 to 29 April 1992. Israel also disrupted classes by carrying out military drills on and near school campuses, invading school buildings, arresting, beating, and shooting at students and teachers. This description by one teacher paints a vivid picture:

> As a teacher, for three years we wake up at 3 o'clock in the morning. And we go out... there isn't streets... The streets are damaged and cut by the bulldozers. There are Israeli soldiers... everywhere. And we move through the mountains. We spend more than two hours. Sometimes we must hide... Sometimes they shoot at the people. It's raining, it's very cold. The women, you see them, shoes have been damaged, their umbrella... the wind took it. We came [to school] very tired. Very tired... Sometimes I hear and I see many people have been injured or killed. You must run or you must disappear. I think I can't say that I did my job well and for my students. If you hear someone killed near you, how can you teach or learn well? You find yourself in a bad condition. So I think the result is that the students will do badly.[49]

When Palestinians responded to these atrocities by setting up makeshift classrooms in their communities – part of a resistance campaign in which Popular Committees assumed responsibility for social services in general – Israel outlawed them. As popular education continued underground, Israel invaded homes and mosques, sometimes arresting children as they walked down streets simply because they held a book in their arms.[50]

That the Israelis were moved to such brutal forms of scholasticide only hardened Palestinians' resolve that education could be a lever of liberation. Rather than Palestinian educators being agent provocateurs of revolution, it is more accurate to suggest that Israeli repression foments resistance. Schools simply provide a conducive space for questioning the status quo because they are institutions that foster the pursuit of meaning and knowl-edge – much of which can take place beyond the ears and eyes of the colonial and capitalist ruling class. They provide time, space, and resources not only for people to socially reproduce themselves as workers or subjects of empire (or nation), but also as individuals and communities pursuing broader horizons, lives worth living. That expansive impulse is ever-present in social reproductive activities. Palestinians have long understood – and the Israeli state has long feared – as much.

Yet, with shifts in the economic and political context come shifts in the form and perceived value of schooling. One year after the signing of the Oslo Accords in 1993, a Transfer Agreement devolved responsibility for education (along with other cultural and social services and limited taxation powers) from the Israeli state to the Palestinian Authority (PA). For the first time ever, Palestinians could exercise "almost full sovereignty" over the West Bank and Gazan public education system.[51] *Almost* because policy and curriculum reforms still require Israeli approval and, most importantly, because schooling takes place on colonised land. As Adam Hanieh writes of the post-Oslo regime, "A Palestinian face may preside over the day-to-day administration of Palestinian affairs, but ultimate power remains in the hand of Israel".[52]

In the early 1990s, educators, politicians, and other intellectuals were already working with UNESCO to develop a specifically Palestinian curriculum. These efforts, now under the auspices of the Palestinian Ministry of Education and Higher Education (MEHE), were ongoing when Palestinians again rose up against their oppressors in 2000. During the Second Intifada, Israel specifically targeted Palestinian schools, colleges, and universities, unleashing even greater damage than earlier.[53] According to ministry and UNESCO figures, 1,125 schools were closed, while military shelling and vandalism inflicted more than $5 million in infrastructural damage. The military also vandalised and confiscated MEHE records kept in Ramallah. Over four years, the Israelis killed 516 Palestinian students, 28 teachers, and 7 school staff. They injured more than 3,000 students and arrested some 670 more.[54] This was followed by Operation Cast Lead: 23 days in 2008–2009 during which Israel killed 250 students and 15 teachers, injuring almost 900 others. Its bombs also destroyed 18 schools and 6 universities, inflicting great damage in another 300 educational facilities. Twenty-nine per cent of the children killed in this period were eight years old or younger.[55] Between and after these periods of heightened tensions, the arrests, harassment, and killings continued, somewhat less intensely, while new separation walls and checkpoints made accessing schools ever more difficult for students and teachers alike.

Not surprisingly, following a boost in school enrolment in the first years of PA-run schooling, trends have reversed. From 1993 to 2011, enrolment in higher education increased by 940 per cent, with greatest gains made by female students. By the early 2010s, dropout rates began ticking upward and enrolment rates trailed off.[56] While there is no question that Israeli settler colonialism (and scholasticide specifically) is to blame for the difficulties Palestinians face in attending school, a more fulsome analysis must consider how these political forces interact with developments in capitalist class dynamics – and the PA's strategies for managing those dynamics since 1994.[57]

Post-Oslo was a period of neoliberalisation across the Middle East, coinciding with a strengthening of the Israeli economy in part because the end of Arab boycotts facilitated greater global investment. Meanwhile, the PA, now a quasi-state, became Israel's abettor, deepening Palestinian dependency on Israeli exports and restructuring the Palestinian workforce such that it was ever more peripheral to Israeli capital: from 1992 to 1996, the number of Palestinians working in Israel fell by 75 per cent (from 116,000 to 28,000, the latter a mere 6 per cent of the Palestinian labour force).[58] One in four workers had a job in the public sector, the rest worked largely in Palestinian-owned small businesses. Unemployment numbers grew, especially among the youth, hovering around 50 per cent.[59] At the same time, the PA fostered the growth of a small but significant Palestinian capitalist class through granting monopolies, import permits, and land on the one hand and using foreign donor monies to develop tourism, agribusiness, and more on the other. Yet, Hanieh notes, "the ability to accumulate was always tied to Israeli debt-based relations… [and] had a conservatizing influence over the latter half of the 2000s, with much of the population concerned with 'stability' and the ability to pay off debt rather than the possibility of popular resistance".[60]

That conservatising influence was also politically cultivated. Along with reordering class relations, the PA aimed "to reorient the Palestinian people toward accommodation, thus limiting their goals of national liberation".[61] To this end, its architects of public schooling steered well clear of the principles outlined in the PLO's 1972 philosophy of education, despite rhetoric to the contrary. Aiming to "modernise" Palestinian society and provide technical training, the PA viewed schooling as a means for integrating students into the post-Oslo economy and promoting Palestinian identity – *outside* the context of settler colonialism.[62] Although the first Palestinian curriculum, completed in 1996, aspired to "the reconstruction of the Palestinian people", it did so without mentioning the long history of the occupation, Zionism, or Jewish settlements. Resistance – or, more aptly, responding to the occupier – was to be entrusted to those in power. In place of resistance, the new curriculum "promote[d] a version of nationalism… that primarily cultivated loyalty to the ruling authority in the West Bank".[63] In 2000, a revised curriculum similarly skirted the fact of the occupation and hued to a neoliberal agenda. It focused on "improving the quality of education, providing vocational education, meeting the needs of girls, and developing human resources".[64] All this was to be achieved within the context of fiscal austerity. Woefully inadequate budgets led to numerous teachers strikes, to which the PA responded by firing and transferring teacher activists.[65]

Textbooks have been a particularly sensitive issue since the PA took over. The Israeli-based Center for Monitoring the Impact of Peace issued a damning report in 1998 suggesting that Palestinian textbooks defame, delegitimise, and encourage violence against Israel.[66] This charge could hardly be further from the truth, according to Nathan Brown whose study of the texts concludes that the earliest texts "stubbornly avoid[ed] treating anything controversial regarding current Palestinian national identity… go[ing] to some lengths to avoid saying anything about Israel at all".[67] Texts published later tread lightly on certain historical and geographical details, treating Israel "with remarkable awkwardness, reticence, and inconsistency".[68] For example, books published in and after 2000 omit Israel from maps (earlier books omitted maps altogether) but similarly fail to demarcate the borders of the Palestinian state and are silent on the issue of borders in the written text. The West Bank and Gaza are indicated with contrasting colours or dotted lines, also without explanation. History texts take a similar approach. While certain issues – Jerusalem is the capital of Palestine, the right of return, Israel's responsibility for refugees – are raised, Brown notes, they are not deeply explored.[69]

Despite the ongoing occupation and devastation Israel has unleashed on the Palestinians since the early 1990s, learning history under the PA is not treated as essential to collective liberation. Indeed, the trend seems to be in the opposite direction. According to a Leibniz Institute report, while textbooks published in the late 2010s portray "the Israeli opponent… as aggressive and hostile", the language is "for the most part, objective in tone and avoids inflammatory expressions". And books published as late as 2020 are described as even less "escalatory", erasing some references to the "conflict" entirely, and removing or altering certain references to the armed resistance.[70] The message of accommodation is not lost on all. As one student laments: "We are not supposed to struggle or raise our voice against Israel because Israel will offer us a 'good life'".[71]

The PA approach to public education is fully in step with its broader cultural politics – which Chandni Desai and Rula Shahwan describe as downplaying the role of the liberation movement and obscuring settler colonialism. This "erased curriculum", they write, "advance[s] the PA's statist project and deepen[s] the stronghold of its neoliberal ideologies within capitalist social relations".[72] In this, the MEHE is not unlike so many other countries' public education systems which, through curriculum design and disciplinary measures, do much more to reinforce the status quo than to challenge it. To some extent, such efforts in Palestine have been rewarded. In a 2018 study, Pherali and Turner observe weaker motivations among the current generation of students, suggesting that education is less valued by them than by their parents who had fewer years of formal schooling. In their view, "the belief that education can contribute to this struggle is losing currency with young people" – a situation they explain by reference to the impact of the occupation's daily grind and high unemployment levels.[73]

Such an explanation is undoubtedly correct but partial. It overlooks that, in past decades (when economic prospects were not much better, and the grind of occupation similarly punishing), Palestinians' motivation for education (formal schooling included) was strong, tied to the strength of and hope in the resistance movement. One wonders then to what extent this generation's possible disillusion with schooling can be attributed to the PA's decision to avoid classrooms discussing the occupation and resistance. When the promise of collective flourishing is repressed, and all hope for change is channelled into officialdom, schools are viewed by the public simply as institutions individual advancement.

That said, it is wrong to lay responsibility for squandering the liberatory potential of public schooling solely or even mostly at the feet of the PA. To begin, the PA is not a state, but a quasi-state, subject to Israel's higher and deadly power. But most importantly, scholasticide is an *Israeli* policy; Israel – not the PA – sets the broad conditions under which any PA policy is enacted. What we learn from this latest chapter in the history of Palestinian schooling is that social reproduction organised from above will either repress or squander liberatory promises of education. It is always and only when there is pressure from below that schooling can serve liberation. And ironically perhaps, in carrying out its deadly policy, Israel does as much, if not more, to stir that pressure from below than it does to quell it.

With every bomb dropped on a Palestinian school or university, with every scholar hunted down and killed, Palestinians are reminded that schools can be unique spaces of social reproduction – unique because they collectivise learning and development, making possible the expansion of horizons while fostering hope in the future. This is true even when a neoliberal agenda dominates. It is true because as Brownson noted about schooling during the Mandate, schools are places where no outside power can "control all… activities all the time".[74]

CONCLUSION

More than anything, Israeli scholasticide targets the collective life-making of Palestinians. The social reproduction of Palestinians as individuals who may or may not be incorporated into a labour market contradicts the eliminationist logic of Israeli settler colonialism. But it is the reproduction of Palestinians *as a collective*, a people who make social and political claims tied to the land they live upon, that in fact holds the potential to overturn the Zionist project. And for Palestinians, education has proven to be a crucial means of collective life-making – one that is as much about surviving as it is about enriching lives. Scholasticide takes aim at that flourishing. The Israeli military relentlessly, if unevenly, targets schools, educators, and students to destroy hope in new horizons – not so much for the individual Palestinian who may become a doctor or a dentist or university professor with relatively little effect on the Zionist project, but for the Palestinian people, who can only win the fight against Zionism if they act collectively.

SRT correctly identifies education systems as essential to the social reproduction of contemporary working classes. But Israel, while capitalist, is only peripherally interested in setting Palestinians to work and not at all interested in reproducing them as self-sufficient subjects (as arguably the British before them were). Although Israel's economic and diplomatic interests have generally prevented it from fully realising its scholasticidal agenda in the past, the current devastation in Gaza (and ominously too in the West Bank) suggests it is closer than ever to doing so. Yet, even now, Palestinians are rebuilding their schools and universities. They are finding places online and, amid the rubble in Gaza, to gather and learn.[75] As Gaza academics and university leaders stated so powerfully in their open letter in May 2024, "We built these universities from tents. And from tents, with the support of our friends, we will rebuild them once again".[76]

NOTES

1. OCHA, "Gaza Strip"; see also UNHR, "UN Experts Deeply Concerned".
2. Ahmed and Vulliamy, "In Gaza". Nabulsi coined this term in 2009, and the genocidal war on Palestine that began in October 2023 has prompted others to develop a deeper understanding of its mechanisms. See Hajir and Qato, "Academia in a Time of Genocide"; Desai, "War in Gaza"; and SAWP, "Scholasticide Definition".
3. See Wind, *Towers of Ivory*, part 2; Mullen, "Building the Palestine International"; and Abu-Saad and Champagne, "Historical Context".
4. DCI, "Under Attack", 22–23.
5. UNRWA stands for the United Nations Relief and Works Agency for Palestine Refugees in the Near East, discussed further below.
6. See Mahshi and Bush, "Palestinian Uprising and Education", 474–75. Popular education carries on a long tradition of Palestinian non-formal education; see Al-zaroo, *Non-Formal Education in Palestine*. For more on Popular Committees, see Robinson, *Building a Palestinian State*, Chapter 5; and Hanbali, "Reimagining Liberation".
7. WBG, "Indicators". For reasons of space, I discuss education in the oPt only; for Palestinian schooling elsewhere, see Shuayb, "Art of Inclusive Exclusions"; and Abu Lughod, "Educating a Community".
8. Pherali and Turner, "Meanings of Education", 572.
9. Cited in Ahmed and Vulliamy, "In Gaza". See also Alzaroo and Hunt, "Education in the Context", 175; Abu Lughod, "Educating a Community"; and Irfan, *Refuge and Resistance*.
10. Although education and schooling are often conflated, the former does not require the latter. This chapter focuses on the evolution of schooling, specifically the public school system, in Palestine.
11. See Ferguson, *Women and Work*, Chapter 8.
12. See Tal-Hi Bitton's Chapter 5 in this volume for a fuller discussion of debates within Settler Colonial Studies and of Israeli settler colonialism considered through the lens of SRT.
13. We need only look to Indigenous land defenders around the world for evidence: from the Sioux Nation of Standing Rock in the US Dakotas to the Māori on Waiheke Island in Aotearoa/New Zealand to the rubber tappers of the Amazon, Indigenous peoples persist and thrive as communities with unique social, ecological, and economic relations despite the odds.
14. It persists alongside and in tension with the capitalist logic of dispossession and accumulation, which is one reason the dynamics of social reproduction differ among and within different settler colonial societies. See Englert, *Settler Colonialism*.
15. Ziadah, "We Teach Life".
16. See Abu-Saad and Champagne, "Historical Context".
17. Another 18 per cent of boys and 8 per cent of girls attended private schools. Abu-Saad and Champagne, "Historical Context", 1036–37.

18. Local Education Councils were disbanded only to be reconstituted in 1939 for purposes of collecting taxes, while the DoE retained control over curriculum, hiring, and so on.
19. The DoE spent 5–7 per cent of its overall budget on education; Schneider, *Mandatory Separation*, 50.
20. According to Britain's Lord Comer, "Education of the [Egyptian] poor has... been too largely and too ambitiously literary. Primary education should... be more concerned with the observation of facts than with any form of speculative reasoning or opinions." Cited in Schneider, *Mandatory Separation*, 60.
21. Abu-Saad and Champagne, "Historical Context", 1038.
22. Schneider, *Mandatory Separation*, 62.
23. Schneider, *Mandatory Separation*, 38. For more on the Mandate-era curriculum, see Furas, *Educating Palestine*; Sabella, "Education in Palestine"; and Abu-Saad and Champagne, "Historical Context".
24. This was also the logic behind establishing residential schools for Indigenous peoples in Canada, the USA, New Zealand, and Australia.
25. See Brownson, "Colonialism, Nationalism".
26. House of Commons Library, "Balfour Declaration".
27. The term is Schneider's; see her *Mandatory Separation*, 38.
28. Furas, *Educating Palestine*, 33.
29. Reports of Arab children's school attendance vary from 30 to 40 per cent. See Schneider, *Mandatory Separation*, 48–50; Furas, *Educating Palestine*, 33; Broco and Trad, "Education in the Palestinian Territories"; and Abu-Saad and Champagne, "Historical Context", 1038.
30. Schneider, *Mandatory Separation*, 49.
31. Furas, *Educating Palestine*, 40. Furas points to one failed attempt to reinstate the ideal by developing a shared (Arab–Jewish) agricultural school in the early 1930s (42); see also, Novick and Dubnov, "Unknown History".
32. Furas, *Educating Palestine*, 51 and 60–67.
33. Furas, *Educating Palestine*, 40.
34. Furas, *Educating Palestine*, 29, 47–60, and 68.
35. Khalidi, *Palestinian Identity*, 150–58.
36. Furas, *Educating Palestine*, 86. Still, according to Furas' analysis of Zionist intelligence gathering from 1918 on, the British and Zionists exaggerated the degree to which Arab teachers encouraged nationalist sentiments.
37. This section draws on the following texts: Furas, *Educating Palestine*, Chapter 3; Mahshi and Bush, "Palestinian Uprising"; Asaad, "Palestinian Educational Philosophy"; Alzaroo and Hunt, "Education in the Context"; Shuayb, "Art of Inclusive Exclusions"; and Alfoqahaa, "Economics of Higher Education".
38. Alzaroo and Hunt, "Education in the Context", 168–69.
39. Asaad, "Palestinian Educational Philosophy", 391.
40. By the mid-1980s that reliance had fallen off as temporary workers from Asia, East Europe, and later East Africa replaced them. See Clarno, "Israel's Lavender Kill List", 21–22; and Al-zaroo, "Non-Formal Education", 111.
41. Cited in Asaad, "Palestinian Educational Philosophy", 391.
42. Asaad, "Palestinian Educational Philosophy", 392–94.

43. PAS, "History of Birzeit University". According to Alfoqahaa ("Economics of Higher Education", 27), Palestinian universities "have never given way to Israeli hegemony" – a reason why it is so important to reconstruct Gazan universities today (see note 76 below).
44. Only one, Islamic University of Gaza, opened in Gaza in 1978. Alfoqahaa ("Economics of Higher Education", 27–30) lists Najah National (1977) and Bethlehem (1973) universities; he omits Hebron (1971) and Palestine Polytechnic (1978) universities.
45. Brownson, "Colonialism, Nationalism", 19.
46. In October 2024, Israel banned UNRWA from operating in Israel and the oPt. As of writing, the legislation had not been fully enforced, largely due to an impasse over a transition plan. See Hasson, "UNRWA Still Operates"; and Makovsky, "Brinkmanship".
47. Mahshi and Bush, "Palestinian Uprising", 471.
48. Pherali and Turner, "Meanings of Education", 571.
49. Cited in Pherali and Turner, "Meanings of Education", 575.
50. See Asaad, "Palestinian Educational Philosophy"; Mahshi and Bush, "Palestinian Uprising"; Al-zaroo, Non-Formal Education; Kelcey, "(A)Political Education?"; and PAS, "History of Birzeit University".
51. Asaad, "Palestinian Educational Philosophy", 393. Arab schools in East Jerusalem are run by the Israeli Ministry of Education and suffer from overcrowding and disproportionately low budgets (UNDP, "Development for Empowerment", 3–4).
52. Hanieh, "Oslo Illusion". Curriculum and teaching are monitored by a joint US–Israeli–Palestinian body; see de Santisteban, "Palestinian Education", 152.
53. Alzaroo and Hunt, "Education in the Context"; Affouneh, "How Sustained Conflict"; and Akesson, "School as a Place", 193.
54. Affouneh, "How Sustained Conflict", 346. See also Akesson, "School as a Place", 193; and Nicolai, "Education and Chronic Crisis".
55. American Muslims for Palestine, Making the Grade.
56. Atamanov and Palaniswamy, "Education for Education's Sake?"; and Bzour, Zuki and Mispan, "Causes and Remedies".
57. Chandni Desai makes this point forcefully; see her "Disrupting Settler Colonial Capitalism". See also Clarno, "Neoliberal Colonization".
58. Hanieh, "Oslo Illusion". See also Clarno, "Neoliberal Colonization", 238.
59. PBS, Press Release.
60. Hanieh, "Oslo Illusion".
61. Samara, "Globalization", 122. See also Desai and Shahwan, "Preserving Palestine".
62. Asaad, "Palestinian Educational Philosophy", 398; and Brown, "Democracy, History".
63. Pherali and Turner, "Meanings of Education", 569.
64. Akesson, "School as a Place", 193; see also Asaad, "Palestinian Educational Philosophy", 397–98.
65. De Santisteban, "Palestinian Education", 153. Teachers strikes continued into the 2020s, with a lengthy, massive and militant wildcat strike rocking Gaza and

the West Bank in the spring of 2023. See Adra, "Defying PA Repression"; and Muaddi, "Palestinian Public School Teachers".

66. The Center changed its name to the Institute for Monitoring Peace and Cultural Tolerance in School Education. Their reports can be found at https://tinyurl. com/3xsy52tr.

67. Brown, "Democracy, History", 2.

68. Brown, "Democracy, History", 8.

69. Brown, "Democracy, History", 9–12.

70. Georg Eckert Institute for International Textbook Research, *Report on Palestinian Textbooks*.

71. Jiménez, "Occupation Wants to Delete Us", 2364.

72. Desai and Shahwan, "Preserving Palestine", 474.

73. Pherali and Turner, "Meanings of Education", 578.

74. Brownson, "Colonialism, Nationalism", 19.

75. Abu Alkas et al., "Gazans Strive to Study"; and Hassan, "Nearly 1 Year". The royalties from this book are being donated to the ISNAD programme of Taawon, a charitable foundation that supports Gazan university students. Their website can be found here: www.taawon.org/en/isnad.

76. Gaza Academics and Administrators, "Open Letter".

7

Checkpoints, the Sexual Division of Labour, and Social Reproduction in the West Bank

Jemima Repo

Checkpoints are a part of Israel's vast colonial security infrastructure that controls the daily movement of Palestinians. They are sites at which colonial power is exercised and normalised through enforced waiting, crowding, intimidation, interrogation, searches, identity checks, and violence.[1] According to 2024 figures, there are 89 staffed checkpoints in the West Bank and a total of 793 obstacles to movement.[2] Rashid Khalidi describes crossing checkpoints as "the quintessential Palestinian experience".[3] As structures that impact the daily life of all Palestinians, they are also "sociotechnical devices" that do more than exert sovereign power by demarcating exclusions and inclusions.[4] In this chapter, I focus on the gendered economic dimensions of checkpoints, specifically approaching the checkpoint as a technology that regulates and controls both production and social reproduction in Palestinian society. Following Yasmin Chilmeran and Nicola Pratt, I approach the depletion of social reproduction not just as an unintended effect of the occupation but rather as a long-term gendered tactic of the project of Zionist settler colonialism.[5] After briefly discussing the ways in which checkpoints directly impact Palestinian people's capacities to socially reproduce themselves – by obstructing access to healthcare, family, and agricultural land, I consider their role in regulating the daily commute of Palestinian (mostly) male waged workers. Through interviews with Palestinian women in the West Bank whose husbands work in Israel, I show that the power exercised at the checkpoint reverberates beyond the physical space of the checkpoint, shaping, in disruptive ways, the daily life-making practices of Palestinian families and communities, that is, social reproduction. In this way, I contend, checkpoints function as colonial technologies that indirectly uphold the sexual division of labour in Palestinian households, regimenting Palestinian social reproduction. I conclude this chapter by considering what happens when that daily commute ends, a situation faced by thousands of Palestinian workers with the onset of the Israeli genocidal war in October 2023.

At their most basic level, checkpoints limit mobility, but they can also be seen as a part of the "slow violence" of settler colonialism that eliminates, through protracted degradation, the conditions necessary to make and sustain life.[6] Historically, settler colonial projects have been structured by the close regulation of mobility in tandem with an "unbounded territoriality" of expansion into the frontier.[7] This is expressed in the facilitated free roaming of settlers across the territories they claim for themselves, and likewise to restrict Indigenous mobilities of natives, circumscribing their land-based claims of possession and belonging.[8] This pattern is apparent in Israel's closure and separation of Palestinian territories through infrastructural and bureaucratic obstructions such as the West Bank Separation Wall, checkpoints, license plates, ID cards, the permit system, and the two-tier road network that work to constrain Palestinian access to lands and livelihoods while simultaneously slowly pushing the frontier forward.[9] It is also a means of elimination by attrition: in Palestine, as in other settler colonial contexts, mobility restrictions work to enable settler colonial dispossession, not only by facilitating the forcible removal of Indigenous populations and depriving them of the right to movement, but also by making basic social reproductive activities extremely difficult or dangerous to carry out.

According to the United Nations Office for the Coordination of Humanitarian Affairs, over half of checkpoints or roadblocks "have a severe impact on Palestinians by preventing or restricting access and movement to main roads, urban centres, services, and agricultural areas".[10] For example, the placement of Israeli checkpoints or the Separation Wall often deliberately renders the vital agricultural land – for subsistence or livelihood – of a Palestinian family inaccessible, or at best accessible only with a hard-to-acquire military permit. The ensuing inability to cultivate the land renders it amenable to appropriation by the Israeli state based on its neglect.[11] Moreover, checkpoints, parallelled by strict residency rights, also enforce the wilful separation of families scattered across historic Palestine, eroding kin relations, weakening support networks, and simply preventing close familial and social relations by making it difficult to attend events like births, weddings, and funerals, as well as everyday visits.[12] Access to medical treatment is also affected. While the checkpoints provide swift access to medical care for the Israeli settlers in the West Bank and East Jerusalem, they hinder access for Palestinians on the other side of the Green Line for whom such access can mean the difference between life and death due to the weakened state of available health services in the West Bank and Gaza.[13] For West Bank Palestinians, permits to seek medical attention in Jerusalem are difficult to obtain.[14] Patients and their companions are regularly delayed at the checkpoint, and their permits can be revoked at any time, even when applications are successful. The added burdens caused by these obstructions are particularly felt by Palestinian women due to their role as primary caregivers responsible for household management, childcare, healthcare, relationships with extended families, and other socially reproductive activities. These obstructions are also directly implicated in the routine reproductive violence targeted at Palestinian women, on occasion even forcing women to give birth at checkpoints, sometimes leading to the death of mothers and newborns.[15] In addition to the reproductive violence against birthing mothers, women who cross checkpoints are regularly subjected to gendered forms of intimidation, humiliation, and violence, such as unveiling and sexual harassment.[16]

In sum, as settler colonial technologies, Israeli checkpoints organise Indigenous elimination by making the reproduction of daily life – family relations, health, subsistence, and so on – extremely difficult in the hope that Palestinians will simply give up and go elsewhere. If the above illustrates some of the daily activities of making and sustaining life that checkpoints hinder or prevent, we might also consider the kinds of activities that checkpoints facilitate. From the perspective of the Israeli state, in addition to spurious claims of "preventing terrorism", the checkpoints also manage Palestinian access to the Israeli labour market. Despite successful efforts by the Israeli state to reduce reliance on Palestinian labour through its replacement with migrant labour, sectors of the Israeli economy, such as construction, have remained dependent on cheap Palestinian labour, often to build illegal settlements on which the social reproduction of Israeli settlers relies.[17] In the next section, I detail how the checkpoint and its accompanying system of permits structure the daily lives of Palestinian men and their families, and by extension, have gendered impacts on the sexual division of labour in the West Bank.

THE COLONIAL PRODUCTION OF THE MALE BREADWINNER MODEL

The terminal-like checkpoints near large urban centres, such as Huwara (Nablus), Qalandiya (Ramallah), and Checkpoint 300 (Bethlehem) are major crossing points for daily labour commuters from the West Bank into Israel. Some of these existed as roadblocks before the Second Intifada (2000–2005) but since that time have been transformed into permanent structures as part of Israel's infamous 712-kilometre-long Separation Wall.[18] These checkpoints are now complex securitised spaces, with numerous corridors, turnstiles, metal detectors, and identity check booths that not only require determination, resilience, and physical stamina for Palestinians to endure but also serve as a daily instrument of their colonial subjugation and humiliation.

While the Israeli government has systematically sought to reduce its reliance of Palestinian labour in the last three decades, for instance by moving manufacturing to neighbouring countries and increasing labour migration to Israel from other countries, especially South and South-East Asia, work in Israel and Jerusalem remains an essential source of income to many Palestinian families and communities in the West Bank.[19] Most checkpoint users are Palestinian men seeking work in Israel or Jerusalem in pursuit of wages that can be as much as five times higher than in the West Bank, making this work difficult for male breadwinners to refuse. Before October 2023, about 93,000 men had permits to work in Israel, with a further 35,000 crossing illegally. A state-controlled quota system determines the sectors in which permits are available, and in what number, based on the needs of Israeli economy. The demand for workers is highest in construction, where 36,000 Palestinian construction workers are employed in settlements, building the encroaching illegal structures that consolidate Israeli settler colonial hold on Palestinian land in the West Bank. Israeli settlement companies exploit the legal ambiguities around settlements in Israeli law to employ Palestinians under worse conditions than they would be able to employ Israelis. For instance, Palestinian employees receive no vacation, sick days, or other benefits, and health and safety regulations are lax.[20] Despite the nature of the work, those fit enough to take it on have little choice because of the deliberately "de-developed" state of the Palestinian economy.[21] As such, by serving as cheap labour to build homes for settlers on Indigenous land, the exploitation of Palestinian labour buttresses the social reproduction of Israeli settlers. As I explain below, this also comes at the expense of the depletion of Palestinian social reproduction.

The nature of much of the work available lends itself to recruiting a commuter workforce composed largely of men, but the requirements for securing a military permit also determine the profiles of viable applicants. Eligibility for an eight-hour work pass is strictly controlled and privileges the labour exploitation of able-bodied men with families. To apply for a permit, a man must be between ages 30 and 50 and be married with children. Furthermore, permits are not issued to those who have been involved in union activity or protests, arrested, imprisoned, or previously dismissed by an Israeli company. The permit system therefore grants privileges of access to male breadwinners who have outgrown young adulthood and have more to lose due to responsibilities towards dependents, and who are without an administrative record of challenging the colonial order of things.

The arduous routine of the checkpoint commute removes men from their families and communities for a large portion of the working day. For instance, at Checkpoint 300 near Bethlehem, a queue starts to form around 4am, with the crowd at its peak around dawn as the men slowly funnel through the first corridors. To get there that early, Palestinian men often wake up as early as 2am. The crowd slowly progresses through the cage-like corridors that eventually lead to security checks. As hundreds of men struggle to get the most advantageous position in the queue, they are tightly packed, and younger men use the tops of walls where the fencing starts to climb over and pass others on the ground. The prolonged and congested waiting required at the checkpoint is therefore physically onerous. Once workers have passed a series of checks including metal detectors and identity checks, they are able to proceed onto buses that take them to their places of work – journeys that add further time to the commute. The workers must return to the West Bank before 7pm, before the expiry of the eight-hour permit, in order to avoid possible arrest. Checks are not carried out or are much less stringent on the way back, but even so some men may only have seven or eight hours at home before having to wake up early again to prepare for the next day's commute.[22]

The male breadwinner norm is therefore reproduced through the permit system, the kind of work in Israel and Israeli settlements available to Palestinians, and the physically demanding, time-consuming commute involving passage through the checkpoint. Moreover, it is a system centred on the labour exploitation of able-bodied, middle-aged, *married* men. The effects of checkpoints on men's lives are highly visible and relatively well documented, but they have an equally significant impact on women's lives. For each man with a work permit, we can assume that there is a wife whose life is affected beyond the space of the checkpoint. In addition to the gendered consequences of directly obstructing social reproduction (as discussed above), in the next section, I discuss how the gendered effects of checkpoints also reach far beyond the physical space of the checkpoint to the intimate space of the home, with the combined effect of reproducing the sexual division of labour. These extended temporalities shape the rhythms of family life and increase women's physical and emotional labour practices and burdens.

CHECKPOINT TIME, THE SEXUAL DIVISION OF LABOUR, AND SOCIAL REPRODUCTION

The geographies of social reproduction literature highlights how labour mobility informs the social reproduction of family and community life.[23] The commuter, whose activity is shaped by the uneven power relations of the economy, is embedded in a web of social relations, including the household, family, and community. The rhythms of commuting – its temporalities and embodied practices – reverberate through these relations, producing and maintaining gendered patterns and experiences of daily life.

This is also the case for commutes across the major checkpoints in the West Bank. As Helga Tawil-Souri emphasises, checkpoints are not just physical spaces but "temporal archipelagos" that "perform temporal work", producing a "time regime" that instructs Palestinians not only on who can travel (and for what purpose) but also when, how long it takes, under what conditions, and for how long.[24] Timekeeping in this context is a technology of "colonial domination over the minutia of everyday life" – a settler colonial mode of "chrononormativity" that both exploits and grinds down Palestinian life, compelling Palestinian commuters to sacrifice their physical and mental well-being, sense of dignity, and family and social relationships in order to access work.[25] In other words, to earn a living and support the life of one's family, Palestinian male commuters are severed from the practices and relationships that constitute and maintain the social life of Palestinian society. By extension, this absence affects those relations and practices at home and elsewhere.

To illustrate these effects, I draw on interviews carried out with married women aged 28 to 50 in the village of Al-Walajah, which lies around two kilometres west of Bethlehem and is within commuter reach of Checkpoint 300.[26] The women, whose husbands undertake the daily commute across the checkpoint, attest to the ways in which the checkpoint regiments everyday life by increasing their responsibilities for social reproduction, including both domestic and emotional labour.

First, the women provide an alternative perspective of the checkpoint and its "temporal archipelago" – the ways in which it structures the daily life of the families of Palestinian commuters. As discussed in the previous section, queues at the checkpoint start to form at night, imposing an incredibly early start to the day. Hayam's husband, for example, wakes up every morning at 2am and leaves for the checkpoint at 3am for a four-hour commute to work, returning home at 7pm after a two-hour journey back from work.[27] As she describes it, "he comes home and barely has time to eat and go to sleep, he has no time to spend at home or do anything other than going to work and coming back, most of his time is wasted on trying to get to work and trying to come home". Her husband has little time to spend at home or see his family. Yet despite his absence, the "time" of the checkpoint dictates the pace, forms, and quantity of domestic work. Another woman, Amani, recalls the duplication of domestic work, especially meal preparation, that the long commute imposes:

My husband wakes up at 4am and I wake up with him to prepare for work. After he leaves, I start working in the house, cleaning, readying the children for school, preparing food before they come back, cooking for my husband when he comes home late. My children want to eat at a certain time, and he comes home late, so I prepare the meals twice.

The gruelling schedule of the checkpoint therefore restructures women's schedules and quantity of domestic labour, even if they do not have to endure the crowds, delays, and humiliation of the checkpoint. Indeed, wives are often not only expected to wake up with their husbands (losing sleep themselves) and prepare meals for the different daily rhythms of household members but also to take care of all household duties, lengthening their working days and adding to their responsibilities. Women consistently stated that the absence of their husband meant that they were responsible for housework, childcare, and maintaining family and community relationships. As Randa states, "I cover for the husband and the wife at the same time", for example, "responsibilities for the children like helping them study, taking them for medical visits, I even look after his in-laws – all these responsibilities are now on me". This was echoed by Hayam: "I alone have to deal with everything… I clean the house, I go shopping, cook, pay electricity bills. Everything that involves the house, I'm responsible for. There's no other way… I have to deal with family duties alone, we can't share responsibilities. I have to organise all family issues, house requirements, deal with the children."

Women's responsibilities for social reproduction are intensified in order to compensate for the reduced contribution of their husbands. In this sense, women are left with the responsibility of not only looking after their husbands, children, and extended families but also of carrying out the essential everyday practices of care required to reproduce Palestinian society. This resonates with existing scholarship that underscores how occupation and the economic conditions of de-development put additional pressures on women to compensate for the declining resources available for social reproduction.[28]

The checkpoint also makes demands on the emotional well-being and endurance of families, both its constituent members and as a whole. Women are often those who find themselves trying to attend to the feelings of everyone – remaining patient while caring for absent, exhausted, stressed, and sometimes angry husbands, attending to children's well-being and juggling the emotional distance between fathers and children caused by the absence and stress foisted upon them by the checkpoint. Karima attests to how the checkpoint causes exhaustion not only for her husband, but also herself:

> For him, he's physically exhausted, because he wakes up early and goes to work for long hours... It makes me also feel nervous and worried about him. Because of lack of sleep I am tired and short-tempered more than usual. I would like to rest and sleep but there is no time for it, because you have to keep up with housework and responsibilities.

The checkpoint, in other words, produces "time poverty" that depletes the temporal and emotional capacities of both husband and wife due to the domino effect it has on domestic responsibilities.[29] This can lead to strains in marital relations, as Amami describes: "When he comes home late, he's stressed, and I've had a long day [too] and I'm also stressed. This creates problems between us, and we don't know how to deal with them... There's no time for you to spend together, to talk about problems. So, you postpone talking and problems pile up."

The translation of physical absence into emotional distance also extends to children. Women were repeatedly saddened by the lack of time available for fathers to spend with their children and the detrimental effects it has on their upbringing. The time that children and fathers did spend together was short and sometimes tense due to the stress caused by the checkpoint. As Amani describes in relation to her children:

> It has a big impact on them. The children don't know their father, they don't understand what he wants, and he doesn't understand what they need... There is not time for them to ask why he's angry and there is not

time for him to ask his children about their day, their problems, about their school, what they did that day. There is not time for that because he only wants to eat, shower, and go to bed, He is already stressed about the next day.

In addition to exhaustion and the prevention of nurturing relation-ships among family members, women were troubled by the impact that the checkpoint and commute had on their husbands' temperaments. Suad, for example, recounted that her husband "wasn't an angry man [before] but with all the pressure and the exhaustion between work and the checkpoint, he has become more angry and short-tempered". This anger was often released at home. Narima, for instance, shared that the checkpoint "affects his mental-ity, if it's crowded, he comes home angry", adding that, "if it is particularly bad, he is irritated… and projects his frustration at everyone in the house". Suad and Narima both understand the anger as an understandable effect of the checkpoint, leaving them also feeling helpless to do anything about it other than to absorb the outbursts and continue to provide their husbands with food and comfort when they are at home.

Much like their husbands, therefore, wives of Palestinian commuters become caught in the temporalities of the checkpoint, adding not only to the extension of their domestic workday and the amount and kinds of tasks they are responsible for but also the mental and emotional exhaustion of this imposed schedule, and the strain and isolation it brings to familial relationships.

CONCLUSION

Feminist scholars point to the two struggles of Palestinian women: coloni-alism and patriarchy.[30] These struggles, and how they are interlinked, are also apparent in the colonial technology of the checkpoint. While Palestin-ian society continues to be deeply patriarchal, the occupation exacerbates and sustains such structures. For instance, land grabs and restricted access to natural resources have diminished the ability of swathes of Palestini-ans to practise agriculture, develop industry, and engage in construction, suffocating the Palestinian economy. With most better-paying jobs avail-able in Israel in male-dominated sectors such as construction, Palestinian women in the West Bank have few opportunities to earn a wage beyond informal labour markets, despite high rates of women's enrolment in higher education.[31] In short, Israeli settler colonial capitalism combined with its segregationist security architecture strengthens rather than destabilises patriarchy. The capitalist demands of the Israeli state, in conjunction with its settler colonial expansionism, produce the demand for cheap Palestinian labour. The checkpoint is required to maintain access to this labour, which supports the social reproduction of Israeli settlers by channelling Palestinians to build Israeli settlements on Palestinian land. The cost for this is borne not only by the exploited and exhausted Palestinian construction workers but also by Palestinian women. Israeli hiring practices for Palestinians, permit regimes, and checkpoint practices reinforce a sexual division of labour among Palestinian communities in the West Bank dependent on access to Israeli labour markets. Moreover, they make women's care of the home, family, relationships and, by extension, Palestinian life as hard as possible to sustain.

The precarity that this system represents for Palestinian life was highlighted during the war on Gaza that began in October 2023. In Gaza, Palestinians are suffering a prolonged genocidal military campaign that not only killed but deliberately destroyed the means of sustaining life.[32] Social reproduction in the West Bank has also been severely impacted. In addition to an escalation of Israeli colonial violence, such as settler attacks, raids, arrests, displacement, home demolitions, and military incursions in the West Bank, movement through checkpoints was heavily restricted, resulting in devastating effects on Palestinian livelihoods. About 150,000 work permits were cancelled and major checkpoints controlling crossings between the West Bank and Israel such as Checkpoint 300, Rantis, Qalandiya, and Wadi Fukin were closed.[33] Israeli wages constitute about 20 per cent of the Palestinian Authority's GDP, and their loss has pushed the West Bank to the brink of economic collapse, leaving many families struggling to purchase basic necessities.[34] The burdens of looking after one's spouse, children, extended family, and neighbours are only aggravated as they are in times of heightened economic hardship and militarised violence.[35] This highlights the double-bind of the checkpoint – the slow violence integral to the highly exploitative labour conditions it facilitates on the one hand, and the accelerated depletion of social reproduction it effects when access to it is severed on the other hand. As such, when we analyse settler colonial control and checkpoints, we should recall not only their restrictions on mobility, but also their deeper role in governing social reproduction and the un/making of Palestinian life.

NOTES

1. Hammami, "On (Not) Surviving"; Mansbach, "Normalizing Violence"; and Rikje, "Checkpoint Knowledge".
2. OCHA, "Movement and Access". The number of roadblocks varies constantly. An updated list is maintained by B'Tselem, "List of Military Checkpoints".
3. Khalidi, *Palestinian Identity*. See also Abourahme, "Spatial Collisions"; and El-Haddad, "Quintessential Palestinian Experience".
4. Pallister-Wilkins, "How Walls Do Work", 152.
5. Chilmeran and Pratt, "Geopolitics of Social Reproduction".
6. Amira, "Slow Violence"; and Nixon, *Slow Violence*.
7. Hughes, "Unbounded Territoriality", 218.
8. Clarsen, "Introduction".
9. Peteet, *Space and Mobility*.
10. In 2023, 339 of 645 obstacles to movement had such an impact. OCHA, "Movement and Access".
11. Fields, "This is Our Land"; and Panosetti and Roudart, "Land Struggle".
12. Chilmeran and Pratt, "Geopolitics of Social Reproduction", 597–98; Griffiths and Joronen, "Marriage under Occupation"; and Peteet, *Space and Mobility*.
13. Dewi, "Health"; and Fahoum and Abuelaish, "Occupation, Settlement".
14. In 2022, 15 per cent of applicants seeking care in East Jerusalem and 20 per cent of applications for their companions were denied, while 9 per cent of ambulance crossings were delayed (OCHA, "Movement and Access").
15. Abdul-Rahim, Abu-Rmeileh, and Wick, "Cesarean Section Deliveries"; Giacaman, Wick, and Abdul-Rahim, "Politics of Childbirth"; Hammami, "Destabilizing Mastery"; and Shalhoub-Kevorkian, "Politics of Birth".
16. Griffiths and Repo, "Women and Checkpoints"; Hammami, "On (Not) Surviving"; and Shalhoub-Kevorkian, "Politics of Birth".
17. Farsakh, *Palestinian Labour Migration*; and Rosenhek, "Political Dynamics".
18. Tawil-Souri, "Qalandia Checkpoint".
19. Clarno, *Neoliberal Apartheid*; and Farsakh, *Palestinian Labour Migration*.
20. Griffiths and Repo, "Biopolitics and Checkpoint".
21. Roy, "De-Development Revisited".
22. Griffiths and Repo, "Biopolitics and Checkpoint".
23. Hanson, "Gender and Mobility"; Mayes, "Mobility, Temporality"; and Walsh et al., "Gendered Mobilities".
24. Tawil-Souri, "Checkpoint Time".
25. Peteet, *Space and Mobility*, 139; and Freeman, *Time Binds*, 3.
26. Griffiths and Repo, "Women's Lives"; and Griffiths and Repo, "Women and Checkpoints".
27. All interviewee names are pseudonyms.
28. Haj, "Palestinian Women"; and Peteet, *Gender in Crisis*.
29. Warren, "Class- and Gender-Based".
30. Alasah, "Palestinian Feminist Movement"; and Darraj, "Palestinian Women".

31. The rate of women's enrolment in higher education was 62 per cent in 2021–2022 (PCBS, "Conditions of the Palestinian Population").
32. Repo, "Genocide and the Destruction".
33. In addition, between October 2023 and May 2024, 44 per cent of 28,292 applications submitted by Palestinians for permits to seek medical care in East Jerusalem or Israel have been denied or remain pending, constituting a 22 per cent decrease in approvals. This can be seen as part of a wider attack on healthcare that extends beyond Gaza. The WHO documented 480 attacks on healthcare in the West Bank between 7 October 2023 and 28 May 2024 (WHO, "WHO Concerned"). Some checkpoints, such as Checkpoint 300 and Qalandiya, reopened in December 2023 and February 2024 but with restricted hours. At the same time, in December 2023 after pressure from Israeli businesses, Israeli authorities permitted 8,000 to 10,000 Palestinian workers – a fraction of the previous 150,000 – to return to work. See B'Tselem, "List of Military Checkpoints".
34. Real GDP in the West Bank has fallen by 23.4 per cent with value added in construction dropping by 47.3 per cent and manufacturing, mining, water, and electricity by 35.4 per cent. Unemployment, in turn, has surged from 14 to 34.9 per cent (ILO, "A Year of War in Gaza").
35. Emejulu and Bassel, "Austerity"; Hedström, "On Violence"; and Pasquetti, Repo, and Shoman, "Settler Colonialism".

8

Insurgent Social Reproduction: The Home, the Barricade, and Women's Work in the 1936 Palestinian Revolution

Mai Taha

There is an image of four Israeli soldiers sitting on the floor of a living room, snacking on some fruits as they're watching television. The image is from a refugee camp near Ramallah in the year 2002. Ariella Azoulay rereads this image when it later makes its way into different family archives marking its rediscovery. One day, she writes, someone recognised "a crime committed, a deed that never should have been done, a violation, a disaster, a horror – something that had been previously ignored and suddenly appeared in a different light".[1] This rediscovery of a crime scene in an image of soldiers watching television – with no blood, no beating, no threats, but only army boots, resting guns, fruits, and a television set – came with a testimony of one of the soldiers:

> It was during the World Cup and we were carrying out searches in a certain village. We had to enter one of the houses. Now you got a really cool platoon commander who's a fan of the Argentinian team too, and he too wants to watch the game. So you tell him, "Listen, bro", you know… this house or that house, it's all the same but this one's got a television set, man". So we went into the house with the TV set, and just took a family out of its home so we could watch the Argentina–Nigeria game.[2]

The rediscovery of that image as a crime scene is one of the many iterations of dispossession since the early days of European settlement in Palestine. A Palestinian family can be displaced out of their home for a few hours so that Israeli soldiers could watch a football game as they raid the fridge for snacks. One can hardly imagine the Palestinian home without this carceral imagery of the settler state. The home has always been a site of the most audacious forms of dispossession. Indeed, home demolition has been a primary tool of settler colonial erasure and the racial hierarchies embedded within urban planning.[3] In Palestine, it has a determinate/indeterminate character, whereby there is always a certainty of demolition that is yet to come at an unknown time.[4] The anticipation of a future violence of home demolition becomes "an affective condition of present".[5] Indeed, the persistent Zionist attack on the home space is "inseparable from attacks on the homeland" and the settler project of dispossession.[6]

While the home has been a target of relentless demolition and displacement from its stable physical structure – as manifested most concretely in the precariousness of the refugee tent from 1948 onwards – it has historically also been a place of care, culture, labour, and resistance. Indeed, the home is always becoming, constantly remade with every demolition and every displacement. In this chapter, I argue that the home embodies these contradictions: both a crime scene and a revolutionary space; a site of colonial surveillance and destruction, and a grounding site of labour and reconstruction. To engage with these tensions within the home, I return to the revolution of 1936–1939 against the British Mandate, a snapshot in the long and ongoing Palestinian revolution. But instead of only looking for revolutionaries in the barricades and the mountains, I look for them in the kitchens, in the bedrooms, and in the living rooms. In that sense, I propose that the production of the home space is itself a conceptual site of theorisation for what can be called *insurgent social reproduction* – from the mundane to the spectacular quotidian details.

There is a long line of Marxist-feminist literature on social reproduction theory. This article pivots off this tradition to argue not only that socially reproductive labour has been historically undervalued, but that it has also played a revolutionary role. I imagine the home as a space of resistance – almost like a battlefield, it harbours weapons, food, water, and rebels. The home became a zone of engagement during the revolution and became a space from which an alternative political imaginary of anticolonialism was assembled and practised. It is hard to find the quotidian details of the home in the traditional state archive; so, instead, I draw primarily on oral history narratives, specifically from the brilliant project led by Faihaa Abdulhadi and a team of researchers who, in the early 2000s, published and archived oral history interviews made with Palestinian women who participated in the 1936 revolution, as well as the Palestine Oral History Archive, which documented the experiences of Palestinians in refugee camps in Lebanon. In addition to oral history, I also draw on literary works and photography, which together form an archive of the home.

In what follows, I first situate the home across time in Palestine within a series of signposts that mark its infrastructure of violence. I think about the constantly mediated relationship between the past and the present, and the ways in which the home today, both as a physical structure and as a social life, mirrors the home during the years when Palestine became a settler colony. Importantly, this mirroring of the past from the present situates the home within a wider set of processes operating during the years of the revolution, framing it as both a political space and an historical one. Second, I go inside the home through thinking with "the minor" – teasing out the daily details, the secrets, and the stories of Palestinian women during the revolution. The article concludes with an examination of some of the broader implications that emerge from this analysis that centres the home as a space that partakes in struggle through the quotidian.

MEMORY AND MIRRORING: SITUATING THE HOME
WITHIN AN INFRASTRUCTURE OF VIOLENCE

The task of remembering from the present is "an active construction of the past".[7] Elias Khoury asks: How do we write a story from a present that does not yet have an ending? When a story ends, it opens up the possibilities for different readings, interpretations, and rereadings, where the ending breathes a second life into the story.[8] But what happens when we can't see the ending yet? Khoury is talking about the ongoing *Nakba*, as not simply an event, but as a structure that changes its meaning across time, operating as a historically differentiated process.[9] Importantly, the *Nakba* has no ending yet, but is constantly reshaped by the present and its memory of the past. If the *Nakba* is not an event, then it also did not start in 1948 either, just as it did not end with the Oslo Accords in 1993; it simply took different forms across time. But it was always in tension with the long Palestinian revolution that has also lived several lives. The 1936–1939 Arab Revolt in Palestine against the settler project is recalled and reassembled from a present shaped by the unremitting viciousness of settler colonialism that feeds off the destruction of Palestinian homes. In that sense, the return to the home in 1936 is not simply out of historical interest, but out of a very present political urgency. Israel's security regime that suffocates and infiltrates Arab homes mirrors that of the British Mandate in the early years of settlement and colonisation. Today, life in Palestine could only be described as a perpetual maze of crossing barriers.[10] The most obvious manifestation of this is the construction of the Separation Wall that runs inside the West Bank, passing through its streets and its homes, separating friends, families, and comrades. This wall operates on both the material and the symbolic registers.[11] Symbolically, the construction of a concrete wall has a completeness to it, as if marking an ending, albeit an unhappy one. The wall represents a fait accompli situation: as if colonialism happened in the past and was resolved by partition. It is as if the temporalities of settler colonialism have been paused or stopped completely to announce a new order governed by this "surreal architecture" of security and checkpoints.[12] But one can see fragments of the past in the image of the wall today, as if recognising some of its features in the security regime founded by the British Mandate during the interwar years. British watchtowers, security walls, checkpoints, and the ransacking of Arab homes during the mandate also yield new meanings as one reads them in light of today's horror, professing a dialectical relationship between the imagery of the past and that of the present.[13] The home continues to be embedded within this securitised and surveilled architecture that imposes itself on the everyday – city and village.

During the early months of the revolution, the mandate government was already instituting an infrastructure of violence across all of Palestine.[14] The revolution itself was sparked by a series of street fights between the two communities in Jaffa and other cities, which eventually culminated in a call for an Arab general strike by 19 April 1936.[15] One of the strike's main drivers was the increase in Jewish immigration and settlement that transformed Palestine's political economy. This was happening in parallel with a slow transfer of agricultural land ownership, alienating Arab peasants from their means of subsistence and creating a growing class of dispossessed peasants who would turn to waged labour.[16] This process had been happening slowly since the turn of the century when early Zionists resorted to American agriculturalists for advice on the best programme for agricultural development based on the perceived similarity between the settler colonial projects in California and in Palestine.[17] These changes in land tenure and labour relations were the material basis for understanding the political economy of the creation of a settler colony.[18]

While the current wall seems very far in time from the arrangements that were present during the 1936 Arab Revolt, there is a strange, even if prophetic, mirroring of the walled present and the tumultuous past. Yet as time passes, there are slightly different reflections of the past – after all, mirrors do break. The partitioning of Palestine would later trigger infinite projects of walling that pass through Palestinian streets, neighbourhoods, homes, and entire cities.[19] The home then is not an insular space but one that mingles and fuses into the street, city, and village life. It is implicated in planning, labour, and security arrangements. To approach the home in this way is to tie it to a set of different processes that operate inside, outside, and through the home. Returning to Palestinian homes in the 1930s means a return to the years in which Palestine became a settler colony, and importantly the years when Palestinians staged a chain of refusals: refusal of the British Mandate and its security apparatus, of increasing numbers of settlers arriving in Palestine, of poor labour conditions, including the creation of a racially segregated labour force, as well as the colonial surveillance of the Arab home, and its constant invasion by everyday acts of violence that arise from this colonial/settler-colonial arrangement of 1930s Palestine.

The years of the 1936–1939 Arab Revolt also witnessed the articulation of one of the earlier partition plans – a decade before the 1947 UN Partition Plan – in the Peel Commission report, which on some level is still present today, acting almost as a palimpsest of the geographies of Israeli apartheid.[20] Lord Peel arrived with his commission in Palestine to investigate the "disturbances" that started with an Arab general strike in 1936, lasting for six months, and turning into a three-year revolution.[21]

More than a year after the Peel Commission, the new Palestine Partition Commission stated that the "Arabs remain inflexibly hostile to partition. During our stay in Palestine, no Arab came forward to submit evidence or to co-operate in any way with us: the boycott was complete".[22] But for the boycott to be truly complete, the home space was used to make up for the lost market from boycotting British commodities. The home was not only a site for plotting and planning, it was also the space from which an alternative market of commercial goods was created within the Arab community during the boycott. The steadfastness of the rebellion for three years, and its rejection of the different "solutions" offered by the mandate government, show that the revolution aimed at dismantling the very logics of settler colonialism. The rebels were not interested in partition. In fact, they imagined an alternative to the colonial state altogether and enacted it on some level during the years of the revolution. Like every revolution, such enactments were mired in contradictions; still, the rebels created an entirely parallel system to that of the mandate: from parallel institutions to rebel courts to the Arab boycott. Without the Palestinian home, this parallel system would not have been possible. The home was also the space for storing weapons, hiding rebels, and for sending secret messages between the revolutionaries. The home reproduced the revolutionaries, making it just as central a space to revolutionary action as the rebels' barricades on the mountains. In that sense, Palestinian women who occupied and managed the homeplace were creative agents who reimagined the Arab home as a space of resistance and repurposed their labour of social reproduction as struggle.

Here, my return to women within the homeplace in Palestine's revolutionary history is not about painting a picture of history *as it really was*, to use Ranke's expression, somehow correcting or completing the literature on the history of the revolution.[23] It is instead about searching for an opening in time, a moment from which to seek refuge.[24] It is about seizing the memory of revolution "as it flashes up at a moment of danger".[25] The return to the home from this perspective then is not really a literal return but a potentiality. It is a way to rethink what is at stake in Palestine.

This entails thinking about capital, class, and gender, as well as racial segregation "at the same time and at once".[26] And the home somehow captures those together. It is a site of labour, reproduction, leisure, rest and recuperation, food, song, culture, and also a site of revolution *and* potentiality. If Marxist-feminists showed that, without women's reproductive labour, workers simply won't go to the factory, then perhaps it also shows that, without women's labour, workers won't "go" to the revolution.[27] But importantly, this poses another underlying question: who indeed is a revolutionary? And what is revolutionary action? In thinking about those two questions, I keep returning to bell hooks' evocative text on the homeplace.[28] She paints a picture of the homeplace as shelter and warmth, as a site of labour: "*feeding our bodies, nurturing our souls*". At the same time, the homeplace is also a site of resistance. Indeed, she recounts how Black people saw the construction of a homeplace, regardless of its fragility and tenuousness (imagine the slave hut or the wooden shack), as having "a radical political dimension".[29] It is precisely this perspective on the home as a space with a "powerful force" that I see in 1930s Palestine.[30] This seemingly erratic spatial-temporal movement is methodological for it is not only the history of Black–Palestinian solidarity that informs this, but it is also informed by approaching Palestine with specificity yet without exceptionality.[31] The long Palestinian revolution has its specific details, but it is also unexceptional – universal, so to speak.[32] Centring women in the homeplace in revolutionary times could create a different history of resistance through what I call *insurgent social reproduction*. In that sense, I build on Marxist-feminist theory to reimagine today's sites of transformative change.

The Home, the Minor, the Secret

Histories of revolutions are often associated with certain forms of actions, affects, sensibilities, and heroisms. Carrying weapons, leading demonstrations, and building clandestine networks of communication rightly populate histories of revolutions. And the 1936 revolution is no exception. Many Palestinian women were revolutionaries in that traditional sense of the term, something which is vastly underrated in the historiography of the revolution and most certainly in state archives and in the archives of international institutions. But here, I am also interested in the role that was, and is, deemed minor. I am interested in the minor because it gets us inside the home, the space often deemed to be outside of history and politics. The minor here is an accumulation of details, reminiscent of the narrative structure of Adania Shibli's novel, *Minor Detail*, which moves across time in Palestine with a grim yet gripping account of quotidian minor details.[33] Shibli inhabits those minor details that become almost like a secret because nobody gives attention to them.[34] The minor in the novel shows the ritualistic, often mundane, sometimes spectacular violence of life under settler colonialism. One could also imagine the minor as a space of freedom and possibility, where "things can be known and seen differently".[35] To "know and see things differently" here is to rearticulate the home within history and politics. The minor details in the home are both ones of colonial violence and revolutionary possibility. The "secrets" or the details recall women, who were neither heroes nor unwitting victims: they were active agents who organically made the homeplace a space of resistance.

Most of the traditional history of the revolution documented that woman had one primary role: provide the revolutionaries with food and water. I engage with this claim on two levels. First, as oral history narratives show, women also contributed to what would be deemed "regular" revolutionary activity, such as handling weapons and leading demonstrations against the mandate. Second, while deemed essential, the labour of "food and water" was considered a mere marginal contribution to the struggle, or indeed minor. But what is it about minor details that could retell the histories of revolutions?

The rebels of Palestine reimagined an alternative to the colonial state. They not only focused their efforts on organising protests, but on reclaiming community autonomy and organisation.[36] It should be noted, however, that none of the leaders from the Palestinian elite supported the movement leading up to the strike initially.[37] It was peasants and workers who established rebel courts instead of the British court system that was under boycott.[38] They established local administrations, guerrilla bands, collected taxes, again in parallel with the Arab boycott and the tax strike against the mandate government, and they developed an impressive intelligence system, which was mostly led by women.[39] Through their appropriation of the traditional symbols of state power, the rebellion "blur[ed] the lines between 'mimicry' and 'mockery'" of the colonial administration, as Ghandour argues.[40] They even stole typewriters from the British government offices to help them go about their business. By "appropriating the paraphernalia of British justice", the rebels marked a new symbolic order where colonial legal structures, from the courts system to the mundane practicality of its typewriters, became up for grabs to be reimagined, repurposed, or simply revolutionised.[41] While appropriating the paraphernalia of British injustice was one side of the story, the repurposing of domestic paraphernalia was the other side. In Arab homes, women would hide the weapons in buckets of wheat and men in wells. They would make flags and protest signs out of bed sheets. And women's dresses with their veil acted as the perfect masquerade for hiding men.[42] Typically, "we are unable to seize the human facts. We fail to see them where they are, namely in humble, familiar, everyday objects".[43] But it was precisely those everyday objects that helped configure the relationship between the home and the struggle. Food itself became a weapon. One of the most common memories of Arab women that was repeated in several oral history accounts, including most recently in Isabella Hammad's family oral history-based novel *The Parisian*, was the following: the protagonist says, "they come into the village, they arrest people and they smash everything. They mix all the food together, the flour with the rice and the sugar... into a pile [and then] they usually add olive oil or petrol".[44] This concocted recipe of flour, uncooked rice, and a pile of sugar all mixed up together with olive oil is but one symbolic manifestation of the infiltration of the infrastructures of colonial violence into the home, whereby even food items get implicated in the fight. Importantly, it reminds us that the fight *is* at home.

The imagery of home destruction that is available to us today is haunting and unsettling. In one instance, Figure 8.1 appears to be incredibly posed with a victimising gaze yet without any trace of the revolution, showing an image of Palestinians sitting in front of their home in ruins with bleak stares after a night raid by British forces in search for weapons. In another instance, the image appears to capture the sheer exhaustion of a life of constant destruction, as if they're pausing to take a breath before they start again. The sheets and blankets lie soiled on the ground, along with scattered pots and pans. The raid has passed. They're still there.

Figure 8.1　Palestine Disturbances 1936: Scene in a Bab Hutta home after an official night raid in search for arms. Photo: Library of Congress, G. Eric and Edith Matson Photograph Collection, American Colony, 2019708835.

Figure 8.2　Palestine Disturbances 1936: Broken pots & pans, said to be the effect of an official raid in an Arab house. Photo: Library of Congress, G. Eric and Edith Matson Photograph Collection, American Colony, 2019708836.

Figure 8.2 is also unsettling, not only because it shows an injured child crying and sitting above the broken pots of his home, clearly frightened by the invasion. It is unsettling also because it appears as if there were no agents orchestrating this raid, as if the child broke the pots, injured himself, and just started crying. Like the image of broken grain bins (Figure 8.3), perhaps the writing on the photo as stored in the Library of Congress today captures enough by its cold description: "Halhul village, near Hebron. Interior of a house showing broken grain bins, said to have been wrecked by army in search of arms. Library of Congress".

Figure 8.3 Palestine Disturbances 1936: In Halhul village, near Hebron. Interior of a house showing broken grain bins, said to have been wrecked by army in search of arms. Photo: Library of Congress, G. Eric and Edith Matson Photograph Collection, 2019708920.

The women would later pick up the broken pots and soiled blankets, wash, fold, and store them back in their places, reversing this spectacle to the mundane order of a household. The repetition of this process would be enacted again with every search party and every night raid. Indeed, the production of the home space is a constant process of making and remaking. While the home is a physical construction of some form, here it is always precarious and subject to threats of invasion and demolition. In resisting that precarity, the home is always becoming, relentlessly reconstituted with every act of violence.

The impressive Marxist-feminist scholarship that has developed from the 1970s until today on social reproduction explains that women's reproductive labour has been historically devalued under capitalism. While this scholarship is particularly instructive in contesting the traditional gendered Marxist analysis of labour, including the history of primitive accumulation, it is intended to nuance the worker–capitalist relationship by highlighting the centrality of women's unpaid reproductive labour in capitalist society. Following the tradition that centres this labour in our analysis of exploitation and oppression, I centre the labour of "food and water" to revolutionary action and argue that socially reproductive labour has indeed played a revolutionary role.[45]

Many women themselves did not consider this as significant enough to be even mentioned in the oral history narratives collected over the years. When asked about the role of women in the revolution, many peasant women said "women did nothing".[46] And in the next breath they would say, "we cooked for the revolutionaries, climbed up the hills to deliver the food in hiding, we would dress the men in women's clothes to hide them from the British and we collected donations for the revolutionaries and their families".[47] One of the women said: "[women] would follow them [the revolutionaries] with water, run with them; the one who falls, they help back up; the one who is thirsty, they give water... and courageous women used to carry weapons. I myself carried weapons".[48] Salimah Abu 'Assaf from Haifa remembers that "the revolutionaries were at [their] home, and [she] had prepared milk and bread for them, then the shooting started, killing them all with British guns".[49] The wife of Abu Raja also remembers that the rebels would come to her house in the evening with "their guns cradled in their arms and their muddy boots on their feet".[50] They would ask for food, so she would get up and cook for them and give them space to sleep the night. In fact, one of the most common memories of the revolution is the celebration of the rebels' visit, sometimes even resembling a wedding feast, where people would sing songs and offer food and drink. Many remember the revolution as an event that "forged new forms of collective struggle" and built solidarity within the Arab community.[51]

Rasmiyya al-Barghouthi known by Umm al-'abd narrates the daily schedule of the household during the revolution: "we have a system: we would wake up earlier... wash and get dressed, and we start distributing [the food items], we finish at 10am, we go out to the demonstration, and at night we deliver the food to the revolutionaries".[52] Kamilia Shnaik and Fatma Khalil also had a rigid schedule of baking and gathering as much food as possible from the surrounding homes to send to the revolutionaries.[53] While those are familiar and regular everyday acts, they are not necessarily known and seen. "It is in the most familiar things that the unknown… is at its richest", writes Lefebvre.[54] Indeed, women were using regular household items to hide their participation in the revolution. In the mountains, and the villages, there was guerrilla fighting, so in places like Bal'a near Tulkarm, a group of women would pass after 10 or 11 at night, carrying bread, water, cheese, and they would ask: "young men, who didn't have dinner yet?"[55] Running the revolution like running the household, women organically created a parallel system that effectively reproduced the revolution for three years. Here, the home becomes a principal site of the social, political, and cultural reproduction of society.

The system was not only about cooking but about devising strategies to circumvent British colonial surveillance of the revolutionaries. For example, Latifa Mahmoud Derbas from Bla'a retold the story of women taking food and water to the revolutionaries. The revolutionaries would eat and move from mountain to mountain, and the women would follow them. When the British army would ask them where they were going with all this water they would say "we are going to the coal mine, we are going to put down the burning coal with the water on our heads… we would put a bundle of firewood together and hide bullets inside it and carry it on our heads so that the revolutionaries could share the ammunitions".[56]

This insurgent reproductive work also entailed financing and budgeting for the revolution. Indeed, peasant women would sell their family jewellery to buy weapons for the revolutionaries.[57] During the early months of the strike, women had to manage the home economics of daily life, cutting the household budget in half by relying more creatively on growing food at home, and on mutual aid support between neighbours and family members. As one narrator puts it: "If I have more of something, I give to my neighbor, if she has more of something, she gives to me".[58] Sometimes it was bread, milk, or any other necessary food item.

The extent to which the rebels relied on the village economy centred the home as a space for hiding, planning, eating, drinking, storing weapons, and building communication networks through the women of the household. Notably also, when the British authorities ordered Arabs to carry identity cards and traffic passes in November 1938, which was one of the early attempts at building a bureaucratic infrastructure of securitisation, in response, the Arabs organised a boycott of all British commercial goods. This boycott meant that they had to avoid the road system that was patrolled by the British army to transport commodities, which were brought to the market on the "heads of women".[59] In women's oral history narratives, they say that once the strike was called for in 1936, all village homes would grow vegetables, grains, and raise chickens, which they would send to the city to avoid buying from the shops and to respect the strike. "Tomatoes, cucumbers, radishes, zucchinis… with rice, some lentils, and burghul. That's it".[60] Figure 8.4 shows fruit baskets being "smuggled" in 1936, demonstrating how women in the villages operated in those parallel networks of self-sufficiency that sustained and reproduced the strike and the revolution that followed. Indeed, peasant women never closed the route between the home and the fields during the strike.

Figure 8.4 Palestine Disturbances 1936: Fruit baskets "smuggled" into the passenger cars. Photo: Library of Congress, G. Eric and Edith Matson Photograph Collection, American Colony, 2019708942.

Thus, the home was connected to the circuit of commercial goods, as it became one of the central fronts of the revolution. See, for example, the temporary vegetable market in Figure 8.5 that created a transitory economy connecting the home to these forms of makeshift exchange. Indeed, as Maria Mies has put it: "without women's responsibility for the continuation of the economy, no successful liberation war can be fought".[61] The revolution helped generate a new infrastructure of social relations, creating different meanings of the homeplace.

Figure 8.5 Palestine Disturbances 1936: New & temporary vegetable market along the Jerusalem Jaffa railroad line. Scene at the Bittir station. Photo: Library of Congress, G. Eric and Edith Matson Photograph Collection, American Colony, 2019708941.

In another narrative, Jamila Badran remembers:

My mother was a messenger between the revolutionaries. My mother would go from 'Aroura to Ramallah to Em-Safa to Birzeit and back to Ramallah to deliver the oral messages. My mother couldn't read and write, so she would only deliver oral messages, such as how to safely move from one place to another, what was the next step, where are the weapons, etc. … My mother was a member of the communication network created to deliver messages during the revolution.[62]

The narrator Khadra al-Sary remembers women who would beat the British with their hands to release the men caught by the officers. Suad Abul Saud spoke about how young women would throw stones at the British army, a role that became emblematic of Palestinian resistance in the First Intifada of 1987.[63] Women were central to the revolution that completely paralysed the country for three years. In fact, the Arab Revolt puzzled people in the meeting of the Permanent Mandates Commission (PMC) at the League of Nations. The PMC claimed that it was "given a task that was entirely new to it". Its task was to evaluate the intentions of the mandatory power on the termination of its then 15-year-old mandate, not because of the "attainment of maturity by the ward" but because of "the difficulties of guardianship".[64] Palestine was in an open rebellion.

On some level, Palestinian women were also part of this open rebellion. "They struggled to create autonomous and beautiful lives... and to live as if they were free".[65] The hesitation is because they did not articulate it in those terms, yet our relationship with the past and how we make sense of it changes as time passes. Perhaps reading the Arab home as a revolutionary space could mean rethinking the agents of transformative change today. The revolution did mark a different form of organising that had to grapple with the complexities of living under patriarchal colonialism as well as local forms of patriarchy in its different manifestations.

In the urban centres, oral history narratives show that there were protests against the forced veil. The rebels had started issuing new ethical and moral edicts that forbade Arab women to follow European hair and dress style, and they imposed on them a forced veil, including the Christian Arab population.[66] In fact, many Christian women remember that the veil marked them as Arabs on the streets and presented them as supporters of the revolution. The narrator Samira Khoury remembers: "Some women, including my own mother, used to wear the veil during the time of the revolution, but at some point they said this [forced] veil is not for us and we have to fight for our rights and our work... at the same time, these same women struggled against colonialism... and protested for women's rights".[67]

The moral edicts forced on women by some of the rebels were also manifested in slogans such as that remembered by Ruqayya Khuri:

Umm al-bunya, al-raqqasa
Bidha bomba wa rasasa.
[The woman who wears a hat, the dancer
Deserves a bomb and a bullet.][68]

This slogan basically threatened women in Haifa with "a bomb and bullet" if one wears a hat, like the Westerners, and behaves promiscuously, like the dancers. Still several accounts describe the women of Haifa going to the market with their children and forcing shopkeepers to observe the strike organised by the rebels. There are clearly class dynamics at play here articulated in the division between the city and the village, but many women were even arrested and charged by the British authorities with "intimidating merchants and smashing shop windows".[69] These class dynamics were articulated in the different memories of women in the village and the city. While peasant woman remembered their role during the revolution through growing vegetables and grains to sustain the strike and later the boycott, in the cities, women's roles included organising demonstrations, working with women's organisations, and supporting detainees. One narrator from a group of urban women said that her father was a trader and, during the strike, they went to Beirut because all Arabs were supporting the strike and no one was working (see Figure 8.6). Her father and mother stayed in Palestine and sent the rest of the family to Lebanon. While this clear class distinction is very present in oral history narratives, some women in the urban centres continued to do reproductive revolutionary labour by opening their homes to the revolutionaries, giving them food, shelter, and a place of hiding.[70]

Figure 8.6 Palestine Disturbances 1936: Deserted scene in Jewellers market, as it has appeared during the months of strike, otherwise a crowded bazaar. Photo: Library of Congress, G. Eric and Edith Matson Photograph Collection, American Colony, 2019708940.

The narrator Ahmed al-Essawy spoke about the role of Jamila Abdul Jawad from 'Anata in monitoring the roads and in alerting the revolutionaries of the close arrival of the British army patrols. She would run from her home and stand in the middle of the village and chant a folk Palestinian riddle to warn the revolutionaries. She would say:

يا سامعين الصوت صلوا على محمد، اللي شاف، اللي قام اللي حط يجعله من قلة الأولاد، من قلة شو! من قلة الصغار يلاعب الغار، من قلة اللي ينط يداعب القط، نط يا قرد نط.

[Those who can hear my voice, pray on Mohammed's soul. The one who sees, who rises, who puts, make him from the few children, from the few what! From the few little ones who play with the laurel, from the few who tease the cat, jump monkey, jump.][71]

That little riddle rescued many rebels, or so they remember.

This memory is almost like a dream sequence that engages the senses, laying claim on this call as a gesture of indigeneity, and as intimacy with the place and its soundscapes. The imagery of Jamila Abdul Jawad, running from her home to the middle of the village, looking up as she uses her voice that echoes riddles to the hidden barracks of the revolutionaries marks the home as an anchor, a corridor that the revolution both relies on and passes through.[72] These fragments of narratives, gestures, and soundscapes of resistance are not in the official state archives. They are assembled as if by montage from family histories, oral narratives, art, and literature.[73] And they show how this archive of the homeplace becomes legible again today in different ways and in a different time. Contemporary dancer Farah Saleh engages with Palestinian memories through an "archive of gestures", a performance which curates hidden stories and movements, a kind of non-linear, subverted mimesis, through dance re-enactments of Palestinian memories of displacement, siege, and partition.[74] Saleh's work makes us imagine that there is a possibility for *life beyond life*, or as Kristin Ross would put it in French, "*survie*", for Jamila's gestures, an opening that starts a conversation with the past from the present. Ross, writing about the Paris Commune, explains that *survie* means not the memory or legacy of the event, "but its *prolongation*... It is a continuation of combat by other means. In the dialectic of the lived and the conceived... the thought of a movement is generated only with and after it: unleashed by the creation and excess of the movement itself. Actions produce dreams and ideas, not the reverse".[75] By re-enacting those gestures from the past, Saleh brings back those openings in history, the moments from which to seek refuge. Perhaps this conversation of bodily gestures from the past to the present and back is an invitation to rethink the role of the home in times of revolution. Acting in and through the home necessarily implicates it in the struggle. Somehow Jamila's gestures and the soundscapes of resistance of 1936 become legible then and today in different ways, and in a different time.

CONCLUSION

Both as a crime scene and as a site of revolution, the Palestinian home is recalled from the past to disrupt a present that is still mired in similar yet new infrastructures of violence. Rediscovering the image of Israeli soldiers watching television as a crime scene is an invitation to rethink our sources of knowledge production that become legible differently as time passes. These rereadings and rediscoveries together assemble a visual and literary archive that not only complicates the traditional narrative of the revolution but also intervenes in a present danger. Indeed, these fragments of narratives remembered by women who witnessed the revolution are recalled from a present that is yet to escape colonialism in its different manifestations. As Khoury reminds us, the story does not yet have an ending. Today's security regime that sends bulldozers for home demolitions and soldiers for search parties essentially holds women at the forefront, and places them as the first line of defence. The home then lies at the heart of this "dispossessive logic" of settler colonialism.[76] But the home, as I have argued, is also central to revolutionary history. And here, I want to return to the question of who is a revolutionary and what is revolutionary action?

The history of the 1936 revolution could be read as universal history in the sense that it redeems the past from what was deemed random and insignificant.[77] The labour of food and water, often seen as marginal or minor, has its specificities in Palestine but is indeed central to the reproduction of any liberation struggle. To see this, "all we need to do", as Henri Lefebvre reminds us, "is simply to open our eyes… and we will discover the immense human wealth that the humblest facts of everyday life contain".[78] The study of the home during the 1936 revolution through the facts of everyday life builds on social reproduction theory to centre the home as a site of theorisation and critique. It also complicates the traditional Marxist understanding of revolutionary subjectivity as embodied solely in the sphere of production, showing how other sites of hybridity between production, reproduction, and consumption – manifested here in the home space – have also been central to revolutionary action. This theoretical and political intervention is as much historical as it is urgent. Perhaps the home could be one space from which we can think about resistance to the gendered division of reproductive labour as a fundamental project of liberation against the colonial technologies of the past and the present: against the British watchtowers and their recipes of uncooked rice and olive oil, and against the realities of settler colonial horror today that, once again, makes it all the way to the Arab kitchen. But also, if the home is the space from which we can rethink historical difference dialectically, we cannot "only accommodate indigenous difference but also arm a critical project against indigenous versions of domination".[79] Maybe only when the home becomes a front of the revolution can it partake in this critical project that is both anticolonial and that rejects Indigenous versions of domination where the home is still tied up with various projects of colonial capital accumulation orchestrated by the ruling class.

ACKNOWLEDGEMENTS

I would like to thank colleagues at the Gendering the Arab Archive Workshop, ACSS, Beirut, 2022; Reassessing the British Mandate in Palestine, the Institute for Palestine Studies Conference, Birzeit University, 2022; the Radical Critical Theory Circle, Nisyros, 2024; the Historical Materialism Conference, London, 2024; and colleagues at LSE Sociology for their valuable engagement with my work. I am also particularly grateful to Hashem Abushama, Mahvish Ahmed, Ayça Çubukçu, Hazem Jamjoum, Rami Rmeileh, and Sara Salem for their feedback on this piece at various stages of writing. I thank Faihaa Abdulhadi for sharing with me the incredible oral history project on the role of women in the 1936 Revolt in Palestine.

NOTES

1. Azoulay, "Getting Rid of the Distinction", 240.
2. See [Breaking the Silence] website: www.breakingthesilence.org.il; and Azoulay, "Getting Rid of the Distinction", 242.
3. Jabareen, "Politics of State Planning".
4. Joronen and Griffiths, "Affective Politics of Precarity", 563.
5. Azoulay and Ophir, "Monster's Tale"; and Joronen and Griffiths, "Affective Politics of Precarity", 566.
6. Shalhoub-Kevorkian and Ihmoud, "Exiled at Home", 380.
7. Hajyahya, "Principle of Return".

8. Khoury, "*Muqadema li Qira'et*", 82.
9. Kēhaulani, "Structure, Not an Event"; and Wolfe, *Settler Colonialism*. Englert (*Settler Colonialism*) has a convincing Marxist critique of Wolfe's analysis, noting that settler colonialism is not only about land and elimination of the native, but also about labour exploitation and the accumulation of capital.
10. Abourahme, "Spatial Collisions".
11. The Wall that the International Court of Justice rejected in its 2004 advisory opinion is the concrete manifestation of the 1947 Partition Plan, the first decision of the then new UN General Assembly on Palestine, which was also, as Walid Khalidi puts it, "the proximate portal of the Nakba [or the Catastrophe]" that birthed the Palestinian diaspora across the world (Khalidi, "Hebrew Reconquista of Palestine", 26).
12. Abourahme, "Spatial Collisions", 454.
13. Khalili, "Continuity of Colonial Control"; and Benjamin, *Arcades Project*.
14. Yassin, *Al-Thawra al-Arabiyaa*, 128, 129.
15. Z'eiter, *Al-Haraka al-Wataniyya al-Filastiniyya*, 64.
16. Kanafani, *Revolution of 1936–1939*; and Mansour, "Arab Worker", 192.
17. Bhandar, *Colonial Lives of Property*.
18. Kanafani, *Revolution of 1936–1939*. The wage differential between Arab and Jewish workers had been developing since the earlier waves of Jewish immigration and settlement in the 1920s and 1930s and created, by the end of the Mandate, a completely partitioned labour force (see Taha, "From Cairo to Jerusalem"; and Englert, *Settler Colonialism*).
19. Dubnov and Robson, *Partitions*. Partition has been traditionally presented as a decolonising method, an exit strategy, a way to move forward towards the blessings of a future postcolonial world. But the truth is that partition has not led to the settlement of conflicts but to eternal "landscapes of long-term geopolitical deferral" (Dubnov and Robson, *Partitions*, 6).
20. For more on apartheid, see Reynolds and Erakat, "We Charge Apartheid?"
21. The Peel Commission concluded its report in 1937, while the revolution continued for another two years. The Commission noted that the Mandate had reached "a deadlock", and that either the Mandate treaty should be amended or "that the mandate should be abrogated" altogether, favouring the latter option. But this option would have meant the division of Palestine into three separate political units (Peel, "Report").
22. Takriti, "Before BDS", 74.
23. Benjamin, *Arcades Project*, 463.
24. Marx, *Eighteenth Brumaire*.
25. Benjamin, *Arcades Project*, 463.
26. Bannerji, *Thinking Through*, 30.
27. Dalla Costa, *Women and the Subversion*; Federici, *Wages against Housework*; and Mies, *Patriarchy and Accumulation*.
28. hooks, "Homeplace", 383.
29. hooks, "Homeplace", 383.
30. Shalhoub-Kevorkian and Ihmoud, "Exiled at Home", 377.

31. Erakat and Hill, "Black–Palestinian Transnational Solidarity"; and Bhandar and Ziadah, "Acts and Omissions".

32. Adorno, *Negative Dialectics*; Buck-Morss, *Hegal, Haiti*; and Tomba, *Insurgent Universality.*

33. Shibli, *Tafsil Thanawi.*

34. Bhutto and Shibli, "When the Present"; and García, "Adania Shibli".

35. Silmi, "Voice and Silence", 73.

36. Anderson, *From Petition to Confrontation*, 629.

37. Abu Rish, "*Dawr al-Riwaya al-Shafawiyya*".

38. Z'eiter, *Al-Haraka al-Wataniyya al-Filastiniyya*, 84.

39. Anderson, *From Petition to Confrontation*, 625.

40. Ghandour, *Discourse on Domination*, 86.

41. Ghandour, *Discourse on Domination*, 102.

42. Abdulhadi, *Adawr al-Mar'a al-Filastiniyya*, 83.

43. Lefebvre, *Critique of Everyday Life*, 132.

44. Hammad, *Parisian*, 533 and 534.

45. Here, I am also intervening in the traditional Marxist reading of revolutionary subjectivity as operating solely within the sphere of production and the creation of value. The vastness of the colonial capitalism infiltrates every aspect of life from the home to the street, to the factory, to nature itself (Taha, "Thinking through the Home").

46. Abdulhadi, *Adawr al-Mar'a al-Filastiniyya*, 30; my translation, here and throughout.

47. Abdulhadi, *Adawr al-Mar'a al-Filastiniyya*, 30 and 47.

48. Abdulhadi, *Adawr al-Mar'a al-Filastiniyya*, 26.

49. Abū 'Assāf, Interview; my translation.

50. Swedenburg, *Memories of Revolt*, 130.

51. Swedenburg, *Memories of Revolt*, 131.

52. Abdulhadi, *Adawr al-Mar'a al-Filastiniyya*, 33.

53. Abdulhadi, *Adawr al-Mar'a al-Filastiniyya*, 33.

54. Lefebvre, *Critique of Everyday Life*, 132.

55. Abdulhadi, *Adawr al-Mar'a al-Filastiniyya*, 35.

56. Abdulhadi, *Adawr al-Mar'a al-Filastiniyya*, 33 and 34.

57. Abdulhadi, *Adawr al-Mar'a al-Filastiniyya*, 36.

58. Abdulhadi, *Adawr al-Mar'a al-Filastiniyya*, 60.

59. Swedenburg, *Memories of Revolt*, 131.

60. Abdulhadi, *Adawr al-Mar'a al-Filastiniyya*, 56 and 61.

61. Mies, *Patriarchy and Accumulation* (2014), 195; and Swedenburg, *Memories of Revolt*, 179.

62. Abdulhadi, *Adawr al-Mar'a al-Filastiniyya*, 46.

63. Abdulhadi, *Adawr al-Mar'a al-Filastiniyya*, 49 and 50.

64. Palestine Royal Commission, *Report*, 1090.

65. Hartman, *Wayward Lives*, xiii.

66. Fleischmann, *Nation and Its "New" Women*, 133.

67. Abdulhadi, *Adawr al-Mar'a al-Filastiniyya*, 43.

68. Swedenburg, *Memories of Revolt*, 181.

69. Swedenburg, *Memories of Revolt*, 177.
70. Abdulhadi, *Adawr al-Mar'a al-Filastiniyya*, 57 and 58.
71. Abdulhadi, *Adawr al-Mar'a al-Filastiniyya*, 48.
72. The gestures of Jamila Abdul Gawad during the revolt are juxtaposed against the imagery of 'Anata today. Today, 'Anata lies in the Israeli Jerusalem municipality. It was occupied in 1967 and now, it is almost completely surrounded by the Wall, separating it from Jerusalem and the surrounding villages. There is one checkpoint that gives access to the rest of the West Bank, but only from dawn to noon, and the passage of Palestinians is forbidden except for those with blue ID cards (see B'Tselem, "List of Military Checkpoints"). It is precisely this architecture that operates on both the spatial and temporal levels: it cements partition and separation on the one hand and imposes a constant status of *waiting* into the lives of Palestinians on the other (Wick, "Practice of Waiting").
73. Benjamin, *Arcades Project*, Konvolut N.
74. Saleh, "Gesturing Refugees".
75. Ross, *Communal Luxury*, 6.
76. Medien, "Palestine in Deleuze", 51.
77. Adorno, *History and Freedom*, Lectures 9 and 10.
78. Lefebvre, *Critique of Everyday Life*, 132.
79. Chaudhary, "Subjects in Difference", 175.

9

"Genocidal Hauntings of Pronatalism": The Dialectics of Assisted Reproduction in Palestine/Israel

Sigrid Vertommen, Weeam Hammoudeh, and Michal Nahman

This chapter aims to situate Israel's "selective pronatalism" on assisted reproductive technologies (ART) within Zionism's century-old, ongoing history of settler colonialism and racial capitalism in Palestine/Israel, to show the intimate links between abortive social reproduction of the settler colonial regime towards the Palestinian people and its own pronatalist reproductive ethos. This has not only resulted in the creation and consolidation of a demographically Jewish state, often at the expense of Palestinian life, but it has also nurtured the emergence of a thriving (trans)national fertility industry. Using ARTs, including surrogacy, egg donation, posthumous sperm-retrieval, and sperm-smuggling as a feminist lens to unpack broader political economies of life and death in Israel/Palestine, we will argue that reproductive technologies materialise through a dialectical mode of capital accumulation on the one hand and demographic elimination on the other – which has taken an explicitly genocidal turn in Gaza post 7 October 2023. This dialectical set of relations and practices requires the enrolment of racially stratified bodies, biologies and un/paid reproductive labours of (potential) mothers, surrogates, egg donors, depending on their global bio-availability and position in Israel's population economy. By bringing in the technologies, labours and markets of life, fertility and biological reproduction in Palestine/Israel into the Marxist feminist debates on social reproduction and value creation under capitalism, we want to emphasise that this process not only necessitates the exploitation of paid reproductive labour and the appropriation of unpaid reproductive labour, but also the demographic and genocidal elimination of Palestinian Indigenous life that is deemed "surplus".

MAKING LIFE THROUGH DEATH

In December 2023, Al Basma IVF Centre, until recently the largest of Gaza's seven fertility clinics, was struck by an Israeli shell. This caused an explosion that destroyed the five liquid nitrogen tanks containing more than 4,000 frozen embryos and 1,000 specimens of sperm and unfertilised eggs of Palestinian intended parents. "We know deeply what these 5,000 lives, or potential lives, meant for the parents, either for the future or for the past," said Bahaeldeen Ghalayini, the Palestinian gynaecologist and obstetrician who founded the famous clinic in 1997.[1] One of those intended parents was Seba Jaafarawi, a 32-year-old woman from Gaza who not only lost her remaining frozen embryos in the blast, but also her long-awaited twins. In what was already a precarious IVF pregnancy, Seba suffered a miscarriage after fleeing from her home that was bombarded by the Israeli army. "The sounds of me screaming and crying at the hospital are still echoing in my ears," she said in an interview. "Whatever you imagine, or I tell you about how hard the IVF journey is, only those who have gone through it know what it's really like."[2]

Seba is one of more than 50,000 pregnant women in Gaza who is unable to receive the needed prenatal, natal, and postnatal care because of the unprecedented destruction of Gaza's hospitals, clinics, and other vital infrastructures of health, care, and life, and the imposed shortage of food, water, medicine, and humanitarian aid.[3] This is materialising as an unrelenting war on pregnant people and their (un)born children.[4] The Palestine Feminist Collective calls it "reproductive genocide", as "the policies, discourses, and practices that delimit, restrict, target, or diminish the life-giving capacities, choices, access, short-term health, long-term health, and life chances of communities made vulnerable by systemic military violence and occupation, besiegement, settler colonialism /or imperial warfare".[5]

In Gaza we are witnessing a 300 per cent reported increase in miscarriages since October 2023.[6] There are reports of acute shortages of antiseptics and of blood products for treating postpartum haemorrhages, resulting in large increases in obstetric complications and premature births. Hysterectomies are performed as a last resort to save pregnant women's lives. C-sections are conducted without anaesthesia, and labouring people are forced to give birth without pain relief.[7] There is also a lack of contraceptives and sanitary products needed for postpartum bleeding and periods. Newborns are increasingly dying because they weigh too little, and mothers are unable to breastfeed their newborns because of critical shortages of food and nutritional supplements for pregnant and breastfeeding women.[8] Dominic Allen, the UNFPA representative for Palestine, stated that doctors in Gaza are no longer seeing any "normal-sized" babies being born. It is hard to consider normality in Gaza after 75 years of occupation, 16 years of siege and 415 days of genocide.

According to updates from Gaza's Ministry of Health in December 2024, Israel's war has killed at least 43,469 Palestinians and injured 102,561 in Gaza since 7 October 2023.[9] Recent findings by the UN Human Rights Office indicate that "women and children" – that troublesome yet troubling category – represent nearly 70 per cent of the fatalities that were counted during the first six months of the onslaught. A further breakdown of these numbers indicate that 44 per cent of the victims are children, with the biggest single category of children aged 5 to 9, followed by those aged 10 to 14, and then those aged up to and including 4.[10] Already in December 2023, UN Secretary-General António Guterres warned that Gaza was rapidly trans- forming into "a graveyard for children", while UNICEF Executive Director Catherine Russell called Gaza "the most dangerous place in the world to be a child". While more than 13,000 Palestinian children have been killed, thousands more have been maimed and orphaned, and now fall under the acronym WCNSF, the gut-wrenching new kinship category that was intro- duced by Gazan hospital workers to account for unaccompanied "Wounded Children who were left with No Surviving Family members".[11]

While the State of Israel is depriving Palestinian women, men, and children of their past, present, and future dreams of (assisted) family- and kinship-making in an unprecedented, live-streamed onslaught, it has been actively mobilising the use of assisted reproductive technologies (ARTs) to reproduce new life among its Jewish citizens. On 7 October, almost immedi- ately after Hamas's deadly attack that killed nearly 1,200 Israelis and foreign nationals, including 36 children, Israel's Ministry of Health announced the implementation of the "Swords of Iron" posthumous sperm retrieval pro- gramme, aimed at harvesting and preserving the sperm of deceased young men, particularly soldiers. Posthumous assisted reproduction has been per- missively regulated in Israel since 2003.[12] However, a new "temporary law order" was freshly introduced to not only allow the surviving partners, but also the parents, of the deceased men to directly request the retrieval process – free of charge and without obtaining the prior consent of the deceased men.[13] The Israeli Knesset is currently voting on an expanded bill on post- humous assisted reproduction that will likely solidify this temporary order into law.

If the law passes, it will make Israel the first country in the world to allow posthumous sperm retrieval upon parental request. The bill stipulates that in cases where the deceased men do not have a partner, the parents could recruit a gestational volunteer who agrees to carry and mother the child by using the retrieved sperm. While the bill is new, the practice is not. The first recorded case of posthumous grandparenthood in Israel dates to 2002 when the parents of Kivan Cohen, a soldier who was killed during a military operation in occupied Gaza, recruited a woman to gestate and mother the child of their deceased son. The Cohen family advertised for potential surrogate/mothers, and from the multiple dozens of women who came forward, they selected a 25-year-old woman to be inseminated.[14]

This inspired Irit Rosenblum, founder and CEO of the Israeli family rights organisation *New Family* to create the Biological Will™, a legal invention to codify the posthumous retrieval of gametes for the purpose of creating a genetic offspring. In the words of Rosenblum, "the Biological Will™ synthesizes psychological, biological, legal, moral and demographic aspects of assisted reproductive technology into an innovative form of legal insurance for genetic continuity".[15] Although the Biological Will™ is not exclusively intended for soldiers, it is particularly popular among them. In their newsletter distributed during Operation Protective Edge, a previous assault on Gaza in 2014, New Family spurred Israeli soldiers to take into consideration the differential in population growth between Palestinians and Israelis before going to war. Israel is not unique in this respect. In Ukraine, since the start of the war with Russia, fertility clinics have been reportedly providing free services to soldiers to freeze their semen through cryopreservation amid "a potentially devastating demographic future".[16]

PARADIGM SHIFTS: FROM SELECTIVE PRONATALISM TO GENOCIDE

The practices described above are often discursively framed as "exceptional" acts of militarised reproduction that are part and parcel of Israel's "pronatalist" climate, in which high birthrates and large families are not only promoted by the state, but equally desired by its citizens.[17] Israelis are indeed known to have the highest fertility rates (2.9) among OECD countries, and to be the biggest consumers of ARTs across the globe, with Israeli women undergoing roughly twice as many IVF cycles as Danish women, the second biggest consumers in the world.[18] Fertility technologies such as in vitro fertilisation (IVF), intracytoplasmic sperm injection (ICSI), prenatal genetic testing

(PGT), preimplantation genetic diagnosis (PGD), posthumous assisted reproduction, surrogacy, and egg donation are not only widely popular, but also permissively regulated and generously sponsored by the state.[19]

Israel's "pronatalist" stance is often justified in Israeli society by referring to cultural paradigms of *Jewishness* that emphasise the importance of fertility and reproduction in Jewish culture, religion, and history. Scholars and policy- and law-makers often reference the Jewish religious commandment to "be fruitful and multiply", the Holocaust trauma to collectively replenish the 6 million Jewish lives that were brutally exterminated by the Nazis, and the belief that having children can not only offer "symbolic immortality" but also "demographic security" in a region marked by war and conflict.[20] These cultural and "exceptionalist" narratives of Jewishness are indispensable for understanding Israel's "resilient pronatalism", as Birenbaum-Cameli calls it.[21] Yet, we insist that this lens is not only incomplete but at times also problematic in the way it obfuscates the necropolitical mechanisms through which the state produces this "pronatalism".[22] These mechanisms are both specific to the Jewish state in how it operationalises the colonial occupation of Palestinian lives and land, and they are also structural features of wider colonial settler states (such as the United States, Australia, Canada) as well as other state-making practices.[23]

Indeed, critical scholars have been arguing for decades that Israel's "pronatalism" is fundamentally "selective".[24] They describe several episodes in Israel's history when the state actively encouraged the fruitful and plentiful reproduction of the European descended Jews to repopulate Eretz Israel, while problematising and even pathologising the higher birthrates of Mizrahi, Yemenite, and Ethiopian Jews and of non-Jewish migrants and Indigenous Palestinians.[25] In particular for Palestinians, on both sides of the Green Line, their so-called "hyperfertility" has been construed as an existential demographic threat to the survival of the Jewish state, and policies and practices to contain this fertility have been enacted since the state's inception.[26]

One famous example of selective pronatalism was the Heroine Mother award that was issued in 1949 by Prime Minister David Ben-Gurion to morally and financially reward Israeli women on the birth of their tenth child. The prize was dropped after ten years though, when it became evident that most of the recipients were Palestinian mothers in Israel. Ben-Gurion clarified that "any future prenatal incentive must be administered by the Jewish Agency and not the state since the aim is to increase the number of Jews and not the population of the state".[27] A more recent example comes from the field of assisted reproduction to which Palestinians with Israeli citizenship have the same legal entitlements as Jewish citizens. However, colonial realities on the ground restrict them from exercising their reproductive rights equally. In 2010, the Israeli Knesset voted in favour of a law to allow egg cell donations. One of the amendments stipulated that the donor and the recipient of the egg cell are required to share the same religion, making it impossible for a Jewish woman to donate an egg cell to a Muslim, Christian, or Druze couple (religious speak for "Palestinians") and vice versa without the approval of an Exception Committee. Since in practice, Palestinian women rarely donate egg cells in Israel, this amendment ensures that they will also be unlikely to benefit from an egg cell donation.[28]

Instead of strictly centring cultural paradigms of Jewishness, which would both inaccurately attribute responsibility to a religion or a people, our research has been prioritising *feminist political economy perspectives* to analyse various technologies and policies of (assisted) reproduction, fertility, family making, and reproductive health in Palestine/Israel as racial biocapitalist and settler colonial practices of Zionist state-building and (trans)national market creation. This paradigm shift exposes the structural race–gender–class stratifications in how the reproductive bodies, biologies, labours, health, and lives of various communities (Israeli, Palestinian, Mizrahi, Ashkenazi, men, women, gay, heterosexual, etc.) are differently "put to work" and "valued" at the crossroads of ongoing histories of settler colonialism and racial capitalism. Weeam Hammoudeh's research in public health focuses on the fragmented relationship between state-building and reproductive practices in the occupied Palestinian territories (oPt).[29] Specifically for assisted reproduction, Michal Nahman and Sigrid Vertommen demonstrated in earlier research that these ARTs "materialise" in Palestine/Israel through dialectical modes of demographic replacement and capital accumulation.[30] In her recent work on surrogacy frontiers, Vertommen makes the argument that (trans)national surrogacy operates as both a "settler colonial frontier" to reproduce a demographically Jewish state at the expense of Palestinian life, and as a "commodity frontier" in which a thriving (trans)national "reproductive-industrial complex" consisting of public and private fertility clinics, governmental agencies, surrogacy and egg donation companies, is capitalising on Israel's selectively pronatalist drive.[31] It is an outsourced labour force of Georgian, American, Colombian, and Indian surrogates as well as Romanian, Ukrainian, and Czech egg cell providers and other reproductive workers who are simultaneously re/producing for the Israeli market and the settler state.

While our previous research aimed to unpack Israel's stratified pronatalism as a structural feature of Zionism's century-old project of state- and
market-building, its post-7 October manifestation is making a qualitatively
different reproductive turn, in which the delimiting of Palestinian life takes
an explicitly genocidal form of erasure in Gaza.[32] Article 2 of the Genocide
Convention, which was conceived largely in response to the Holocaust
horrors with the aim to prevent the "intentional destruction, in whole or in
part, of a national, ethnical, racial or religious group", considers measures that
are *intended* to prevent births within that group as a modality of genocide.[33]
In some of Settler Colonial Studies' earlier theorisations on erasure, the
question of intention is somehow "bypassed" for its irrelevance from the
Indigenous people's perspective. Patrick Wolfe, for instance, famously wrote
that "Indigenous dispossession is not altered by absent-mindedness", arguing
that Palestinian erasure was a consistent outcome of Zionism's settler colonial
"Project Europe" in Palestine rather than an intended or unintended conse-
quence.[34] However, some scholars of Indigenous Studies and Settler Colonial
Studies, like Al-Asaad, noted repeatedly that settler colonialism indicates the
plausibility of genocide, precisely because while it is not invariably genocidal
it is inherently eliminatory.[35] In Palestinian terms, these nuanced understandings of erasure and replacement are captured in the term *Nakba*.[36] In our
statement "Resistance is Fertile: No Reproductive Justice without Freedom
for Palestine" (December 2023), we echoed these warnings and those of
Palestinian, Black, and anticolonial feminist scholars against "reproductive genocide" in Gaza, and called on all scholars, practitioners, and people
of conscience in our fields of obstetrics, reproductive health, and the social
study of (assisted) reproduction to not only bear witness and analytically
unpack Israel's technologies of reproductive warfare, but also to vehemently
oppose its deadly dialectics of, on the one hand, pronatalism and, on the
other hand, plausible genocide. This call garnered a global swell of over 400
signatures and support from some of the most prominent scholars and practitioners of reproduction.[37] More than a year, and many thousands of deaths
and prevented and compromised births later, we are burdened with an even
greater feminist scholarly duty to further scrutinise the reproductive-demographic relations between pronatalism and genocide, and to critically analyse
how settler colonialism's past and present haunts contemporary imaginaries,
policies, and markets of assisted reproduction and family making. The term
"genocidal pronatalism" is not intended to imply that Israeli state pronatalism
is in itself genocidal – we have neither the ethnographic data nor the desire
to make such a leap. Rather, the dialectical relations between the eliminatory

and the re/productive forces of reproduction and war, and the specificities of these in relation to the genocide in Gaza and resistance in the OPT are highlighted by this term.

Our focus on the dialectics of assisted reproduction in Palestine/Israel allows us to expand Marxist understandings of state-making reproductive practices to see what is both general and particular about "genocidal pronatalism". With this, we want to make three pertinent interventions in the Marxist and feminist debates on social reproduction that become visible by taking Palestine as our epicentre of praxis. First, to bring in stratified processes, practices, and labours of biological reproduction (including fertility, pregnancy, obstetrics, postpartum, and assisted reproduction) into debates around the "value" and labours of social reproduction in capitalist modes of accumulation.[38] Second, to emphasise that capital accumulation not only requires the exploitation of paid reproductive labourers (in our case of surrogates, egg cell providers, fertility doctors, nurses, nannies, etc.) and the appropriation of unpaid reproductive labour of (intended) parents, grandparents, and other caretakers, but also that global capital relies on the demographic and genocidal elimination of Indigenous life that is deemed "surplus".[39] This is not an "Israeli exception", we suggest, nor a long gone, "primitive" stage of capital accumulation, but rather a structural feature of global capitalism. Third, to insist that (assisted) reproduction is not only deployed as a site of capitalist profiteering and settler colonial demographic control but has also been appropriated as a site of anticolonial resistance or survival.

In the remainder of this chapter, we illustrate these three interventions by briefly introducing two case studies of assisted reproduction in Palestine/Israel that emerged from our empirical studies. Each illustrates ART's dialectical entanglements between life- and death-making, capital accumulation and genocidal replacement, and control and resistance. The first case study stems from Nahman's research on the transnational oocyte industry between Israel and Romania in the early 2000s. The second draws on the research by Vertommen and Hammoudeh on sperm-smuggling as a re-humanising and life-affirming practice of reproductive resistance by Palestinian political prisoners and their spouses.

TRANSNATIONAL EGG DONATION FROM SECOND INTIFADA TO TODAY

To decouple Israeli state practices of assisted reproduction from the destructive force of the occupation of Palestine that began over 75 years ago is to tell an incomplete story.[40] It leaves out an account of the ways that the vital politics of the IVF industry depend on a stratified, carceral, and even violently eliminatory logic with a long history. Thus, we turn to the example of Romanian eggs imported to Israel in 2002. At that time, the Israeli Ministry of Health had shut down all domestic egg donations due to a series of "human egg thefts" that had taken place in public hospitals. This was a highly publicised story in which the liberal media decried, and the judicial system punished two physicians who had opted to extract eggs from women, many more eggs than the women were aware of, and offer them at a profit to women and couples seeking egg donation in the private clinics of these doctors. A two-tiered medical system facilitated the exploitation of the reproductive substances and embodied labour of women in Israel, who ended up being unpaid donors effectively. While this was shut down and the doctors arrested, a new reproductive market "frontier" outside the state's borders opened up, on this occasion, in Romania – one of the earliest and most prolific sites of cross-border egg donation.

In that particular locale, egg providers were recruited via word of mouth by the local staff, mostly women, who ran the clinic's day-to-day activities. In this manner, young women working in the lower rungs of Romania's newly forming IVF industry reached out to friends, sisters, and acquaintances to grow a pool of donors that made this Israeli IVF outpost into a well-working business of extracting oocytes, fertilising them with sperm brought over from Israel, cryopreserving it, and taking it "back" to Israel. The women providing the eggs spoke of their egg provision candidly and openly though at the time this kind of reproductive work was still considered a legal grey area.[41] The 21 egg providers Nahman interviewed were factory workers, students, retail workers, and women employed in the country's unregulated informal economy. They wanted a better life, dreamt of leaving Romania and had a wish that their eggs might help some other woman to have the dream of a family. Collectively, their theorising of their own reproductive labour in providing eggs reflected the complexity of being a worker and reproducer who is situated in the highly uneven and stratified global (bio)economy.

The profitability of this market was enabled by the historic oppressive practices in Romania that prevented women from having abortions under Ceausescu, coupled with high unemployment rates at the time of the research and an eagerness among young women to get ahead using whatever means they could. Several Israeli physicians opened remote IVF clinics in Romania, with full Israeli Ministry of Health support and oversight, to extract and fertilise eggs, cryopreserve and bring them to Israel where they were implanted into wombs of commissioning prospective mothers. This in itself may be seen as a fascinating account of some of the earliest cases of what's now benignly referred to as "cross-border reproductive care" (CBRC) by the medical and bioethical world, a form of extended privatised social reproduction relying on underpaid reproductive labourers in what was, in the early 2000s, a highly unregulated global economy of oocytes. Today, there are several private fertility agencies that broker egg cells for the Israeli and global fertility market, some of them with a specialisation in recruiting Jewish egg cell providers such as A Jewish Blessing or The Chosen One.[42]

However, even more pertinent to the issue of how Israeli state pronatalism is intimately tied to the necropolitical, is the fact that at the very same time as these clinics were operating in the early 2000s, the Al-Aqsa Intifada (Second Intifada) was taking place. While Israeli citizens (including some 1948 Palestinians, Druze, and reproductive tourists from abroad) were accessing this privatised and open-border travel of reproductive commodities, Palestinian people, many of whom were ethnically cleansed from their homes in Palestine and relegated to the West Bank and Gaza with little access to reproductive technologies, were experiencing a highly oppressive form of reproductive repression governed by a necropolitical rather than pronatalist logic.[43] Specifically, from 2000 to 2004, 61 women were detained at checkpoints while pregnant and in labour. Of those who gave birth at Israeli military checkpoints along the roads separating 1948 borders and the West Bank, 36 babies died as a result of being born in conditions unfit for birthing.[44] To understand this more simply, to travel by car from the site where women were accessing highly specialised and "world-leading" treatment for infertility with IVF and donated eggs that had crossed over 2,000 kilometres to where women were giving birth at a checkpoint took under 20 minutes. Overall, the infant mortality rates are almost five times higher in the West Bank and more than six times higher in Gaza than in Israel.[45] Similarly, maternal mortality rates in 2020 were eight times higher, 28.5 per 100,000 live births in Palestine, versus three per 100,000 live births in Israel.[46]

In addition to this differential in birth outcomes and mortality rates caused by the structures of occupation, further segregational scaffolding was created and promoted, this time in the realm of the law. While cross-border egg donation was beginning between Israel and Romania, legal authorities and policymakers were in the early stages of drafting and debating what would become the law around the permissibility of cross-religious egg donation. This law, eventually coming into effect in 2010, prevented cross-religious egg donation and coincided with the proposal of five Citizenship and Nationality Laws which deepened the ethnic divides. These overlaps in time of different regimes of colonial segregational power, though not a coordinated effort in any way, are notable and linked through the existing social ethos that simultaneously devalued Palestinian life and valued Jewish reproduction.

In the case of assisted reproductive practices in the early 2000s, a capitalist market and pronatalist logic for the settler population operated along porous borders on the one hand, while an eliminatory, limiting, carceral necropolitical logic operated for the Palestinian population on the other. This example, taken from more than two decades ago still holds resonance for us now in understanding the ways that border and frontier making and unmaking are deeply embedded in settler colonial modes of social reproduction.

RESISTANCE IS FERTILE

In August 2012, local Palestinian and regional news stations aired a story about a Palestinian woman, Dalal, giving birth to a baby boy after successful artificial insemination with her husband's sperm. She has not seen her husband, Ammar, in over ten years, as he is serving a life-sentence conviction in an Israeli military prison. Ammar was able to smuggle his sperm out of prison where it reached an IVF facility in Nablus, West Bank, within twelve hours, despite heavy monitoring by prison authorities. Local press and political leaders presented this unusual narrative as a victory against the Israeli occupation and another example of Palestinian abilities to invent ways to carry out one of the functions of a "normal" life, reproduction, under extremely difficult and "abnormal" circumstances. The happy mother explained in an interview that this was her husband's idea: he didn't want her to be alone; he wanted her to have a son who would be with her when her daughters grew up.[47] Dalal was the first woman to successfully use ARTs in order to have a child with her imprisoned husband's smuggled sperm. The birth of this baby was praised as a political victory for the nation, an act of defiance to Israel, an extension of the prisoner's family name, and a source of old-age security for the "single" mother.[48]

Since Dalal's and Ammar's success with IVF using smuggled sperm, over 100 children have been born to at least 76 prisoners as of May 2023.[49] One of the most famous of these cases is that of the late Walid Daqqa and his wife Sana. Walid and Sana married while Walid was in prison, and though they are both Palestinians with Israeli citizenship, they do not have the same rights as imprisoned Jewish Israelis (including conjugal visits, which are often considered as a threat to Israel's national security). Like other political prisoners, Walid smuggled his sperm to Sana, leading to the birth of their daughter, Milad, whose name means birth in Arabic. In all these cases, Israeli authorities have consistently refused to acknowledge these children and their paternity. However, prisoners have continued to smuggle their sperm to have children with their wives. In addition to the ingenuity of what has often been highlighted as an act of resistance, the success in being able to have children has also been facilitated by the availability (and often pro bono provision of IVF services) as well as a social and religious infrastructure that clears the way for this act to be facilitated and accepted in Palestinian society.

In the media accounts of Dalal and Sana, as well as in research interviews conducted with other women who have had children with their husbands' smuggled sperm, the insistence on life and the making of life under conditions that try to prevent it are salient.[50] Some of the women described the birth of their child in ways that highlighted a renewal of life and bringing in of life energy that had been absent for a long period of time. The life of the family was made more lively with the birth of a new child; the bond between husband and wife separated by prison walls was renewed through the conception and birth of a new child; and hope for the future given a new breath of life. This hope is embodied in the lines of the poem titled "I write to a child, yet unborn" that Daqqa penned for Milad before she was born:

> I write to a child, yet unborn...
> I write to an idea or a dream that intentionally or unintentionally
>   frightens the jailer; even before becoming a reality,
> I write to any child,
> I write to my child that has not been born yet,
> I write to the birth (Milad) of the future.
> This is how we want to name our child,
> and this is exactly how I would like for the future to recognize us [...]
> Will I stop dreaming?
> I'll continue to dream despite this cruel reality,
> I'll search for a meaning for life despite what I have already lost.
> They dig ancestors' cemeteries searching for a delusional authenticity,
> while we search for a better future for our grandchildren; one certain to
>   come.
> Salaam Milad, salaam my dear.[51]

Walid's words recognise the context of the prison (and by extension the occupation) and the threat that the unborn child poses to the Israeli establishment. Yet, the birth of Milad is an insistence on life, despite the sacrifices and the prison walls.[52] It is an insistence on dreaming. In the last few lines, he juxtaposes Israelis digging cemeteries "searching for a delusional authenticity" to Palestinians who are more focused on a better future for their grandchildren. This insistence on life through birth, which is being made possible by the defiant use of ARTs by Palestinians living under a regime predicated on their destruction, can be read as an important act of resistance through the guarantee of a future.

GENOCIDAL HAUNTINGS OF PRONATALISM

How do pregnant women like Seba Jaafarawi, intended grandparents like the Cohens, sperm-smuggling prisoners and their spouses like Walid and Sana Daqqa, fertility brokers like the New Family Organisation and A Jewish Blessing, fertility doctors like Bahaeldeen Ghalayini and Zion Ben-Raphael, government officials of Ministries of Health, and Romanian egg cell providers and Georgian surrogates become "related" to each other? In our account, they are all protagonists in Palestine/Israel's global fertility chain, that is powered by capitalist-colonial modes of accumulation and elimination, in which the reproductive bodies, labours, biologies, lives, and dreams of these protagonists are "valued" in differential, distributed, uneven, and selective ways. Our insistence on their dialectical relationality is crucial. The Israeli state's Zionist biopolitics of assisted reproduction comes to life through its genocidal hauntings of the pasts and presents.

In her research on the (queer) necropolitics of transnational surrogacy and adoption in the war- and conflict-ridden borderlands between Mexico and Guatemala, Silvia Posocco introduced the term "genocide de/kinning" to describe family-making practices that are predicated on the exertion of genocidal violence against Indigenous communities and individuals, and the forced removal and abduction of children.[53] Similarly, we analyse how ARTs materialise in Palestine/Israel as a reproductive-demographic zero-sum, in which the policies to reproduce Jewish life are shaped in relation to the erasure of Indigenous Palestinian life. Israeli pronatalism is haunted by past, present, and ongoing histories of genocide and *Nakba* – from the Shoah that obliterated Jewish life to the current genocide in Gaza that is targeting Palestinian life. Beyond the personal subjectivities and wishes of individual (intended) parents or grandparents to reproduce life, which we do not aim to question, judge, nor romanticise here, our feminist political economy account of ARTs aims to make visible the capitalist-colonial power dynamics in which these reproductive desires materialise and are capitalised on – in fertility clinics, egg cell and surrogacy companies, Ministry of Health offices, pharmaceutical and biotech companies. These not only rely on the labours and biologies of both paid and unpaid reproductive workers, but also on what Shalhoub-Kevorkian terms the "Ashla'a", the "scattered body parts and dismembered flesh" of people – children, men and women alike – who are deemed 'surplus'".[54]

It is from the "Ashla'a" and Gaza's dismembered ruins and body-territories that resurfaces the moral and political imperative for all of us, academics and non-academics alike, to think, act, and revolt with that crucial Marxist feminist insight, that is, that reproduction's "dual characteristic" makes it a fertile site of oppression *and* resistance.[55] Maybe it is also a good time to reckon with Hannah Arendt's concept of "natality" that conceives of birth as a political opening, a potential for a radically different future.[56] Arendt writes that the "miracle that saves the world, the realm of human affairs, from its normal, 'natural' ruin is ultimately the fact of natality, in which the faculty of action is ontologically rooted. It is, in other words, the birth of new men and the new beginning, the action they are capable of by virtue of being born".[57] So while we mourn the loss of "natality" and life infrastructures in Palestine and Lebanon, let us not lose sight of the imperative of nurturing new political communities who struggle for the total liberation of all peoples.

NOTES

1. In relation to other feminist discussions on reproduction and abortion, we want to emphasise that we do not perceive embryos, sperm, and egg cells as human lives but as potential human lives, in this case potential Palestinian lives.
2. Salem, Creidi, and Mills, "Gaza's IVF Embryos".
3. This is meticulously documented by numerous international health and human rights organisations such as the World Health Organization, International Planned Parenthood Federation, Save the Children, UN Population Fund, UNICEF, and by the Institute for Palestine Studies' newly established database that documents the targeting and destruction of the health sector in the Gaza Strip (see Ferguson and Desai, "Sexual and Reproductive Health"; and Hanbali, "Reimagining Liberation").
4. See Irfan, Abu Shammala, and Saleh, "Will There Be a Future".
5. Palestine Feminist Collective, "Palestinian Feminist Collective Condemns".
6. See UNFPA, "Over 300 Days".

7. See Al-Mughrabi, "In Gaza"; and Limaye, "Giving Birth".

8. See Ferguson and Desai, "Sexual and Reproductive Health".

9. Al Jazeera, "Nearly 70 Percent".

10. See Farge, "Gaza Women, Children".

11. See *Al Jazeera*, "Over 13,000 Children".

12. See Hashash, "Medicine and the State".

13. Between 7 October 2023, and 28 August 2024, 187 posthumous sperm retrieval procedures were completed on deceased men, 171 of whom were soldiers, and most of which were initiated by parents (Savitsky, Eldar-Geva, and Shvartsur, "Israeli Men's Attitudes").

14. See Araj, "Rush to Preserve"; and Sinclair, "Israeli Court Allows".

15. These quotes can be found on the Biological Will website: biologicalwill. com/?page_id=194.

16. See Min, "Soldiers in Ukraine".

17. The term "militarised reproduction" gained traction during Operation Protective Edge, Israel's war on Gaza in 2014, when a profound militarisation of the discourses and practices of assisted reproduction took place, such as the targeting of Gazan women's sexual and reproductive capacities, Israeli fertility clinics reporting increased selection of Israeli sperm donors with a combat background in the army, and Israeli soldiers freezing their sperm before going to war (see Shalhoub-Kevorkian, Ihmoud, and Dahir-Nashif, "Sexual Violence"; and Vertommen, "From the Pergonal Project").

18. See Birenbaum-Carmeli, "Thirty-Five Years".

19. See Kahn, *Reproducing Jews*.

20. See, for instance, the work of Kahn, *Reproducing Jews*; Teman, "Embodying Surrogate Motherhood"; and Ivry, *Embodying Culture*.

21. Birenbaum-Carmeli, "Thirty-Five Years".

22. See, for instance, the work of Kanaaneh, *Birthing the Nation*; Nahman, *Extractions*; Shalhoub-Kevorkian "Politics of Birth"; and Vertommen "From the Pergonal Project".

23. See, for instance, Weinbaum, *Afterlives of Reproductive Slavery*; Keaney, *Making Gaybies*; and the special issue of *Catalyst: Feminism, Theory and Technoscience* on "Global Fertility Chains and the Colonial Present of Assisted Reproductive Technologies", see Vertommen, Parry, and Nahman (2022).

24. See, for instance, Yuval-Davis and Stasiulis, *Unsettling Settler Societies*; Portugese, *Fertility Policy in Israel*; and Kanaaneh, *Birthing the Nation*.

25. Famous cases include Depo Provera, the Stolen Yemenite Children and the legal restrictions of migrant care workers to build a family and have children in Israel. See, for instance, the work of Weiss, *Chosen Body*; Madmoni-Gerber, *Israeli Media*; and Shohat, "Sephardim in Israel". As this chapter focuses on the stratified fertility regimes between Palestinians and Israelis, we do not have space to further discuss these cases, but we underline the necessity of developing a *relational* approach in understanding the reproductive management of different racialised communities and populations under Israeli sovereign control.

26. See Portuguese, *Fertility Policy in Israel*.

27. Quoted in Kanaaneh, *Birthing the Nation*, 35.

28. See Hashash, "Medicine and the State"; and Vertommen, "From the Pergonal Project".
29. See Hammoudeh and Hogan. "Proximate Determinants"; and Hammoudeh et al., "In Search of Health".
30. See Nahman, "Materializing Israeliness"; and Nahman, *Extractions*.
31. See Vertommen, "From the Pergonal Project"; and Vertommen, "Surrogacy at the Fertility Frontier".
32. See Segal, "Textbook of Genocide"; Albanese, "Anatomy of a Genocide"; Shalhoub-Kevorkia, "There Is So Much Love"; Ihmoud, "On Love"; and Ihmoud, "Countering Reproductive Genocide".
33. United Nations General Assembly, "Convention on the Prevention".
34. For the relation between elimination and settler colonialism in Palestine, see Sayegh "Zionist Colonialism"; Said, *Pen and the Sword*; and Wolfe, "Structure and Event". In his discussion on the relation between genocide, genocidal agency, and settler colonialism, Wolfe explained that the term "logic of elimination" "avoids both the Scylla of reified social systems and the Charybdis of spontaneous individual voluntarism" (Wolfe, "Structure and Event", 103). For critiques on the inherently eliminatory logic of settler colonialism, see, for instance, Englert, *Settler Colonialism*.
35. Similar to Wolfe, Al-Asaad ("Elimination") emphasises the genocidal plausibility of settler colonialism. Other scholars have critiqued the one-sided analytical focus of settler colonialism as a form of rule based on Indigenous elimination by foregrounding a more dynamic understanding of settler colonialism that makes more epistemic and ontological space for Indigenous life-making, resistance, and survival (Bhandar and Ziadah, "Acts and Omissions"; and Desai, "Disrupting Settler Colonial Capitalism").
36. See, for instance, Eghbariah, "Toward Nakba".
37. Reprosist, "Resistance is Fertile".
38. See, for instance, Franklin and Lock, *Remaking Life & Death*; Cooper and Waldby, *Clinical Labor*; and Vora, *Life Support*.
39. See Salamanca et al., "Past is Present"; Clarno, *Neoliberal Apartheid*; and Wolfe, *Traces of History*.
40. See Nahman, "Nodes of Desire", and Nahman, *Extractions*.
41. See Nahman, "Nodes of Desire".
42. See the websites of A Jewish Blessing: ajewishblessing.com; and The Chosen One: tcoeggdonation.com.
43. See Shalhoub-Kevorkian, "Politics of Birth".
44. OHCHR. "Issue of Palestinian".
45. In 2013, the neonatal mortality rate was estimated at 15.8 per 1,000 live births in the occupied Palestinian territories, compared with 3.5 in Israel (van den Berg, et al., "Increasing Neonatal Mortality"). In Gaza, the infant mortality rate among Palestinian refugees in 2015 was 22.7 per 1,000 live births (UNRWA, "Infant Mortality").
46. See UNFPA, "Over 300 Days." See also World Bank figures in "Israel".
47. Dalal and Ammar's son was born through pre-implantation genetic diagnosis (PGD), which allowed them to select the desired sex of the embryo. In an

interview with Vertommen, Dalal mentioned: "For my husband Ammar, having a boy is a way of prolonging his line, since his mother, father, and brother have died, and a second brother is living overseas." Vertommen's account of sperm smuggling foregrounds the dual character and ambivalence of reproductive technologies such as IVF and PGD. On the one hand, they serve as a last resort for Palestinian women to abide with the cultural traditions and societal imperatives of motherhood in what is still a patriarchal society. On the other hand, they permeate the political arena as a vexed site through which Palestinians are negotiating and claiming their reproductive rights in an act of embodied sabotage. See Vertommen, "Babies from Behind Bars".

48. See Donnison, "Palestinians Born".
49. Seventy-six Palestinian prisoners had children through smuggled sperm. Middle East Monitor, "Report".
50. See Vertommen, "Babies from Behind Bars"; Hamdan, "Every Sperm is Sacred"; Rexer, "Materiality of Power"; and Ftouni, "They Make Death".
51. Farraj, "We Don't Want".
52. See Ftouni. "They Make Death".
53. See Posocco, "Harvesting Life".
54. Shalhoub-Kevorkian, "There Is So Much Love".
55. See Federici, *Revolution at Point Zero*.
56. See Lee and Mykitiuk, "Surviving Difference".
57. See Arendt, *Human Condition*, 247.

Onwards

A Glass of Water, A Burning Boy[1]

Fady Joudah

A young man burning alive in his makeshift hospital bed singed the unspeakable into world memory—a short memory, a hyperactive memory with attention-deficit, a deliberately porous memory backed by industrial chronicity—so why would the executioners care? Culture of the aftermath of images and the lives they contain. *National Geographic* with blazing green eyes. Gender and the environment. A Pulitzer for a vulture objectively giving a moribund child his space to die of starvation. A corpse is a corpse. A naked girl screaming in pain on the road of her forced displacement, half-her body burnt by an army of a people who perpetually protest what they refuse to topple. The risk-benefit ratio demands it. How many genocides were not called by their names? Anachronism or denial?

And on that Monday morning—in the courtyard of Al-Aqsa Martyrs hospital in *The Orchard of Palm Dates* where my family settled their expulsion seventy-plus years ago—this young man burning alive. The fire starting at his feet and moving cephalad—the drama of a head spared to the last, as if the fire was doing us a favour, granting us the memory we desire for when the genocidaires' dream finally ended them. They would have had it coming. A final solution boomerangs a version of a pyrrhic victory with no victor. Burning alive, the man had no name, only titles of what he was and was not to us. A Palestinian in Gaza. Age unknown. His arms raised stiff to guard his face. His arms raised stiff because the fire had engulfed his torso so fast it contracted him into a narrative that wasn't there.

Will you allow me the vulgarity of saying that his arms were a zombie dance pose of Michael Jackson's *Thriller*? Are we not the beast with forty eyes? Is the language of his killers not part of our life? Is there a death we have not cheapened? There is, the chorus quickly replies. The man burning alive could not scream. A physiologic thing at that point. He in total shock. We in total awe. He beyond nociception. Irrelevant larynx.

After his murder, his name came alive, his vital face and beautiful black hair, the stories about his genius at school, his ambition to become a physician— and he might have become a gifted trauma surgeon serving in a state of the art burn unit somewhere civilised. This wouldn't be possible without your resistance in a system that keeps alive, by proxy, those it chars by proxy. We keep them alive in our name, though not in our name we char them. Your Intifada. Mine emerges against a horror on a wheel of conditioned call and response.

A charred soul, like invisible ink, once burned, becomes visible in lieu of the body it once illuminated. Also, the charred soul soots the killer's soul. Yet the killer's body goes on being, washing, exfoliating, doing things to advance life on Earth. Does the camera make the unspeakable more speakable in the digital age? Is that a good thing or just a thing? The horror not subject to live-streamed narration versus the horror that is.

More books. In search of a clarity hellbent on extracting the categorical imperative out of the universal. Until what remains of the universal is life as autonomous thing ticking away indifferent, reproducing itself whatever the form. It drives humans insane that they can't be better than life. All that talk and cortical thinking. All of it extraneous to life that reproduces recurrence. Do you think the universe cares about lifeforms according to our definition of what constitutes a living thing? But time is long, and time is now. If you convince yourself that now is long and yours, you own time.

Billions of us on the planet living in conditions better than in any other era in human history, we're told. As if humans before us did not understand the meaning of life as we do. Or did understand but were unable to attain the means to that meaning as we have. For example, I love detours as much as the next pronoun. What did efficiency ever do for life that inefficiency didn't? The word for pronoun in Arabic doubles for the word for conscience. The root shrivels within. On the day of the footage of the burning young man.

Did you know his younger brother, who was also burning, was saved from the fire by their father but then died a few days later from his wounds? What was his name? Their father asked the eldest for forgiveness because he made no attempt to save him. He spoke the words, *Same'ni Yaba* into the blaze. The father did not shout them. The roaring fire like a raging ocean no sound penetrates.

When I first saw the video, a man out of the frame was shouting: "Pull him out, your religion be damned." He was talking to the panicked group of young men darting around the blaze looking for an opening that permits their courage to slink away from their fear—a couple tossed a blanket over the burning body, but the flames devoured it at the moment of contact. One less blanket, the winter approaching. And the blasphemous phrase the man shouted in renunciation of the divine as a renunciation of the human or the self in the human. "Your religion be damned." When the phrase enters English, it lives, if it lives at all, inside a mirror. The body from which it came disappears. The image in the mirror casts no shadow. I watched the flames and listened, urging the past that had already happened to remain unaltered. I spoke back to the blasphemer and the confused young men in search of a window for rescue: "Let him burn", I snapped at the screen, my reflex at their reflex, code red for code blue: "Leave him be, let mercy in, your religion be damned."

The hospital I work in, at, or for spends millions of dollars to drag a single American life out of imminent death. This spring a retired physician wouldn't let his wife go, for three weeks of instrumentation, so that they would get reconciled with futility on their own terms. The diagnosis doesn't matter. And then one day, past his delusion, he started demanding more hydromorphone to be administered to her more frequently. As patron of the arts, she learned "only about beauty", not mortality, she said to me one day before she called me Dr Death. She couldn't know I was in the middle of my genocide.

From one medical team to another, we passed the baton of patient rights, knowing fully well we were attending to a miserable endgame. The machinery of technology routinises my numbness and reliance on what numbs me. What neutralises my ethics? A healthcare system borne of a system that spends gazillions to annihilate other lives in wars. To say nothing of who gets what control over their body, the life that is the life within, and when? Who gets to override another's body, domestic or foreign? The autoimmune can go eat itself. In Gaza, pregnancy has become a threat to two lives in one body. Attritional to more than two.

Sha'ban, the man burning alive, named after the month that precedes Ramadan in the Islamic lunar calendar. His brother also perished. What was his name? Their sister hung on by the skin of her teeth. Then perished. What will become of their father, mother, and other siblings? What is your memory a slave to? And then another footage came through. A young girl wailing over the wholesome corpse of her father laid before her in his house thobe. Yet to be shrouded, he looked asleep. Perhaps a shrapnel killed him without disfiguring him, or the force of impact, an internal translational injury, finished him off. She looked like she was nine years old but could have been six, now orphaned and "unchilded".

Her little brother was also conjoined with her, no mother or woman around them. He was crying, though less intensely than she was. That's how young he was. Absorbing his sister's wailing but unable to match it. Stuttering his cries. His mind unsure which route his body should take. And his sister's eyes darting up and down her father's corpse, refusing to settle her gaze on his face, addressing his abdomen and legs, and screaming: "Will you wake up, Yaba, just for one minute, you'll be okay, you need to wake up." As if he was in one of his lazy moods, and she was ready to be driven to her favourite cousin's house to go to the beach as promised.

She kept scanning him up and down in sync with her screams that recalled another girl, Huda, whose father, along with seven family members, were gunned down by Israeli forces while they were having a family day on the beach 18 years earlier. Darwish wrote about it. The footage reached the far corners of the world. And here we are. She abruptly turns to her father's serene, departed face and says: "How about a glass of water, Yaba? Shall I bring you some water, Yaba, a sip of water?" Her tone softening into tender negotiation. Countless times during her few years, he'd been thirsty and looked beat, and she offered him water, or he asked her for it. Sometimes it was after he woke up from a nap on the couch or before bedtime. And she loved it, and would cherish watching her little brother, who had reached the glass-of-water carrying age, get in on the action. Water mapping love in their brains before she or he knew what that beautiful thing was that was mapping itself inside them. She had been soaking it all up.

A categorical imperative. I still get my parents water before they ask for it. And when I ask my kids for water, I feel my parents in me and feel my kids feeling good. Haven't you recited back to your parents this verse of water they had recited to you?

NOTE

1. An earlier version of "A Glass of Water, A Burning Boy" first appeared in *Lit Hub*.

Contributors

Asmaa AbuMezied is a gender and economic justice expert with more than 13 years of experience addressing labour rights, economic inclusion, and unpaid care work in fragile and conflict-affected settings. She has worked with the ILO, IFC, and Oxfam, leading research and programmes on inclusive labour markets and gender-sensitive economic policies. Currently pursuing an MPA in Development Practice at Columbia University, her research focuses on the annihilation of care structures in genocide, post-conflict reconstruction, and feminist economic frameworks. Her work has been published in *Oxfam Policy & Practice, Development and Gender Journal*, *Al-Shabaka*, and the *World Economic Forum*.

Mai Abu Moghli is an assistant professor at the Human Rights Program of the School of Social Sciences and Humanities at the Doha Institute for Graduate Studies. She specialises in critical human rights and development studies, comparative and international education in emergencies, and refugee studies with a focus on Arabic-speaking countries.

Tithi Bhattacharya is a professor of South Asian History at Purdue University, in West Lafayette, Indiana. She is the author of *The Sentinels of Culture: Class, Education, and the Colonial Intellectual in Bengal* (Oxford University Press, 2005) and the editor of the now classic study, *Social Reproduction Theory: Remapping Class, Recentering Oppression* (Pluto Press, 2017). Her co-authored book includes the popular *Feminism for the 99%: A Manifesto* (Verso, 2019), which has been translated into over 30 languages. Her new book, *Ghostly Past, Capitalist Presence: A Social History of Fear in Colonial Bengal* (Duke University Press, 2024) is the first study of the relationship between capitalism and the uncanny in the context of colonial Bengal. She writes extensively on Marxist theory, gender, and the politics of Islamophobia. Her work has been published in the *Journal of Asian Studies*.

Tal-Hi Bitton is a doctoral candidate in Philosophy at the University of Oregon. He studies historical materialist philosophy, particularly social reproduction theory, and anticolonial theory.

Susan Ferguson is associate professor emerita at Wilfrid Laurier University, Ontario, and affiliated researcher at the University of Houston, Texas. She researches and writes about feminist theory, childhood and capitalism, and Canadian political discourse on Palestine, and is the author of *Women and Work: Feminism, Labour, and Social Reproduction* (Pluto Press, 2020). She is a long-time Marxist feminist activist and member of Faculty for Palestine in Canada. She is on the editorial board of *Midnight Sun* and co-edits the Mapping Social Reproduction book series for Pluto Press.

Weeam Hammoudeh is an assistant professor at the Institute of Community and Public Health at Birzeit University, Palestine. She works on the structural and political determinants and political economy of health and well-being.

Fady Joudah is a physician and poet based in Houston, Texas. He has received a PEN award, the Griffin Poetry Prize, and a Guggenheim fellowship. He has translated several collections of poetry from Arabic, including *The Butterfly's Burden* by Mahmoud Darwish. His 2024 poetry collection composed after 7 October 2023, *[...]* (Milkweed, 2024), was a National Book Awards finalist. He was awarded the Jackson Poetry Prize in 2024.

Michal Nahman is Associate Professor in Social Anthropology at the University of the West of England, Bristol. She works on reproductive labour, value and reproductive justice, "race", and nationalisms. Her work on global reproductive politics centres the sites of primary value creation in global reproductive markets, namely, Romanian egg donors to Israel/Palestine, migrant egg providers in Spain, and women providing milk to privatised human milk corporations in India.

Jemima Repo is Reader in Political and Feminist Theory at Newcastle University. Her research is mainly in feminist theory and biopolitics. She is author of *The Biopolitics of Gender* (Oxford University Press, 2015). Her current research is on the commodification of feminist activism, as well as social reproduction in the West Bank, and generational experiences of violence in Gaza.

Rachel Rosen is a professor of Sociology at University College London. Her research focuses on marginalised childhoods and social reproduction in neoliberal and racialised border regimes. She is co-author of *Bordering Social Reproduction: Migrant Mothers and Children Making Lives in the Shadows* (Manchester University Press, 2025) and co-editor of *Feminism and the Politics of Childhood: Friends or Foes?* (UCL Press, 2018). She is a member of BDS@UCL (https://bdsatucl.com) and Sociologist in Solidarity with Palestinians (https://socispal.wordpress.com/). Her work on this chapter was part of a fellowship generously supported by the Independent Social Research Foundation.

Mai Taha is an Assistant Professor at the Department of Sociology, London School of Economics and Political Science (LSE). She has written on law, colonialism, labour, class and gender relations, and social reproduction in the Middle East. Using film, literature, oral history, and sound archives, Mai's research explores the different scales of revolution that draw out historical tensions arising in anticolonial liberation struggles, workers' movements, and struggles over social reproduction.

Sigrid Vertommen works as a lecturer and researcher in gender studies at the University of Amsterdam and at Ghent University. Her research focuses on the global politics of (assisted) reproduction from Israel/Palestine to Georgia and Belgium, using various materialist, anti-/de-colonial, and techno-feminist lenses.

Ruth Wilson Gilmore is professor of earth and environmental sciences at the Graduate Center of the City University of New York. Co-founder of many grassroots organisations, she is author of *Abolition Geography: Essays Towards Liberation* (Verso, 2022).

Bibliography

Abdo, Nahla. "Colonial Capitalism and Agrarian Social Structure: Palestine: A Case Study". *Economic and Political Weekly* 26, no. 30 (1991): PE73–PE84. www.epw.in/journal/1991/30/review-political-economy-review-issues-specials/colonial-capitalism-and-agrarian.

Abdo, Nahla. "Gender and Politics under the Palestinian Authority". *Journal of Palestine Studies* 28, no. 2 (1999): 38–51. https://doi.org/10.2307/2537933.

Abdulhadi, Faihaa. *Adawr al-Mar'a al-Filastiniyya fi el-thalatheeniyyat: Al-Musahama al-Siyasiyya lelmar'a al-Filastiniyya: Ruwayat al-Nisaa', Nusus al-Muqabalat al-Shafawiyya* [*The Roles of Palestinian Women in the 1930s: The Political Contribution of Palestinian Women: Women's Narratives, the Texts of the Oral History Interviews*]. Ramallah: Gender Policy Institute, 2005.

Abdul-Rahim, Hanan F., Niveen "Mohammed Elias" Abu-Rmeileh, and Laura Wick. "Cesarean Section Deliveries in the occupied Palestinian territory (oPt): An Analysis of the 2006 Palestinian Family Health Survey". *Health Policy* 93 (2009): 151–6. https://doi.org/10.1016/j.healthpol.2009.07.006.

Abourahme, Nasser. "Spatial Collisions and Discordant Temporalities: Everyday Life between Camp and Checkpoint". *International Journal of Urban and Regional Research* 35, no. 2 (2011): 453–61. https://doi.org/10.1177/02632764251324134.

Abraham, Yuval. "'Lavender': The AI Machine Directing Israel's Bombing Spree in Gaza". *+972 Magazine*, 3 April 2024. www.972mag.com/lavender-ai-israeli-army-gaza/.

Abu Alkas, Dalwoud, et al., "Gazans Strive to Study as War Shatters Education System". *Reuters*, 13 May 2024.

Abu Al-Namel, Hussein. *Gaza Strip, 1948–1967: Economic, Political, Sociological and Military Development*. Beirut: Palestine Research Center, 1979.

Abu Hussein, Hadeel S. *The Struggle for Land under Israeli Law: An Architecture of Exclusion*. London: Routledge, 2021.

Abu Lughod, Ibrahim. "Educating a Community in Exile: The Palestinian Experience". *Journal of Palestinian Studies* 2, no. 3 (Spring 1973): 94–111. https://doi.org/10.2307/2535750.

Abu Moghli, Mai, and Yamila Hussein Shannan. "Childhood, (Im)Mobility and Care in Palestine: A Crisis of Institutional Violence". In *Crisis for Whom? Critical Global Perspectives on Childhood, Care, and Migration*, edited by Rachel Rosen, Elaine Chase, Sarah Crafter, Valentina Glockner, and Sayani Mitra. London: UCL Press, 2023.

Abu Moghli, Mai, and Mezna Qato. "A Brief History of a Teacher's Strike". *Middle East Research and Information Project (MERIP)*, 5 June 2018. https://merip.org/2018/06/a-brief-history-of-a-teachers-strike/.

Abu Rish, Raf'a. "*Dawr al-Riwaya al-Shafawiyya li al-Mar'a al-Filastiniyya fi al-Hifadh 'ala al-Hawiyya al-Wataniyya*" ["The Role of Oral History Narratives of Palestinian Women in Protecting the National Identity"]. *Jaridat Haq al-'Awda* [*The Journal of the Right of Return*] 36 (2007).

Abu-Saad, Ismael, and Duane Champagne. "A Historical Context of Palestinian Arab Education". *American Behavioral Scientist* 49, no. 8 (April 2006): 1035–51. https://doi.org/10.1177/0002764205284717.

Abu-Sittah, Ghassan. "Gaza Hospital Bombing: 'Every Western Politician Has the Blood of These Children on Their Hands'". *Middle East Eye*, 18 October 2023. www.middleeasteye.net/opinion/israel-palestine-war-gaza-hospital-bombing-western-politician-blood-children-hands.

Addameer. "Imprisonment of Children". *Addameer: Prisoner Support and Human Rights Association*, December 2017. www.addameer.org/the_prisoners/children.

Adorno, Theodor. *History and Freedom: Lectures 1964–1965 [Lectures 9 and 10]*. Cambridge: Polity, 2006.

Adorno, Theodor. *Negative Dialectics*. London: Continuum, 2007.

Adra, Basel. "Defying PA Repression Palestinian Teachers Lead Biggest Strike in Years". *+972 Magazine*, 18 April 2023.

Affouneh, Saida Jaser. "How Sustained Conflict Makes Moral Education Impossible: Some Observations from Palestine". *Journal of Moral Education* 36, no. 3 (2007): 343–56. https://doi.org/10.1080/03057240701553321.

Ahmed, Ameera, and Ed Vulliamy. "In Gaza, the Schools are Dying Too". *Guardian*, 10 January 2009.

Akesson, Bree. "School as a Place of Violence and Hope: Tensions of Education for Children and Families in Post-Intifada Palestine". *International Journal of Education Development* 41 (2015): 192–9. https://doi.org/10.1016/j.ijedudev.2014.08.001.

Akram-Boshar, Shireen. "Recentering Indigenous Resistance in the Settler Colonial Analysis of Palestine". Paper presented to the Twenty-First Annual Conference of Historical Materialism. London. 7–10 November 2024.

Al-Asaad, Faisal. "Elimination in Settler Colonialism". *Critical Legal Thinking*, 1 July 2024. https://criticallegalthinking.com/2024/07/01/key-concept-elimination-in-settler-colonialism/.

Alasah, Eman. "The Palestinian Feminist Movement and the Settler Colonial Ordeal: An Intersectional and Interdependent Framework". *Meridians* 23, no. 1 (2024): 110–32. https://doi.org/10.1215/15366936-10926920.

Albanese, Francesca. "Anatomy of a Genocide: Report of the Special Rapporteur on the Situation of Human Rights in the Palestinian Territories Occupied Since 1967". *United Nations Human Rights, Office of the High Commissioner*, A/HRC/55/73, 25 March 2024.

Alfoqahaa, Sam Abd Al-Qadir. "Economics of Higher Education under Occupation: The Case of Palestine". *Journal of Arts & Humanities* 4, no. 10 (2015): 25–43. https://doi.org/10.18533/journal.v4i10.820.

Al-Hamdani, Laila. "Palestinian Women in the Occupied Territories: An Interview with Laila al-Hamdani". Interview by Ehud Ein-gil, *Matzpen*, 10 February 1989. https://matzpen.org/english/1989-02-10/palestinian-women-in-the-occupied-territories-an-interview-with-laila-al-hamdani/.

Al Jazeera, "Life Under Siege: Palestinians in Gaza Speak Out". YouTube video, 28 October 2023. www.youtube.com/watch?v=ZbPdR3E4hCk.

Al Jazeera. "Nearly 70 Percent of Deaths in Gaza are Women and Children: UN". *Al Jazeera*, 8 November 2024.

Al Jazeera. "Our Nakba Repeats, and Our North Is Exterminated". *Al Jazeera Blogs*, 28 October 2024.

Al Jazeera. "Over 13,000 Children Killed in Gaza, Others Severely Malnourished: UNICEF". *Al Jazeera*, 17 March 2024.

Al Jazeera. "They Broke My Teeth: A Palestinian Doctor Recounts His Torture at the Hands of the Israeli Army". *Al Jazeera*, 13 October 2024.

Allen, Lori. *The Rise and Fall of Human Rights: Cynicism and Politics in Occupied Palestine*. Stanford, CA: Stanford University Press, 2013.

Al-Mughrabi, Nidal. "In Gaza, Hospital Procedures without Anesthetics Prompted Screams, Prayers". *Reuters*. 10 November 2023.

Al-zaroo, Salah H. *Non-Formal Education in Palestine: A Response to School Exclusion*. Doctoral dissertation. University of Warwick, 1998.

Alzaroo, Salah, and Gillian Lewando Hunt. "Education in the Context of Conflict and Instability: The Palestinian Case". *Social Policy & Administration* 37, no. 2 (April 2003): 165–80. http://hdl.handle.net/2345/1961.

American Muslims for Palestine. "Making the Grade: The State of Education in Palestine". *American Muslims for Palestine*, 2009.

Amira, Saad. "The Slow Violence of Israeli Settler-Colonialism and the Political Ecology of Ethnic Cleansing in the West Bank". *Settler Colonial Studies* 11, no. 4 (2021): 512–32. https://doi.org/10.1080/2201473X.2021.2007747.

Anderson, Charles. *From Petition to Confrontation: The Palestinian National Movement and the Rise of Mass Politics, 1929–1939*. Doctoral dissertation. New York University, 2013.

Araj, Izzeddin. "The Rush to Preserve the Sperm of Slain Soldiers Exposes the Deep Militarism of Israeli Society". *Mondoweiss*, 10 December 2023. https://mondoweiss.net/2023/12/the-rush-to-preserve-the-sperm-of-slain-soldiers-exposes-the-deep-militarism-of-israeli-society/.

Arda, Lama, and Subhabrata Bobby Banerjee. "Governance in Areas of Limited Statehood: The NGOization of Palestine". *Business & Society* 60, no. 7 (2021): 1675–707. https://doi.org/10.1177/0007650319870825.

Arendt, Hannah. *The Human Condition*. Chicago, IL: University of Chicago Press, 1998.

Arruzza, Cinzia. "Functionalist, Determinist, Reductionist: Social Reproduction Feminism and Its Critics". *Science & Society* 80, no. 1 (2016): 9–30. https://doi.org/10.1521/siso.2016.80.1.9.

Asaad, Denise. "Palestinian Educational Philosophy between Past and Present". *Studies in Philosophy and Education* 19 (2000): 387–403. https://doi.org/10.1023/A:1005263010833.

Asad, Talal. "Class Transformation under the Mandate". *MERIP Reports*, no. 53 (1976): 3–23. https://doi.org/10.2307/3011204.

Atamanov, Aziz, and Nethra Palaniswamy. "Education for Education's Sake? The Conundrum Facing Palestinian Youth". *World Bank Blogs: Arab Voices*, 16 August 2017. https://blogs.worldbank.org/en/arabvoices/education-education-s-sake-conundrum-facing-palestinian-youth.

Ayyash, Muhannad. "Colonial Racial Capitalism and Violence: Theorising the Relationship between Empire and Israeli Settler Colonialism". *Journal of Holy Land and Palestine Studies* 23, no. 2 (2024): 205–20. https://doi.org/10.3366/hlps.2024.0339.

Azoulay, Ariella. "Getting Rid of the Distinction between the Aesthetic and the Political". *Theory, Culture & Society* 27, no. 7–8 (2010): 239–62. https://doi.org/10.1177/0263276410384750.

Azoulay, Ariella, and Adi Ophir. "The Monster's Tail". In *Against the Wall*, edited by Michael Sorkin. New York: W.W. Norton, 2005.

Bannerji, Himani. *Thinking Through: Essays on Feminism, Marxism and Anti-Racism*. Toronto: Canadian Scholars' Press, 1995.

Barnea, Yuval. "From Crisis to Prosperity: Netanyahu's Vision for Gaza 2035 Revealed Online". *Jerusalem Post*, 3 May 2024.

Ben-Bassat, Yuval. "Rural Reactions to Zionist Activity in Palestine before and after the Young Turk Revolution of 1908 as Reflected in Petitions to Istanbul". *Middle Eastern Studies* 49, no. 3 (May 2013): 349–63. https://doi.org/10.1080/00263206.2013.783823.

Benjamin, Walter. *The Arcades Project*. Translated by Howard Eiland and Kevin McLaughlin. Cambridge, MA: Harvard University Press, 2002.

Best, Beverley. *The Automatic Fetish: The Law of Value in Marx's Capital*. London: Verso, 2024.

Bhandar, Brenna. *Colonial Lives of Property: Law, Land, and Racial Regimes of Ownership*. Durham, NC: Duke University Press, 2018.

Bhandar, Brenna, and Rafeef Ziadah. "Acts and Omissions: Framing Settler Colonialism in Palestine Studies". *Jadaliyya*, 14 January 2016. www.jadaliyya.com/Details/32857/Acts-and-Omissions-Framing-Settler-Colonialism-in-Palestine-Studies.

Bhattacharya, Tithi. "Explaining Gender Violence in the Neoliberal Era". *International Socialist Review*, no. 91 (2013): 25–47. https://isreview.org/issue/91/explaining-gender-violence-neoliberal-era/index.html.

Bhattacharya, Tithi. "How Not to Skip Class: Social Reproduction of Labor Power and the Global Working Class". In *Social Reproduction Theory: Remapping Class, Recentering Oppression*, edited by Tithi Bhattacharya. London: Pluto Press, 2017.

Bhattacharya, Tithi. "I Forgot to Die: Thinking through the Social Reproduction of Palestinian Life". *Spectre* (online), 22 March 2024. https://spectrejournal.com/i-forgot-to-die/.

Bhattacharya, Tithi. "Introduction: Mapping Social Reproduction Theory". In *Social Reproduction Theory: Remapping Class, Recentering Oppression*, edited by Tithi Bhattacharya. London: Pluto Press, 2017.

Bhattacharya, Tithi, ed. *Social Reproduction Theory: Remapping Class, Recentering Oppression*. London: Pluto Press, 2017.

Bhutto, Fatima, and Adania Shibli. "When the Present is Haunted by the Past. Edinburgh International Book Festival, YouTube video, 26 August 2020. www.youtube.com/watch?v=2TJ1jpTYQcU&t=2941s.

Birenbaum-Carmeli, Daphna. "Thirty-five Years of Assisted Reproductive Technologies in Israel". *Reproductive Biomedicine & Society Online* 2 (June 2016): 16–23. https://doi.org/10.1016/j.rbms.2016.05.004.

Birenbaum-Carmeli, Daphna, and Yoram S. Carmeli, eds. *Kin, Gene, Community: Reproductive Technologies among Jewish Israelis*. Vol. 19. New York: Berghahn Books, 2010.

Black, Ian. "Doctor Admits Israeli Pathologists Harvested Organs without Consent". *Guardian*, 21 December 2009.

Bohrer, Ashley J. *Marxism and Intersectionality: Race, Gender, Class and Sexuality under Contemporary Capitalism*. Bielefeld: transcript Verlag, 2019.

Breaking the Silence. "Out of the Entire Neighborhood, Only Two Houses Remained Standing". *Breaking the Silence*, 6 May 2015. www.breakingthesilence.org.il/testimonies/videos/97738.

Brown, Nathan J. "Democracy, History, and the Contest over the Palestinian Curriculum". Adams Institute Papers, November 2001. www.mideastweb.org/Democracy in the Palestinian Curriculum.pdf.

Brownson, Elizabeth. "Colonialism, Nationalism, and the Politics of Teaching History in Mandate Palestine". *Journal of Palestine Studies* 43, no. 3 (Spring 2014): 9–25. https://doi.org/10.1525/jps.2014.43.3.9.

B'Tselem. "List of Military Checkpoints in the West Bank and Gaza Strip". *B'Tselem*. Updated 5 June 2024. tinyurl.com/2s36sx7n.

Buck, Daniel. "On Primitive Accumulation and Its Shadowy Twin, Subsumption". *Human Geography* 2, no. 3 (November 2009): 97–100. https://doi.org/10.1177/194277860900200311.

Buck-Morss, Susan. *Hegel, Haiti, and Universal History*. Pittsburgh, PA: University of Pittsburgh Press, 2009.

Busk, Larry Alan, and Elizabeth Portella. "The Contradiction between Use-Value and Exchange-Value: Ecology, Imperialism, and the Telos of Production".

Emancipations: A Journal of Critical Social Analysis 3, no. 1 (2024). https://doi.org/10.55533/2765-8414.1080.

Bzour, Mahyoub, Fathiah Mohamed Zuki, and Muhamad Mispan. "Causes and Remedies for Secondary School Dropout in Palestine". *Improving Schools* 26, no. 1 (2022): 52–64. https://doi.org/10.1177/13654802211004067.

Cabral, Amílcar. "The Weapon of Theory: On Presuppositions and Objectives of National Struggle in Relation to Social Structure". In *Unity and Struggle: Speeches and Writings*, edited by Amílcar Cabral. New York: Monthly Review Press, 2016.

Cali, Massimiliano, and Sami H. Miaari. "The Labor Market Impact of Mobility Restrictions: Evidence from the West Bank". *World Bank*. Policy Research Working Paper, No. 6457, 2013.

Chak, Tings. "Not Only to Stay Alive, But to Stay Human: An Interview with Pavel Eguez". *Tricontinental Institute of Social Research*, 23 June 2020. https://thetricontinental.org/interview-2-2020-pavel-eguez/.

Chaudhary, Zahid. "Subjects in Difference: Walter Benjamin, Frantz Fanon, and Postcolonial Theory". *Differences* 23, no. 1 (2012): 151–83. https://doi.org/10.1215/10407391-1533556.

Chilmeran, Yasmin, and Nicola Pratt. "The Geopolitics of Social Reproduction and Depletion: The Case of Iraq and Palestine". *Social Politics* 26, no. 4 (2019): 586–607. https://doi.org/10.1093/sp/jxz035.

Chughtai, Alia, and Muhammet Okur. "One Year of Israel's War on Gaza". *Al Jazeera*, 8 October 2024.

Clarno, Andy. "Israel's Lavender Kill List: A Joint Imperial Production". *Spectre* 10 (Fall 2024): 18–32.

Clarno, Andy. *Neoliberal Apartheid: Palestine/Israel and South Africa after 1994*. Chicago, IL: Chicago University Press, 2017.

Clarno, Andy. "Neoliberal Colonization in the West Bank". *Social Problems* 65, no. 3 (2018): 323–41.

Clarsen, Georgine. "Introduction: Special Section on Settler-Colonial Mobilities". *Transfers* 3, no. 5 (2015): 41–48.

Cooper, Melinda, and Catherine Waldby. *Clinical Labor: Tissue Donors and Research Subjects in the Global Bioeconomy*. Durham, NC: Duke University Press, 2014.

Coulthard, Glen. *Red Skin, White Masks: Rejecting the Colonial Politics of Recognition*. Indigenous Americas. Minneapolis, MN: University of Minnesota Press, 2014.

Dalla Costa, Maria-Rosa. *Women and the Subversion of the Community: A Mariarosa Dalla Costa Reader*. London: PM Press, 2019.

Darraj, Susan Muaddi. "Palestinian Women: Fighting Two Battles". *Monthly Review* 56, no.1 (2004): 25–36. https://doi.org/10.14452/MR-056-01-2004-05_3.

Darwish, Mahmoud. "In Jerusalem". In *The Butterfly's Burden*. Translated by Fady Joudah. Port Townsend, WA: Copper Canyon Press, 2007.

Darwish, Mahmoud. *Journal of an Ordinary Grief*. Translated by Ibrahim Muhawi. Brooklyn, NY: Archipelago Books, 2010 (1973).

Davies, Jack. "The World Turned Outside In: Settler Colonial Studies and Political Economy". *Historical Materialism* 31, no. 2 (2023): 197–235. https://doi.org/10.1163/1569206x-bja10015.

Davis, Angela Y., Brenna Bhandar, and Rafeef Ziadah. "Angela Y. Davis". In *Revolutionary Feminisms: Conversations on Collective Action and Radical Thought*, edited by Brenna Bhandar and Rafeef Ziadah. London: Verso, 2020.

DCI. "Arbitrary by Default: Palestinian Children in the Israeli Military Court System". *Defence for Children International* (Palestine), 31 May 2023.

DCI. "Under Attack: Settler Violence against Palestinian Children in the Occupied Territory". *Defence for Children International* (Palestine), July 2010.

Delphy, Christine. *Close to Home: A Materialist Analysis of Women's Oppression*. Translated by Diana Leonard. London: Verso Books, 2016.

Desai, Chandni. "Disrupting Settler Colonial Capitalism: Indigenous Intifadas and Resurgent Solidarity from Turtle Island to Palestine". *Journal of Palestine Studies* 50, no. 2 (2021): 43–56. https://doi.org/10.1080/0377919X.2021.1909376.

Desai, Chandni. "The War in Gaza is Wiping Out Gaza's Education and Knowledge Systems". *Conversation*, 8 February 2024. https://theconversation.com/the-war-in-gaza-is-wiping-out-palestines-education-and-knowledge-systems-222055.

Desai, Chandni, and Rula Shahwan. "Preserving Palestine: Visual Archives, Erased Curriculum, and Counter-Archiving Amid Archival Violence in the Post-Oslo Period". *Curriculum Inquiry* 52, no. 4 (2022): 469–89. https://doi.org/10.1080/03626784.2022.2114778.

de Sicilia, Andrés Saenz. "Being, Becoming, Subsumption". *Radical Philosophy* 2, no. 12 (2022): 35–47. www.radicalphilosophy.com/wp-content/uploads/2022/05/rp212_de-sicilia.pdf.

de Santisteban, Agustín Velloso. "Palestinian Education: A National Curriculum against All Odds". *International Journal of Educational Development* 22 (2002): 145–54. https://doi.org/10.1016/S0738-0593(01)00009-8.

Dewi, Sharmila. "Health in the West Bank". *Lancet* 370 (2007): 1405–6. https://doi.org/10.1016/S0140-6736(07)61591-8.

Donnison, Jon. "Palestinians Born 'From Prisoners' Smuggled Sperm'". *BBC*, 15 March 2013.

Douthat, Ross. "Five Rules for an Aging World". *New York Times*, 21 January 2023.

Dubnov, Arie, and Laura Robson, eds. *Partitions: A Transnational History of Twentieth-Century Territorial Separatism*. Stanford, CA: Stanford University Press, 2019.

Dunbar-Ortiz, Roxanne. *An Indigenous Peoples' History of the United States*. Boston, MA: Beacon Press, 2014.

EHRM. "Gaza: Israel Deliberately Militarizes Civilian Objects, Turns Schools into Military Bases". *Euro-Med Human Rights Monitor*, 1 May 2024.

Eghbariah, Rabea. "Toward Nakba as a Legal Concept". *Columbia Law Review* 124, no. 4 (May 2024): 887–991. https://columbialawreview.org/content/toward-nakba-as-a-legal-concept/.

El Dabbagh, Mustafa M. *Palestine, Our Homeland: First Series, Part Two: Al Dyar Al Gazia*. Kufr Qari': Dar El-Huda Publication, 1991.

El-Haddad, Laila. "The Quintessential Palestinian Experience". *The Electronic Intifada*, 14 April 2009.

Elia, Nada. *Greater than the Sum of Our Parts: Feminism, Inter/Nationalism, and Palestine*. London: Pluto Press, 2023.

Elia, Nada. "75 Years of Sumud". *Mondoweiss*, 13 May 2023. https://mondoweiss.net/2023/05/75-years-of-sumud/.

El-Kurd, Mohammed. The Israeli military drops new messages. @m7mdkurd. X. 21 October 2023. twitter.com/m7mdkurd/status/1715764117145784734.

Emejulu, Akwugo, and Leah Bassel. "Austerity and the Politics of Becoming". *Journal of Common Market Studies* 56, no. S1 (2018): 109–19. https://doi.org/10.1111/jcms.12774.

Englert, Sai. "Hebrew Labor without Hebrew Workers: The Histadrut, Palestinian Workers, and the Israeli Construction Industry". *Journal of Palestine Studies* 52, no. 3 (2023): 23–45. https://doi.org/10.1080/0377919X.2023.2244188.

Englert, Sai. *Settler Colonialism: An Introduction*. London: Pluto Press, 2022.

Englert, Sai. "Settlers, Workers, and the Logic of Accumulation by Dispossession". *Antipode* 52, no. 6 (November 2020): 1647–66. https://doi.org/10.1111/anti.12659.

Englert, Sai. "Smoke and Mirrors: Rising Israeli 'Fascism' or Forgetting the Labour Zionist Past". *Middle East Critique* 28, no. 3 (2019): 289–305.

Englert, Sai, and Gargi Bhattacharyya. "Capital's Genocide: A Conversation on Racial Capitalism, Settler Colonialism, and Possible Worlds after Gaza". *Journal of Holy Land and Palestine Studies* 23, no. 2 (2024): 165–86. https://doi.org/10.3366/hlps.2024.0337.

Englert, Sai, Michal Schatz, and Rosie Warren, eds. *From the River to the Sea: Essays for a Free Palestine*. London: Verso Press, 2023.

Erakat, Noura. *Justice for Some: Law and the Question of Palestine*. Stanford CA: Stanford University Press, 2019.

Erakat, Noura, and Marc Lamont Hill. "Black–Palestinian Transnational Solidarity: Renewals, Returns, and Practice". *Journal of Palestine Studies* 48, no. 4 (2019): 7–16. https://doi.org/10.1525/jps.2019.48.4.7.

Euromed. "Israel's Herbicide Spraying: Palestinian Farmers' Means of Subsistence Jeopardised". *Euromed Rights*, 22 April 2020.

Euronews. "Israel 'Stealing Organs' from Bodies in Gaza, Alleges Human Rights Group". *Euronews*, 27 November 2023.

Fahoum, Khalid, and Izzeldin Abuelaish. "Occupation, Settlement, and the Social Determinants of Health for West Bank Palestinians". *Medicine, Conflict, and Survival* 35, no. 3 (2019): 265–83.

Fakhri, Michael. "Starvation and the Right to Food, with an Emphasis on the Palestinian People's Food Sovereignty". *United Nations General Assembly*, 17 July 2024.

Fanon, Frantz. *The Wretched of the Earth*. Translated by Richard Philcox. Revised ed. New York: Grove Press, 2021.

Farge, Emma. "Gaza Women, Children are Nearly 70% of Verified War Dead, UN Rights Office Says". *Reuters*. 8 November 2024.

Farraj, Basil. "'We Don't Want to Receive Them as Martyrs': The Red Cross Is Failing in Its Duty to Palestinian Prisoners". *The New Arab*, 10 January 2024.

Farsakh, Leila. *Palestinian Labour Migration to Israel: Labour, Land and Occupation*. London: Routledge, 2005.

Federici, Silvia. *Re-Enchanting the World: Feminism and the Politics of the Commons*. Kairos. Oakland, CA: PM Press, 2019.

Federici, Silvia. *Revolution at Point Zero: Housework, Reproduction, and Feminist Struggle*. Oakland, CA: PM Press, 2012.

Federici, Silvia. *Wages against Housework*. Bristol: Falling Wall Press, 1975.

Feierstein, Daniel. *Genocide as Social Practice: Reorganizing Society under the Nazis and Argentina's Military Juntas*. New Brunswick, NJ: Rutgers University Press, 2014.

Feiglin, Moshe. "Moshe Feiglin: The Only Solution Is the 'Complete Destruction of Gaza'". *Middle East Eye*, YouTube video, 26 October 2023. www.youtube.com/watch?v=rjLW847tvig.

Ferguson, Laura, and Sapna Desai. "Sexual and Reproductive Health and Rights in Palestine: Securing Spaces to Speak Out." *Sexual and Reproductive Health Matters* 32, no. 1 (2024): 1–5. https://doi.org/10.1080/26410397.2024.2397956.

Ferguson, Susan. *Women and Work: Feminism, Labour, and Social Reproduction*. London: Pluto Press, 2020.

Fields, Gary. "'This is *Our* Land': Collective Violence, Property Law, and Imagining the Geography of Palestine". *Journal of Cultural Geography* 29, no. 3 (2021): 267–91. https://doi.org/10.1080/08873631.2012.726430.

Fleischmann, Ellen. *The Nation and Its "New" Women: The Palestinian Women's Movement, 1920–1948*. Berkeley, CA: University of California Press, 2003.

Forensic Architecture. "The Killing of Hind Rajab". *Forensic Architecture*. 21 June 2024. https://forensic-architecture.org/investigation/the-killing-of-hind-rajab.

Franklin, Sarah, and Margareth Lock. *Remaking Life & Death: Toward an Anthropology of the Biosciences*. Sante Fe, NM: Sar Press, 2003.

Freeman, Elizabeth. *Time Binds: Queer Temporalities, Queer Histories*. Durham, NC: Duke University Press, 2010.

Ftouni, Layal. "'They Make Death, and I'm the Labor of Life': Palestinian Prisoners' Sperm Smuggling as an Affirmation of Life". *Critical Times* 7, no. 1 (April 2024): 94–109. https://doi.org/10.1215/26410478-11082977.

Furas, Yoni. *Educating Palestine: Teaching and Learning History under the Mandate*. Oxford: Oxford University Press, 2020.

García, José. "Adania Shibil on Writing Palestine from the Inside". *Literary Hub*, 6 February 2017. https://lithub.com/adania-shibli-on-writing-palestine-from-the-inside/.

Gaza Academics and Administrators. "Open Letter Gaza Academics and University Administrators to the World". *Al Jazeera*, May 29, 2024.

Georg Eckert Institute for International Textbook Research. *Report on Palestinian Textbooks*. Leibniz Institute for Educational Media, 2021.

Ghandour, Zeina. *A Discourse on Domination in Mandate Palestine: Imperialism, Property and Insurgency*. London: Routledge-Cavendish, 2010.

Ghanim, Honaida. "Thanatopolitics: The Conceptualization of Power over Death in Settler Colonialism". In *Biopolitics and Necropolitics*, edited by Marina Gržinić and Šefik Tatlić. Novi Sad: AMEU-ISH, 2019.

Giacaman, Rita, Laura Wick, and Hanan Abdul-Rahim. "The Politics of Childbirth in the Context of Conflict: Politics or De Facto Practices?" *Health Policy* 72 (2005): 129–39. https://doi.org/10.1016/j.healthpol.2004.06.012.

Gilmore, Ruth Wilson. *Golden Gulag: Prisons, Surplus, Crisis, and Opposition in Globalizing California*. Berkeley, CA: University of California Press, 2007.

Gimenez, Martha. *Marx, Women, and Capitalist Social Reproduction: Marxist Feminist Essays*. Leiden: Brill, 2019.

Griffiths, Mark, and Mikko Joronen. "Marriage under Occupation: Israel's Spousal Visa Restrictions in the West Bank". *Gender, Place & Culture* 26, no. 2 (2018): 153–72. https://doi.org/10.1080/0966369X.2018.1551784.

Griffiths, Mark, and Jemima Repo. "Biopolitics and Checkpoint 300 in Occupied Palestine: Bodies, Affect, Discipline". *Political Geography* 65 (2018): 17–25. https://doi.org/10.1016/j.polgeo.2018.04.004.

Griffiths, Mark, and Jemima Repo. "Women and Checkpoints in Palestine". *Security Dialogue* 52, no. 3 (2021): 249–65. https://doi.org/10.1177/0967010620918529.

Griffiths, Mark, and Jemima Repo. "Women's Lives beyond the Checkpoint in Palestine". *Antipode* 52, no. 4 (2020): 1104–21. https://doi.org/10.1111/anti.12627.

Guillaumin, Colette. *Racism, Sexism, Power and Ideology*. London: Routledge, 2002.

Haaretz. "Israeli Army Appears to Be Using Gaza Hospital, School as Bases, Washington Post Reports". *Haaretz*, 17 May 2024.

Hackl, Andreas. "Occupied Labour: Dispossession through Incorporation among Palestinian Workers in Israel". *Settler Colonial Studies* 13, no. 1 (2023): 96–114. https://doi.org/10.1080/2201473X.2022.2032545.

Hage, Ghassan. "Waiting Out the Crisis: On Stuckedness and Governmentality". In *Waiting*, edited by Ghassan Hage. Melbourne: Melbourne University Press, 2009.

Haj, Samira. "Palestinian Women and Patriarchal Relations". *Signs* 17, no. 4 (1992): 761–78. https://doi.org/10.1086/494763.

Hajir, Basma, and Mezna Qato. "Academia in a Time of Genocide: Scholasticidal Tendencies and Continuities". *Globalisation, Societies and Education* (2025): 1–9. https://doi.org/10.1080/14767724.2024.2445855.

Hajyahya, Adam. "The Principle of Return: The Repressed Ruptures of Zionist Time". *Parapraxis* (2024). www.parapraxismagazine.com/articles/the-principle-of-return.

Hamdan, Mohammed. "Every Sperm is Sacred: Palestinian Prisoners, Smuggled Semen and Derrida's Prophecy". *International Journal of Middle East Studies* 51, no. 4 (2019): 525–45. https://doi.org/10.1017/S0020743819000680.

Hammad Isabella. *The Parisian*. New York: Random House, 2019.

Hammami, Rema. "Destabilizing Mastery and the Machine: Palestinian Agency and Gendered Embodiment at Israeli Military Checkpoints". *Current Anthropology* 60, no. S19 (2019): S87–97. https://doi.org/10.1086/699906.

Hammami, Rema. "On (Not) Surviving at the Checkpoint: Palestinian Narrative Strategies of Surviving Israel's Carceral Geography". *Borderlands* 14, no. 1 (2015): 1–17. www.borderlands.net.au/vol14no1_2015/hammami_checkpoint.pdf.

Hammoudeh, Weeam, and Dennis P. Hogan. "Proximate Determinants of Palestinian Fertility: A Decomposition Analysis". *Lancet* 380 (2012): S20. https://doi.org/10.1016/S0140-6736(13)60201-9.

Hammoudeh, Weeam, Awad Mataria, Laura Wick, and Rita Giacaman. "In Search of Health: Quality of Life among Postpartum Palestinian Women". *Expert Review of Pharmacoeconomics & Outcomes Research* 9, no. 2 (April 2009): 123–32. https://doi.org/10.1586/erp.09.8.

Hanafi, Sari, and Linda Tabar. "The Intifada and the Aid Industry: The Impact of the New Liberal Agenda on the Palestinian NGOs". *Comparative Studies of South Asia, Africa and the Middle East* 23, no. 1 (2003): 205–14. https://doi.org/10.1215/1089201X-23-1-2-205.

Hanbali, Layth. "Reimagining Liberation through the Popular Committees". *Al-Shabaka* (Policy Brief), February 2022. https://al-shabaka.org/briefs/reimagining-liberation-through-the-popular-committees/.

Hanegbi, Haim, Moshe Machover, and Akiva Orr. "The Class Nature of Israeli Society". *New Left Review* 65 (January–February 1971): 3–26.

Hanieh, Adam. "Class, Economy, and the Second Intifada". *Monthly Review* 54, no. 5 (2002): 29–41. https://doi.org/10.14452/MR-054-05-2002-09_3.

Hanieh, Adam. "Framing Palestine: Israel, the Gulf States, and American Power in the Middle East". *Transnational Institute*, 13 June 2024. www.tni.org/en/article/framing-palestine.

Hanieh, Adam. *Lineages of Revolt: Issues of Contemporary Capitalism in the Middle East*. Chicago, IL: Haymarket Books, 2013.

Hanieh, Adam. "The Oslo Illusion". *Jacobin*, 21 April 2013. https://jacobin.com/2013/04/the-oslo-illusion.

Hanson, Susan. "Gender and Mobility: New Approaches for Informing Sustainability". *Gender, Place & Culture* 17, no.1 (2010): 5–23. https://doi.org/10.1080/09663690903498225.

Harb, Samir. "Exhausted Circulation: The Limits to Cement Transportation and Urban Metabolism in the West Bank". *Journal of Palestine Studies* 51, no. 4 (2022): 45–67. https://doi.org/10.1080/0377919X.2022.2133969.

Harnecker, Marta. "Ideas for the Struggle". 2nd ed., translated by Federico Fuentes. *Old and New Project Archive*, 2016.

Hartman, Sadiya. *Wayward Lives, Beautiful Experiments: Intimate Histories of Social Upheaval*. Fleischmann, NY: W.W. Norton, 2019.

Hashash, Yali. "Medicine and the State: The Medicalization of Reproduction in Israel". In *Kin, Gene, Community: Reproductive Technology among Jewish Israelis*, edited by Daphna Birenbaum-Carmeli and Yoram S. Carmeli. New York: Berghahn Books, 2010.

Hassan, Yasmeen. "Nearly 1 Year into the War, Some Students Go Back to School". CBC News, 16 September 2024.

Hasson, Nir. "UNRWA Still Operates in Jerusalem, West Bank and Gaza Despite Israeli Law Banning Agency". *Haaretz*, 9 February 2025.

Hedström, Jenny. "On Violence, the Everyday, and Social Reproduction: Agnes and Myanmar's Transition". *Peacebuilding* 9, no. 4 (2021): 371–86. https://doi.org/10.1080/21647259.2021.1881329.

Hennessy, Rosemary, and Chrys Ingraham. "Socialist Feminism and the Limits of Dual Systems Theory". In *Materialist Feminism: A Reader in Class, Difference, and Women's Lives*, edited by Rosemary Hennessy and Chrys Ingraham. New York: Routledge, 1997.

Herzl, Theodor. *The Jewish State. Jewish Virtual Library*. Translated by Sylvie D'Avigdor. American Zionist Emergency Council, 1946 [1896]; and Jewish Virtual Library.

hooks, bell. "Homeplace: A Site of Resistance". In *Undoing Place? A Geographical Reader*, edited by Linda Mcdowell. London: Routledge, 2020 [1997].

House of Commons Library. "Balfour Declaration". Briefing Paper, No. CBP 7766, *HCL, UK Parliament*. 14 November 2016.

Hughes, Sara Salazar. "Unbounded Territoriality: Territorial Control, Settler Colonialism, and Israel/Palestine." *Settler Colonial Studies* 10, no. 2 (2020): 216–33. https://doi.org/10.1080/2201473X.2020.1741763.

Human Rights Watch. "Middle East and North Africa". *World Report*, 2001. www.hrw.org/legacy/wr2k1/.

Human Rights Watch. "Ripe for Abuse: Palestinian Child Labor in Israeli Agricultural Settlements in the West Bank". *Human Rights Watch*, 13 April 2015. www.hrw.org/report/2015/04/13/ripe-abuse/palestinian-child-labor-israeli-agricultural-settlements-west-bank.

Ihmoud, Sarah. "Countering Reproductive Genocide in Gaza: Palestinian Women's Testimonies". Consortium on Gender, Security and Human Rights, YouTube video, 5 November 2024. youtube.com/watch?v=htW_1OXKlBk.

ILO. "A Year of War in Gaza: Impacts on Employment and Livelihoods in the West Bank and Gaza Strip". *International Labour Organization*, ILO Brief, Bulletin No. 1, 2024. www.ilo.org/publications/year-war-gaza-impacts-employment-and-livelihoods-west-bank-and-gaza-strip.

Inlakesh, Robert. "Hussam Abu Safyia: The Doctor Who Stood Up to an Army – Profile". *Palestine Chronicle*, 31 December 2024.

IPC. "IPC Global Initiative Special Brief: The Gaza Strip". *Integrated Food Security Phase Classification*, 18 March 2024.

Irfan, Anne. *Refuge and Resistance: Palestinians and the International Refugee System*. New York: Columbia University Press, 2023.

Irfan, Bilal, Abdallah Abu Shammala, and Khaled Saleh. "Will There Be a Future for Newborns in Gaza?" *Lancet* 404, no. 10464 (2 November 2024): 1725–6. https://doi.org/10.1016/S0140-6736(24)02249-9.

Ivry, Tsipy. *Embodying Culture: Pregnancy in Japan and Israel*. New Brunswick, NJ: Rutgers University Press, 2010.

Jabareen, Yosef Rafeq. "The Politics of State Planning in Achieving Geopolitical Ends: The Case of the Recent Master Plan for Jerusalem". *International Development Planning Review* 32, no. 1 (2010): 27–43. https://doi.org/10.3828/idpr.2009.11.

Jaffe, Aaron. "From Social Reproduction Theory to Social Reproduction Strikes". *Socialism and Democracy* 36, nos. 1–2 (2022): 157–79. https://doi.org/10.1080/08854300.2023.2170671.

Jaffe, Aaron D. "The History and Afterlife of Marx's 'Primitive Accumulation'". *Historical Materialism* 32, no. 3 (2024): 188–215. https://doi.org/10.1163/1569206x-bja10030.

Jiménez, Erika. "The Occupation Wants to Delete Us: Palestinian Youth's Interpretation of and Resistance to Settler Colonialism". *Third World Quarterly* 44, no. 11 (2023): 2351–69. https://doi.org/10.1080/01436597.2023.2230901.

Joffe, Lawrence. "Fadwa Tuqan: Palestinian Poet Who Captured Her Nation's Sense of Loss and Defiance". Obituary. *Guardian*, 15 December 2003.

Joronen, Mikko, and Mark Griffiths. "The Affective Politics of Precarity: Home Demolitions in Occupied Palestine". *Environment and Planning D: Society and Space* 37, no. 3 (2019): 561–76. https://doi.org/10.1177/0263775818824341.

Kahn, Susan Martha. *Reproducing Jews: A Cultural Account of Assisted Conception in Israel*. Durham, NC: Duke University Press, 2000.

Kanaaneh, Rhoda Ann. *Birthing the Nation: Strategies of Palestinian Women in Israel*. Vol. 2. Berkeley, CA: University of California Press, 2002.

Kanafani, Ghassan. *The Revolution of 1936–1939 in Palestine: Background, Details, & Analysis*. New York: 1804 Press, 2023.

Keaney, Jaya. *Making Gaybies: Queer Reproduction and Multiracial Feeling*. Durham, NC: Duke University Press, 2023.

Kēhaulani, Kauanui J. "'A Structure, Not an Event': Settler Colonialism and Enduring Indigeneity". *Lateral* 5, no. 1 (Spring 2016). https://csalateral.org/issue/5-1/forum-alt-humanities-settler-colonialism-enduring-indigeneity-kauanui/.

Kelcey, Joe. "An (A)Political Education? UNRWA, Humanitarian Governance, and Education for Palestinian Refugees During the First Intifada (1987–1993)". *Harvard Educational Review* 92, no. 3 (2022): 391–412. https://doi.org/10.17763/1943-5045-92.3.391.

Kelley, Robin D.G. "The Rest of Us: Rethinking Settler and Native". *American Quarterly* 69, no. 2 (2017): 267–76. https://doi.org/10.1353/aq.2017.0020.

Khalidi, Muna H. "'This Land, My Sister, Is a Woman': Fadwa Tuqan's Legacy as a Feminist Icon". *Institute of Palestine Studies* (Blog), 30 September 2022. www.palestine-studies.org/en/node/1653278.

Khalidi, Raja. "Nation and Class: Generations of Palestinian Liberation". *Rethinking Marxism* 30, no. 3 (2018): 368–92. https://doi.org/10.1080/08935696.2018.1525967.

Khalidi, Raja, and Sobhi Samour. "Neoliberalism as Liberation: The Statehood Program and the Remaking of the Palestinian National Movement". *Journal of Palestine Studies* 40, no. 2 (2011): 6–25. https://doi.org/10.1525/jps.2011.XL.2.6.

Khalidi, Rashid. *Palestinian Identity: The Construction of Modern National Consciousness*. New York: Columbia University Press, 1997.

Khalidi, Walid. "The Hebrew *Reconquista* of Palestine: From the 1947 United Nations Partition Resolution to the First Zionist Congress of 1897". *Journal of Palestine Studies* 39, no. 1 (2009): 24–42. https://doi.org/10.1525/jps.2010.XXXIX.1.24.

Khalili, Laleh. "The Continuity of Colonial Control Mechanisms in Palestine". SOAS Palestine Society Annual Conference, Vimeo video, 14 November 2013 (2014). https://vimeo.com/channels/soaspalestine/80685204.

Khatib, Rasha, Marin McKee, and Salim Yusuf. "Counting the Dead in Gaza: Difficult but Essential". *Lancet* 404, no. 10449 (July 20, 2024): 237–8. https://doi.org/10.1016/S0140-6736(24)01169-3.

Khoury, Elias. "*Muqadema li Qira'et al-Nakba al-Mustamirra*" ["An Introduction to Reading the On-Going Nakba"]. *Majallat al-Dirasat al-Falastiniyya* [*The Palestine Studies Magazine*] 135 (2023).

Khoury, Jack, et al. "Five-Year Plan for Israel's Arab Community: $9 Billion Won't Bridge a Gap Decades in the Making". *Haaretz*, 28 October 2021.

Kuttab, Eileen S. "Palestinian Women in the 'Intifada': Fighting on Two Fronts". *Arab Studies Quarterly* 15, no. 2 (1993): 69–85.

Law for Palestine. "Law for Palestine Releases Database with 500 Instances of Israeli Incitement to Genocide – Continuously Updated". *Law for Palestine*, 4 January 2024.

Lazzarini, Philippe. Staggering. @UNLazzarini. X. 12 March 2024. x.com/UNLazzarini/status/1767618985397272831?lang=en&mx=2.

Lebowitz, Michael A. *Between Capitalism and Community*. New York: Monthly Review Press, 2020.

Lefebvre, Henri. *Critique of Everyday Life: The One-Volume Edition*. London: Verso Books, 2014.

Lefebvre, Henri. *The Production of Space*. Translated by Donald Nicholson-Smith. Oxford: Blackwell, 1991.

Library of Congress. "Israel: Supreme Court Affirms Constitutionality of Basic Law: Israel–Nation State of the Jewish People". *Global Legal Monitor*, 4 October 2021.

Limaye, Yogita. "Giving Birth with No Painkillers under the Bombs in Gaza". *BBC News*. 24 November 2023.

Lindroth, M., and H. Sinevaara-Niskanen. *Colonial Emotions: Affective States and the Political Economy of Hope*. London: Routledge, 2022.

Lukács, Georg. *History and Class Consciousness: Studies in Marxist Dialects*. Translated by Rodney Livingstone. Cambridge, MA: MIT Press, 2000.McAlevey, Jane. *No Shortcuts: Organizing for Power in the New Gilded Age*. New York: Oxford University Press, 2016.

McGinn, Jack. "Non-Hierarchical Revolution: Grassroots Politics in the First Palestinian Intifada". *Oxford Middle East Review* (2021): S33–43.

Madmoni-Gerber, Shoshana. *Israeli Media and the Framing of Internal Conflict: The Yemenite Babies Affair*. New York: Palgrave Macmillan, 2009.

Maharmeh, Ihab. "Israel's Exploitation of Palestinian Labor: A Strategy of Erasure". *Al-Shabaka: The Palestinian Policy Network*, January 2025.

Mahshi, Khalil, and Kim Bush. "The Palestinian Uprising and Education for the Future". *Harvard Educational Review* 59, no. 4 (November 1989): 474–5.

Makdisi, Ussama Samir. *Age of Coexistence: The Ecumenical Frame and the Making of the Modern Arab World*. Oakland, CA: University of California Press, 2019.

Makovsky, David. "Brinkmanship Over Israel's Ban on UNRWA". *Washington Institute for Near East Policy*, 28 January 2025.

Mansbach, Daniela. "Normalizing Violence: From Military Checkpoints to 'Terminals' in the Occupied Territories". *Journal of Power* 2, no. 2 (2009): 255–73. https://doi.org/10.1080/17540290903072591.

Mansour, George. "The Arab Worker under the Palestine Mandate (1937)". *Settler Colonial Studies* 2, no. 1 (2012): 190–205. https://doi.org/10.1080/2201473X.2012.10648832.

Marx, Karl. *Capital: A Critique of Political Economy*. Vol. 1. Edited by David Fernbach. Translated by Ben Fowkes. London: Penguin Books, 1981.

Marx, Karl. *Capital: A Critique of Political Economy*. Vol. 3. Translated by David Fernbach. London: Penguin Classics, 1991.

Marx, Karl. *The Economic and Philosophic Manuscripts of 1944*, edited by Dirk J. Struik. Translated by Martin Milligan. New York: International Publishers, 1964.

Marx, Karl. *The Economic and Philosophical Manuscripts*. Moscow: Progress Publishers, 1977.

Marx, Karl. *The Eighteenth Brumaire of Louis Napoleon*. DigiCat, 2023.

Marx, Karl. *Grundrisse: Foundations of the Critique of Political Economy*. London: Penguin Classics, 1993.

Mayes, Robyn. "Mobility, Temporality, and Social Reproduction: Everyday Rhythms of the 'FIFO Family' in the Australian Mining Sector". *Gender, Place & Culture* 27, no. 1 (2020): 126–42. https://doi.org/10.1080/0966369X.2018.1554555.

Mbembe, Achille. "Necropolitics". *Public Culture* 15, no. 1 (2003): 11–40.

Mbembe, Achille. *Necropolitics*. Durham, NC: Duke University Press, 2019.

Meari, Lena. "Sumud: A Palestinian Philosophy of Confrontation in Colonial Prisons". *South Atlantic Quarterly* 113, no. 3 (2014): 547–78. https://doi.org/10.1215/00382876-2692182.

Meari, Lena, and Rula Abu-Duhou. "The Palestinian Student Movement and the Dialectic of Palestinian Liberation and Class Struggles". In *The University and Social Justice: Struggles across the Globe*, edited by Aziz Choudry and Salim Vally. London: Pluto Press, 2020.

Medien, Kathryn. "Palestine in Deleuze". *Theory, Culture & Society* 36 no. 5 (2019): 49–70. https://doi.org/10.1177/0263276418816369.

Metzer, Jacob. *The Divided Economy of Mandatory Palestine*. Cambridge: Cambridge University Press, 1998.

Middle East Monitor. "11,000 Palestinian Students Killed since 7 October". *Middle East Monitor*, 18 September 2024. www.middleeastmonitor.com/20240918-11000-palestinian-students-killed-since-7-october/.

Middle East Monitor. "Report: 76 Palestinian Prisoners had Children through Smuggled Sperm". *Middle East Monitor*. 17 May 2023. www.middleeastmonitor.com/20230517-report-76-palestinian-prisoners-had-children-through-smuggled-sperm/.

Mies, Maria. *Patriarchy and Accumulation on a World Scale: Women in the International Division of Labour*. London: Bloomsbury, 2014.

Min, Roselyne. "Soldiers in Ukraine are Freezing Sperm to Have Families in Case They Don't Return Home from the War". *Euronews*. 22 February 2023.

Mohammad, Linah. "Children Make Up Nearly Half of Gaza's Population. Here's What It Means for the War". *NPR*, 19 October 2023.

Mohandesi, Salar, and Emma Teitelman. "Without Reserves". In *Social Reproduction Theory: Remapping Class, Recentering Oppression*, edited by Tithi Bhattacharya. London: Pluto Press, 2017.

Muaddi, Qassam. "Palestinian Public School Teachers on 'Largest General Strike since 2016' for the 10th Day". *The New Arab*, 27 April 2022.

Mullen, Bill V. "Building the Palestine International". *Social Text Online*, 5 July 2012. https://socialtextjournal.org/periscope_article/mullen/.

Nahman, Michal Rachel. *Extractions: An Ethnography of Reproductive Tourism*. Basingstoke: Palgrave Macmillan, 2013.

Nahman, Michal. "Materializing Israeliness: Difference and Mixture in Transnational Ova Donation". *Science as Culture* 15, no. 3 (2006): 199–213. https://doi.org/10.1080/09505430600890669.

Nahman, Michal. "Nodes of Desire: Romanian Egg Sellers 'Dignity' and Feminist Alliances in Transnational Ova Exchanges". *European Journal of Women's Studies* 15, no. 2 (2008): 65–82. https://doi.org/10.1177/1350506807088068.

Narotzky, Susana, and Niko Besnier. "Crisis, Value, and Hope: Rethinking the Economy". *Current Anthropology* 55, no. S9 (2014): S4–16. https://doi.org/10.1086/676327.

New Arab Staff & Agencies. "Indian Workers Replace Palestinians in Israel's Construction Sector". *The New Arab*, 31 December 2024. www.newarab.com/news/indian-workers-replace-palestinians-israels-building-sector.

Nicolai, Susan. "Education and Chronic Crisis in Palestine". *Forced Migration Review*, n.d. www.fmreview.org/nicolai-palestine/.

Nixon, Rob. *Slow Violence and the Environmentalism of the Poor*. Cambridge, MA: Harvard University Press. 2013.

Novick, Tamar, and Arie M. Dubnov. "The Unknown History of the Palestinian School Funded by an Iraqi Jew". *+972 Magazine*, 25 February 2017. www.972mag.com/the-unknown-history-of-the-palestinian-school-funded-by-an-iraqi-jew/.

Nye, Naomi Shihab. "A Palestinian Might Say". *Tiny Journalist*. Rochester, NY: BOA Editions, 2019.

OCHA. "Gaza Strip". *United Nations Office for the Coordination of Humanitarian Affairs* (Reported Impact Snapshot), 11 September 2024.

OCHA. "Movement and Access in the West Bank, September 2024". *United Nations Office for the Coordination of Humanitarian Affairs* (Fact Sheet), August 2024.

OECD. "Better Life Index". *Organization for Economic Co-operation and Development Forum*, 2020.

OHCHR. "Attacks on Hospitals During the Escalation of Hostilities in Gaza (7 October 2023–30 June 2024)". *United Nations Human Rights Office of the High Commissioner* (Thematic Report), 31 December 2024.

OHCHR. "Issue of Palestinian Pregnant Women Giving Birth at Israeli Checkpoints". *United Nations Office of the High Commissioner for Human Rights* (Report), 14 April 2005.

OHCHR. "'More than a Human Can Bear': Israel's Systematic Use of Sexual, Reproductive and Other Forms of Gender-Based Violence Since 7 October 2023". *United Nations Human Rights Office of the High Commissioner*, 13 March 2025.

OHCHR. "UN Experts Condemn 'Flour Massacre,' Urge Israel to End Campaign of Starvation in Gaza". *United Nations Human Rights Office of the High Commissioner* (Press Release), March 2024.

Ollman, Bertell. *Alienation: Marx's Conception of Man in Capitalist Society* [1971]. Cambridge: Cambridge University Press, 1996.

Othman, Orouba. "*Gaza wa-Tahawwulat Bunya al-Mawt*" ["Gaza and the Transformations of the Structure of Death"]. *7iber*, 15 October 2023. 7iber.com/society/غزة-وتحولات-بنية-الموت/.

Oxfam. "The Humanitarian Impact of the Gaza Blockade". *Oxfam International*, 2018.

Oxfam. "Palestinian Women Working in Illegal Israeli Settlements: Dependencies, Exploitation and Opportunity Costs". Oxfam Briefing Paper, March 2025.

Palestine Feminist Collective. "The Palestine Feminist Collective Condemns Reproductive Genocide in Gaza". *Palestine Feminist Collective*, n.d. https://palestinianfeministcollective.org/the-pfc-condemns-reproductive-genocide-in-gaza/.

Palestine Royal Commission. *Report*. London: His Majesty's Stationary Office, 14 September 1937. National Library of Scotland. tinyurl.com/5bb5p4jb.

Pallister-Wilkins, Polly. "How Walls Do Work: Security Barriers as Devices of Interruption and Data Capture". *Security Dialogue* 47, no. 2 (2016): 151–64. https://doi.org/10.1177/0967010615615729.

Panosetti, Fadia, and Laurence Roudart. "Land Struggle and Palestinian Farmers' Livelihoods in the West Bank: Between De-Agrarianization and Anti-Colonial Resistance". *Journal of Peasant Studies* 51, no. 5 (2024): 1079–101. https://doi.org/10.1080/03066150.2023.2277748.

Pappe, Ilan. *Ten Myths about Israel*. London: Verso, 2017.

Pappé, Ilan, and Richard Falk. *The Gaza Strip: The Political Geography of Deprivation*. London: Pluto Press, 2014.

PAS. "History of Birzeit University". *Palestine and Arabic Studies Program, Birzeit University*, n.d.

Pasquetti, Silvia, Jemima Repo, and Hala Shoman. "Settler Colonialism and Mortal Dangers: Affective Responses to COVID-19 and the 2021 Israeli Bombings among Young Palestinians in Gaza". *International Political Sociology* 18, no. 3 (September 2024): 1–20. https://doi.org/10.1093/ips/olae031.

PBS. Press Release. *Palestinian Bureau of Statistics*, 11 August 2024.

PCBS. "The Conditions of the Palestinian Population on the Occasion of World Population Day, 11/07/2023". *Palestinian Central Bureau of Statistics*, 2023.

Peel, William. "The Report of the Palestine Commission". *International Affairs (Royal Institute of International Affairs 1931–1939)* 16, no. 5 (1937): 761–79. https://doi.org/10.2307/2603820.

Peteet, Julie. *Gender in Crisis: Women and the Palestinian Resistance Movement*. New York: Columbia University Press, 1991.

Peteet, Julie. *Space and Mobility in Palestine*. Bloomington, IN: Indiana University Press, 2017.

Pherali, Tejendra, and Ellen Turner, "Meanings of Education under Occupation: The Shifting Motivations for Education in Palestinian Refugee Camps in the West

Bank". *British Journal of Sociology of Education* 39, no. 4 (2018), 567–89. https://doi.org/10.1080/01425692.2017.1375400.

Polman, Linda. *The Crisis Caravan: What's Wrong with Humanitarian Aid?* Translated by Liz Waters. New York: Metropolitan Books, 2010.

Portella, Elizabeth, and Larry Alan Busk. "The Formal and Real Subsumption of Gender Relations". *Historical Materialism* 32, no. 3 (2024): 353–84. https://doi.org/10.1163/1569206x-bja10039.

Portugese, Jacqueline. *Fertility Policy in Israel: The Politics of Religion, Gender and Nation*. Westport, CT: Praeger, 1998.

Posocco, Silvia. "Harvesting Life, Mining Death: Adoption, Surrogacy and Forensics across Borders". *Catalyst: Feminism, Theory, Technoscience* 8, no. 1 (2022): 1–19. https://catalystjournal.org/index.php/catalyst/article/view/35071/29025.

Post, Charles. "Explaining Imperialism Today". *Spectre*, no. 7 (Spring 2023): 54–67.

Povinelli, Elizabeth. *Geontologies: A Requiem to Late Liberalism*. Durham, NC: Duke University Press, 2016.

Prashad, Vijay. "The Only Right that Palestinians have not been Denied Is the Right to Dream". *Tricontinental Institute of Social Research Newsletter* 5, 1 February 2024.

Puar, Jasbir K. *The Right to Maim: Debility, Capacity, Disability*. Durham, NC: Duke University Press, 2017.

Rai, Shirin M. *Depletion: The Human Costs of Caring*. Oxford: Oxford University Press, 2024.

Reidy, Eric. "'More People Will Die': How Israel's UNRWA Ban Affects Palestinians in Gaza and Beyond". *The New Humanitarian*, 7 November 2024.

Repo, Jemima. "Genocide and the Destruction of the Means of Social Reproduction in Gaza". *European Journal of Politics and Gender* 8, no. 2 (2024): 492–9. https://doi.org/10.1332/25151088Y2024D000000061.

Reprosist. "Resistance is Fertile: No Reproductive Justice without Freedom for Palestine". *Reprosist*, 19 December 2023, tinyurl.com/mwvj62fc.

Rexer, Gala. "The Materiality of Power and Bodily Matter(ing): Embodied Resistance in Palestine". *Body & Society* 29, no. 4 (2023): 3–28. https://doi.org/10.1177/1357034X231201950.

Reynolds, John, and Noura Erakat. "We Charge Apartheid? Palestine and the International Criminal Court". *Third World Approaches to International Law Review (TWAIL Review)*, 20 April 2021. https://ssrn.com/abstract=3998126.

Rikje, Alexandra. "Checkpoint Knowledge: Navigating the Tunnels and Al Walaja Checkpoints in the Occupied Palestinian Territories". *Geopolitics* 26, no. 5 (2020): 1589–607. https://doi.org/10.1080/14650045.2020.1737020.

Rijke, Alexandra, and Claudio Minca. "Inside Checkpoint 300: Checkpoint Regimes as Spatial Political Technologies in the Occupied Palestinian Territories". *Antipode* 51, no. 3 (June 2019): 968–88. https://doi.org/10.1111/anti.12526.

Rizzi, Alberto. "The Infinite Connection: How to Make the India-Middle East-Europe Economic Corridor Happen". *European Council on Foreign Relations*, April 2024.

Robinson, Glenn E. *Building a Palestinian State: The Incomplete Revolution*. Bloomington, IN: Indianapolis University Press, 1997.

Robyn, Lee, and Roxanne Mykitiuk. "Surviving Difference: Endocrine-disrupting Chemicals, Intergenerational Justice and the Future of Human Reproduction". *Feminist Theory* 19, no. 2 (2018): 205–21. https://doi.org/10.1177/1464700118764080.

Rodney, Walter. *How Europe Underdeveloped Africa*. London: Verso, 2018.

Rosen, Rachel, and Eve Dickson. "The Exceptions to Child Exceptionalism: Racialised Migrant 'Deservingness' and the UK's Free School Meal Debates". *Critical Social Policy* 44, no. 2 (2024): 201–21. https://doi.org/10.1177/02610183231223948.

Rosenhek, Zeev. "The Political Dynamics of a Segmented Labour Market: Palestinian Citizens, Palestinians from the Occupied Territories and Migrant Workers in Israel". *Acta Sociologica* 46, no. 3 (2003): 231–49.

Ross, Andrew. *Stone Men: The Palestinians Who Built Israel*. London: Verso, 2019.

Ross, Kristin. *Communal Luxury: The Political Imaginary of the Paris Commune*. London: Verso Books, 2016.

Roy, Sara. "De-Development Revisited: Palestinian Economy and Society Since Oslo". *Journal of Palestine Studies* 28, no. 3 (1999): 64–92.

SAWP. "Scholasticide Definition". *Scholars against the War in Palestine*, n.d.

Sabbagh-Khoury, Areej. "'But If I Don't Steal It, Someone Else Is Gonna Steal It': Israeli Settler-Colonial Accumulation by Dispossession". *Middle East Report*, no. 302 (Spring 2022).

Sabella, Bernard. "Education in Palestine and British Policies 1917–1948". *Bethlehem University Journal* 2, no. 1 (1983): 63–79.

Said, Edward W. *The Pen and the Sword: Conversations with David Barsamian*. Monroe, ME: Common Courage Press, 1994.

Said, Hashem, and Zahriyeh Ehab. "Gaza's Kids Affected Psychologically, Physically by a Lifetime of Violence". *Al Jazeera*, 31 July 2014.

Salamanca, Omar Jabary. "Asphyxiation: The Gaza Strip and the Violence of Three-Dimensional Colonialism". *Geopolitics* 19, no. 3 (2014): 708–35.

Salamanca, Omar Jabary, Mezna Qato, Kareem Rabie, and Sobhi Samour. "Past is Present: Settler Colonialism in Palestine". *Settler Colonial Studies* 2, no. 1 (2012): 1–8.

Salem, Saleh, Imad Creidi, and Andres Mills. "Gaza's IVF Embryos Destroyed by Israeli Strike". *Reuters*. 14 April 2024.

Saleh, Farah. (2018) "Gesturing Refugees". *Saleh Farah* (2018). www.farahsaleh.com/gesturing-refugees.

Samara, Adel. "Globalization, the Palestinian Economy and the 'Peace Process'". *Social Justice* 27, no. 4 (2000): 117–32.

Samour, Sobhi. "Covid-19 and the Necroeconomy of Palestinian Labor in Israel". *Journal of Palestine Studies* 49, no. 4 (196) (Summer 2020): 53–64.

Sánchez Broco, Félix, and Jumana Trad. "Education in the Palestinian Territories". *Centre for Middle Eastern Studies of the Foundation for the Social Promotion of Culture*, Round Table 2011, 28 April 2011.

Savitsky, Bella, Talia Eldar-Geva, and Rachel Shvartsur. "Israeli Men's Attitudes toward Posthumous Reproduction and Prior Consent amid Ongoing Armed Conflict". *Andrology* 13, no. 4 (2025): 763–72. https://doi.org/10.1111/andr.13757.

Sayegh, Fayez. "Zionist Colonialism in Palestine (1965)". *Settler Colonial Studies* 2, no. 1 (2012): 206–25. https://doi.org/10.1080/2201473X.2012.10648833.

Sayigh, Rosemary. "Palestinian Women: Triple Burden, Single Struggle". In *Palestine: Profile of an Occupation*, edited by 'Ādil Samārah. *Khamsin*, no. 14 (1989); and London: Zed Books, 1989.

Schneider, Suzanne. *Mandatory Separation: Religion, Education, and Mass Politics in Palestine*. Stanford, CA: Stanford University Press, 2018.

Schölch, Alexander. "The Economic Development of Palestine, 1856–1882". *Journal of Palestine Studies* 10, no. 3 (1981): 35–58. https://doi.org/10.2307/2536459.

Schölch, Alexander. *Palestine in Transformation, 1856–1882*. Translated by William C. Young and Michael C. Gerrity. Washington, DC: Institute for Palestine Studies, 1993.

Segal, Raz. "A Textbook of Genocide". *Jewish Currents*. 13 October 2023.

Seikaly, Sherene. "Men of Capital in Mandate Palestine". *Rethinking Marxism* 30, no. 3 (2018): 393–417. https://doi.org/10.1080/08935696.2018.1525968.

Shafir, Gershon. *Land, Labor, and the Origins of the Israeli–Palestinian Conflict, 1882–1914*. Updated ed. Berkeley, CA: University of California Press, 1996.

Shalhoub-Kevorkian, Nadera. "The Biopolitics of Israeli Settler Colonialism: Palestinian Bedouin Children Theorise the Present". *Journal of Holy Land and Palestine Studies* 15, no. 1 (2016): 7–29. https://doi.org/10.3366/hlps.2016.0127.

Shalhoub-Kevorkian, Nadera. *Incarcerated Childhood and the Politics of Unchilding*. Cambridge: Cambridge University Press, 2019.

Shalhoub-Kevorkian, Nadera. "The Politics of Birth and the Intimacies of Violence against Palestinian Women in Occupied East Jerusalem". *The British Journal of Criminology* 55, Shalhoub-Kevorkian, Nadera. "There is So Much Love in Palestine". Interview by Karim Makdisi, Saree Makdisi, and Ussama Makdisi. *Makdisi Street*, podcast video, 9 March 2024.

Shalhoub-Kevorkian Nadera, and Sarah Ihmoud. "Exiled at Home: Writing Return and the Palestinian Home". *Biography* 37, no. 2 (2014): 377–97. https://doi.org/10.1353/bio.2014.0029.

Shalhoub-Kevorkian, Nadera, Sarah Ihmoud, and Suhad Dahir-Nashif. "Sexual Violence, Women's Bodies and Israeli Settler Colonialism". *Jadaliyya*, 17 November 2014. www.jadaliyya.com/Details/31481.

Shaul, Yehuda. Do not leave stone upon stone. @YehudaShaul. X. 11 November 2023. twitter.com/YehudaShaul/status/1723375961394000090.

Shibli, Adania. *Tafsil Thanawi* [*Minor Detail*]. Beirut: Dar Al-Adab, 2017.

Shohat, Ella. "Sephardim in Israel: Zionism from the Standpoint of Its Jewish Victims". *Social Text*, no. 19-20 (Autumn 1988): 1-35. https://doi.org/10.2307/466176.

Shuayb, Maha. "The Art of Inclusive Exclusions: Educating the Palestinian Refugee Students in Lebanon". *Refugee Survey Quarterly* 33, no. 22 (2014): 20-37. https://doi.org/10.1093/rsq/hdu002.

Silmi, Amirah. "Voice and Silence in Assia Djebar and Adania Shibli". *Critical Times* 6, no. 1 (2023): 58-84. https://doi.org/10.1215/26410478-10235943.

Sinclair, Katy. "Israeli Court Allows Use of Dead Soldier's Sperm". *Progress Educational Trust: BioNews* 393, 29 January 2007. www.progress.org.uk/israeli-court-allows-use-of-dead-soldiers-sperm/.

Swedenburg, Ted. *Memories of Revolt: The 1936-1939 Rebellion and the Palestinian National Past*. Fayetteville, AR: University of Arkansas Press, 2003.

Taha, Mai. "From Cairo to Jerusalem: Law, Labour, Time and Catastrophe". *Law and Critique* 30, no. 3 (2019): 243-64. https://doi.org/10.1007/s10978-019-09248-5.

Taha, Mai. "Thinking through the Home: Work, Rent, and the Reproduction of Society". *Social Research: An International Quarterly* 90, no. 4 (2023): 837-58. https://doi.org/10.1353/sor.2023.a916356.

Takriti, Abdelrazzak. "Before BDS: Lineages of Boycott in Palestine". *Radical History Review* 2019, no. 134 (May 1, 2019): 58-95. https://doi.org/10.1215/01636545-7323408.

Tawil-Souri, Helga. "Checkpoint Time". *Qui Parle: Critical Humanities and Social Sciences* 26, no. 2 (2017): 383-422. https://muse.jhu.edu/article/689615.

Tawil-Souri, Helga. "Qalandia Checkpoint as Space and Nonplace". *Space and Culture* 14, no. 1 (2011): 4-26. https://doi.org/10.1177/1206331210389260.

Tayeb, Sami. "The Palestinian McCity in the Neoliberal Era". *Middle East Report*, no. 290 (Spring 2019): 24-8.

Teman, Elly. 2009. "Embodying Surrogate Motherhood: Pregnancy as a Dyadic Body-Project". *Body and Society* 15, no. 3 (2009): 47-69. https://doi.org/10.1177/1357034X09337780.

Thier, Daphna. "Not an Ally: The Israeli Working Class". In *Palestine: A Socialist Introduction*, edited by Sumaya Awad and brian bean. Chicago, IL: Haymarket Books, 2020.Ticktin, Miriam. *Casualties of Care: Immigration and the Politics of Humanitarianism in France*. Berkeley, CA: University of California Press, 2011.

Tomba, Massimiliano. *Insurgent Universality: An Alternative Legacy of Modernity (Heretical Thought)*. Oxford: Oxford University Press, 2019.

UNDP. "Development for Empowerment: The 2014 Palestine Human Development Report". *United Nations Development Program*, April 2015.

UNFPA. "Over 300 Days of Israel's War on Gaza: UNFPA's Humanitarian Response in the OPT 2024". *United Nations Population Fund*, August 2024.

UN General Assembly. Convention on the Prevention and Punishment of the Crime of Genocide, United Nations, Treaty Series, vol. 78, p. 277, 9 December 1948, www.refworld.org/legal/agreements/unga/1948/en/13495.

UNHR. "UN Experts Deeply Concerned Over 'Scholasticide' in Gaza". *United Nations Human Rights, Office of the High Commissioner*, 18 April 2024.

UNOSAT. "Gaza Strip Comprehensive Damage Assessment". *United Nations Satellite Centre*, 8 November 2023.

UNRWA. "Health". *United Nations Refugee Works Association*, n.d. unrwa.org/what-we-do/health.

UNRWA. "Infant Mortality No Longer in Decline: 'Alarming Trend' According to New Report by UNRWA". *United Nations Refugee Works Association*, 13 June 2018.

UNRWA. "UNRWA Situation Report #152 on the Humanitarian Crisis in the Gaza Strip and the West Bank, Including East Jerusalem". *United Nations Refugee Works Association*, 22 December 2024.

United Nations. "الأمم المتحدة تحذر من تدهور الوضع الإنساني في غزة" ["United Nations Warns of the Deterioration of the Humanitarian Situation in Gaza"]. *UN News Arabic*, November 2024. news.un.org/ar/story/2024/11/1136276.

United Nations General Assembly. "Children and Armed Conflict: Report of the Secretary-General". *United Nations Security Council*, A/77/895-S/2023/363, 5 June 2023.

United Nations General Assembly. "Convention on the Prevention and Punishment of the Crime of Genocide". *International Committee of the Red Cross*, IHL Database, 9 December 1948.

van den Berg, Maartje M., et al. "Increasing Neonatal Mortality among Palestine Refugees in the Gaza Strip". *PLOS ONE* 10, no. 8 (4 August 2015). https://doi.org/10.1371/journal.pone.0135092.

Varela, Paula. "Women Workers at the Heart of Social Reproduction Struggles: Theoretical Debates and Political Battles". *Workers of the World* 1 (December 2023): 44–51. https://doi.org/10.5281/zenodo.10581469.

Veracini, Lorenzo. *Israel and Settler Society*. London: Pluto Press, 2006.

Veracini, Lorenzo. "'Settler Colonialism': Career of a Concept". *Journal of Imperial and Commonwealth History* 41, no. 2 (2013): 313–33. https://doi.org/10.1080/03086534.2013.768099.

Vertommen Sigrid. "Babies from Behind Bars: Stratified Assisted Reproduction in Palestine/Israel". In *Assisted Reproduction Across Borders: Feminist Perspectives on Normalizations, Disruptions and Transmissions*, edited by Merete Lie and Nina Lykke. New York: Routledge, 2016.

Vertommen Sigrid. "From the Pergonal Project to Kadimastem: A Genealogy of Israel's Reproductive-industrial Complex". *BioSocieties* 12 no. 2 (2017): 282–306. https://doi.org/10.1057/biosoc.2015.44.

Vertommen Sigrid. "Surrogacy at the Fertility Frontier: Rethinking Surrogacy in Israel/Palestine as an (Anti)Colonial Episteme". *History of the Present* 14, no. 1 (2024): 108–37. https://doi.org/10.1215/21599785-10898374.

Vertommen, Sigrid, Bronwyn Parry, and Michal Nahman. "Introduction: Global Fertility Chains and the Colonial Present of Assisted Reproductive Technologies". *Catalyst: Feminism, Theory and Technoscience* 8, no. 1 (2022): 1–17. https://doi.org/10.28968/cftt.v8i1.37920.

Vogel, Lise. "Domestic-Labour Debate". *Historical-Critical Dictionary of Marxism* 16, no. 2 (2008): 237–43.

Vora, Kalindi. 2015. *Life Support: Biocapital and the New History of Outsourced Labor*. Minneapolis, MN: University of Minnesota Press, 2015.

WBG. "Indicators: Education". *World Bank Group*, n.d. data.worldbank.org/indicator.

WHO. "Casualties: Conflict-Related Direct Casualties as Reported by the Palestinian Ministry of Health (since October 7, 2023)". *World Health Organization*, Unified Health Dashboard, Version 2.0. Updated 28 December 2024.

WHO. "WHO Concerned about Escalating Health Crisis in West Bank". *World Health Organization*, News, 14 June 2024. www.who.int/news/item/14-06-2024-who-concerned-about-escalating-health-crisis-in-west-bank.

Walsh, Deatra, Halldis Valestrand, Siri Gerrard, and Marit Aure. "Gendered Mobilities in the North: Advancing an International Comparative Perspective". *Norwegian Journal of Geography* 67, no. 5 (2013): 260–5. https://doi.org/10.1080/00291951.2013.847857.

Warren, Tracey. "Class- and Gender-Based Working Time? Time Poverty and the Division of Domestic Labour". *Sociology* 37, no. 4 (2003): 733–52. https://doi.org/10.1177/00380385030374006.

Weinbaum, Alys Eve. *Afterlives of Reproductive Slavery*. Durham, NC: Duke University Press, 2019.

Weinberger, Teddy. "Maternity Leave in Israel". *Jewish Herald Voice*, 28 December 2023.

Weinstock, Nathan. "The Impact of Zionist Colonization on Palestinian Arab Society Before 1948". *Journal of Palestine Studies* 2, no. 2 (1972): 49–63.

Weiss, Meira. *The Chosen Body: The Politics of the Body in Israeli Society*. Stanford, CA: Stanford University Press, 2002.

Wick, Livia. "The Practice of Waiting under Closure in Palestine". *City & Society* 23 (2011): 24–44. https://doi.org/10.1111/j.1548-744X.2011.01054.x.

Wilkins, Brett. "'Cashing in on Genocide': Israeli Firm Pitches Beachfront Real Estate in Leveled Gaza". *Common Dreams*, 19 December 2023.

Wind, Maya. *Towers of Ivory and Steel: How Israeli Universities Deny Palestinian Freedom*. London: Verso, 2024.

Wolfe, Patrick. "Settler Colonialism and the Elimination of the Native". *Journal of Genocide Research* 8, no. 4 (2006): 387–409. https://doi.org/10.1080/14623520601056240.

Wolfe, Patrick. *Settler Colonialism and the Transformation of Anthropology: The Politics and Poetics of an Ethnographic Event.* London: Cassell, 1999.

Wolfe, Patrick. "Structure and Event: Settler Colonialism, Time and the Question of Genocide". In *Empire, Colony, Genocide: Conquest, Occupation and Subaltern Resistance in World History*, edited by Dirk Moses. New York: Berghahn Books, 2008.

Wolfe, Patrick. *Traces of History: Elementary Structures of Race.* London: Verso, 2016.

World Bank. "Israel: Gender Data Portal". genderdata.worldbank.org/en/economies/israel.

Yassin, Subhi. *Al-Thawra al-Arabiyaa al-Kubra fi Filastin* [*The Great Arab Revolution in Palestine*]. Damascus: Dar Al-Hana, 1961.

Young, Iris Marion. "Beyond the Unhappy Marriage: A Critique of the Dual Systems Theory". In *Women and Revolution: A Discussion of the Unhappy Marriage of Marxism and Feminism*, edited by Lydia Sargent. Montreal: Black Rose Books, 1981.

Yuksul, Cagdas. "Israel Needs to Face Trial for Organ Trafficking: Claims and Confessions". *Anadolu Agency*, 27 September 2024.

Yuval-Davis, Nira. "National Reproduction and the Demographic Race in Israel". In *Woman-Nation-State*, edited by Yuval-Davis and Floya Anthias. London: Palgrave Macmillan, 1989.

Yuval-Davis, Nira, and Daiva Stasiulis, eds. *Unsettling Settler Societies: Articulations of Gender, Race, Ethnicity and Class.* London: Sage Publication, 1995.

Z'eiter, Akram. *Al-Haraka al-Wataniyya al-Filastiniyya (1935–1939): Yawmiyyat Akram Z'eiter* [*The Palestinian National Movement (1935–1939): The Diary of Akram Z'eiter*]. Beirut: Institute for Palestine Studies, 1981.

Ziadah, Rafeef. "We Teach Life". *Rafeef Ziadah*, video, 23 November 2015. rafeefziadah.net/js_albums/we-teach-life/.

Zu'bi, Nahla. "The Development of Capitalism in Palestine: The Expropriation of the Palestinian Direct Producers". *Journal of Palestine Studies* 13, no. 4 (1984): 88–109. https://doi.org/10.2307/2536992.

The Pluto Press Newsletter

Hello friend of Pluto!

Want to stay on top of the best radical books
we publish?

Then sign up to be the first to hear about our
new books, as well as special events,
podcasts and videos.

You'll also get 50% off your first order with us
when you sign up.

Come and join us!

Go to bit.ly/PlutoNewsletter